Population Geography

POPULATION GEOGRAPHY

Girish Chopra

Commonwealth

Population Geography

Edition : 2024

ISBN 81-7169-998-7

Published by :

Commonwealth Publishers
4831/24, Prahlad Street,
Ansari Road, Darya Ganj,
New Delhi - 110002
Ph. : 23275511, 23257835
e-mail : campusbooks@hotmail.com

Typesetting by :
Rishu Computers
Delhi - 110092

Printed at :
Royal Digital Press
Delhi 110053

Preface

The role of population trends in human welfare has been the subject of long-standing debate. When the modern expansion of the human population began in the late 18th century, Thomas Malthus argued that unrestrained population growth would be limited by constraints on food production. Instead, world population has expanded much more rapidly than Malthus envisioned, growing from 1 to 6 billion over the past two centuries. Only very recently has population growth approached or actually reached zero in much of the industrial world and has rapid population growth begun to wind down in developing countries.

The trends in population size, age structure, births, and other demographic variables are of interest to a wide range of analysts, including policy-makers, scientists, and planners in industry and government. For example, global and national trends in population size are needed to project the future demand for food, water, and energy and the environmental impact of rising consumption of natural resources. Subnational projections help planners decide where to build new schools and where investments in roads and other infrastructure are required. Reliable estimates of the number of retired people in need of pensions and health care are essential to the optimal design of social security systems.

The present book examines the population growth and change of small and large area of the planet and investigates the demographic components of the population. It covers spatial characteristics of population such as distribution, density, growth, sex ratio, religion, caste, literacy, economic structure, house hold, etc. Besides students and teachers, demographers, policy-makers, and general public alike will find this work of utmost use.

Girish Chopra

Contents

1

Dimensions of Population Trends

Population dynamics are one of the key factors to consider when thinking about development. In the past 50 years the world has experienced an unprecedented increase in population growth.

A "natural population increase" occurs when the birth rate is higher than the death rate. While a country's population growth rate depends on the natural increase and on migration, world population growth is determined exclusively by the natural increase.

Around the world, death rates gradually decreased in the late 19th and the 20th centuries, with death rates in the developing world plummeting after World War II thanks to the spread of modern medicine. In much of the developing world the decline in death rates preceded the decline in birth rates by 20 years or more, resulting in record-high rates of population growth of 3 percent or even 4 percent a year. Since the 1960s birth rates have also been declining rapidly in most developing countries except those in Sub-Saharan Africa and the Middle East. This trend in birth rates in the developing world is comparable to what took place in Europe and the United States in the 19th century.

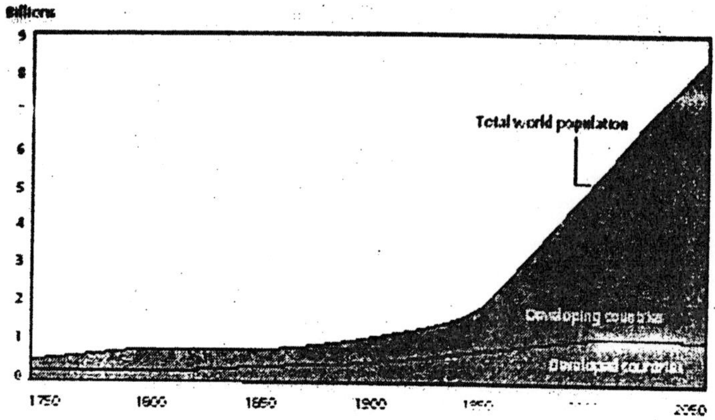

Figure 1. World population, 1750–2050

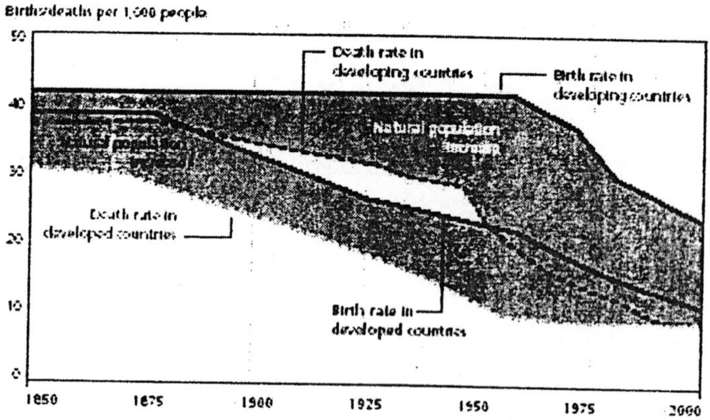

Figure 2.Trends in birth and death rates, 1850–2000

Today's low-income countries still have the world's highest birth rates, although women tend to have fewer children than before. The reasons for lower fertility are varied, but most are related to developing countries' economic growth and human development. Parents choose to have smaller families when health conditions improve so that they no longer have to fear that many of their babies might die, and when they do not have to rely on their children to work on the family farm or business or to take care of them in their old age. In addition, more parents are sending their daughters to school, which is important also because women with basic education tend to produce healthier children and smaller families.

More women now have opportunities to work outside the home, so they are starting their families later and having fewer children. On top of all that, access to family planning is improving, so parents can control the number and spacing of their children.

A lower fertility rate may not immediately lead to a lower birth rate and lower population growth if a country has a larger number of men and women in their reproductive years than before. Population growth caused by more women giving birth even though each has the same number of or fewer children is called "demographic momentum." Demographic momentum is particularly significant in developing countries that had the highest fertility rates 20–30 years ago.

The decline in birth rates over the past few decades has lowered population growth rates in developing countries despite a continuing decline in death rates. Population growth is even slower in developed countries. Stabilizing birth rates and increasing death rates have already led to a natural population decrease in Italy and Germany. Japan and Spain are expected to follow soon.

Over the past 30 years the worldwide population growth rate fell from more than 2.0 percent to 1.5 percent a year, and experts expect this trend to continue. But in absolute numbers the world's population is growing faster than ever before—by about 230,000 people a day in mid-

1995. This is happening because of the larger than ever population base.

In 1995 there were about 5.7 billion people on earth, almost twice as many as in 1970. The next 35 years are projected to add another 2.5 billion people—90 percent of them in developing countries.

The share of developing countries in the world population is expected to increase from 84 percent to 88 percent.

In the short run, rapid population growth in poor countries leads to lower GNP per capita, allowing fewer resources to be invested in each person's human capital—the key to increasing labor productivity. But in the long run, provided that labor productivity does in fact increase, having more workers could contribute to the economic strength of developing countries.

STATE OF WORLD POPULATION

World Population

Table 1. World Population 2003

Ranking	Economy	(thousands)
1	China	1,288,400
2	India	1,064,399
3	United States	291,044
4	Indonesia	214,471
5	Brazil	176,596
6	Pakistan	148,439
7	Russian Federation	143,425
8	Bangladesh	138,066
9	Nigeria	135,632
10	Japan	127,210

Ranking	Economy	(thousands)
11	Mexico	102,291
12	Germany	82,551
13	Philippines	81,503
14	Vietnam	81,314
15	Turkey	70,712
16	[illegible]	68,613
17	Egypt, Arab Rep.	67,559
18	[illegible]	66,392
19	Thailand	62,014
20	France	59,725
21	United Kingdom	59,280
22	Italy	57,646
23	Congo, Dem.Rep.	53,153
24	Myanmar	49,362
25	Ukraine	48,356
26	Korea, Rep.	47,912
27	South Africa	45,294
28	Colombia	44,402
29	Spain	41,101
30	Argentina	38,377
31	Poland	38,195
32	Tanzania	35,889
33	Sudan	33,546
34	Kenya	31,916
35	Algeria	31,833
36	Canada	31,630
37	Morocco	30,113
38	Afghanistan	28,766[a]
39	Peru	27,148
40	Uzbekistan	25,604
41	Venezuela,RB	25,549
42	Uganda	25,280

Ranking	Economy	(thousands)
44	Iraq	24,700
45	Nepal	24,660
46	Korea, Dem. Rep.	22,612
47	Saudi Arabia	22,528
48	Romania	22,200
49	Ghana	20,426
50	Australia	19,890
51	Sri Lanka	19,193
52	Yemen, Rep.	19,173
53	Mozambique	18,791
54	Syrian Arab Republic	17,384
55	Madagascar	16,894
56	Côte d'Ivoire	16,835
57	Netherlands	16,215
58	Cameroon	16,087
59	Chile	15,774
60	Kazakhstan	14,908
61	Angola	13,522
62	Cambodia	13,404
63	Zimbabwe	13,102
64	Ecuador	13,029
65	Guatemala	12,307
66	Burkina Faso	12,109
67	Niger	11,762
68	Mali	11,652
69	Cuba	11,299
70	Malawi	10,962
71	Greece	10,680
72	Zambia	10,403
73	Belgium	10,348
74	Czech Republic	10,202
75	Portugal	10,191
76	Hungary	10,120

Ranking	Economy	(thousands)
77	Senegal	10,048
78	Tunisia	9,895
79	Belarus	9,881
80	Somalia	9,626
81	Bolivia	8,980
82	Sweden	8,956
83	Dominican Republic	8,739
84	Chad	8,582
85	Haiti	8,440
86	Rwanda	8,251
87	Azerbaijan	8,233
88	Serbla and Montenegro	8,104[b]
89	Austria	8,059
90	Guinea	7,909
91	Bulgaria	7,824
92	Switzerland	7,344
93	Burundi	7,206
94	Honduras	6,969
95	Hong Kong, China	6,816
96	Benin	6,720
97	Israel	6,688
98	El Salvador	6,533
99	Tajikistan	6,305
100	Lao PDR	5,660
101	Paraguay	5,643
102	Libya	5,559
103	Papua New Guinea	5,502
104	Nicaragua	5,480
105	Denmark	5,387
106	Slovak Republic	5,381
107	Sierra Leone	5,337
108	Jordan	5,308
109	Finland	5,210

Ranking	Economy	(thousands)
110	Georgia	5,126
111	Kyrgyz Republic	5,052
112	Turkmenistan	4,863
113	Togo	4,861
114	Norway	4,560
115	Lebanon	4,498
116	Croatia	4,456
117	Eritrea	4,389
118	Singapore	4,250
119	Moldova	4,238
120	Bosnia and Herzegovina	4,140
121	United Arab Emirates	4,041
122	New Zealand	4,009
123	Costa Rica	4,005
124	Ireland	3,947
125	Puerto Rico	3,898
126	Central African Republic	3,881
127	Congo, Rep.	3,757
128	Lithuania	3,454
129	Uruguay	3,380
130	Liberia	3,374
131	West Bank and Gaza	3,367
132	Albania	3,169
133	Armenia	3,056
134	Panama	2,984
135	Mauritania	2,693
136	Jamaica	2,640
137	Oman	2,599
138	Mongolia	2,480
139	Kuwait	2,382
140	Latvia	2,321
141	Macedonia, FYR	2,049
142	Namibia	2,015

Ranking	Economy	(thousands)
143	Slovenia	1,964
144	Lesotho	1,793
145	Botswana	1,722
146	Guinea-Bissau	1,489
147	Gambia, The	1,421
148	Estonia	1,350
149	Gabon	1,344
150	Trinidad and Tobago	1,313
151	Mauritius	1,225
152	Swaziland	1,106
153	Bhutan	874
154	Fiji	835
155	Timor-Leste	810
156	Cyprus	770
157	Guyana	769
158	Bahrain	712
159	Djibouti	705
160	Qatar	624
161	Comoros	600
162	Equatorial Guinea	494
163	Cape Verde	470
164	Solomon Islands	457
165	Luxembourg	448
166	Macao, China	444
167	Suriname	438
168	Malta	399
169	Brunei	356
170	Bahamas, The	317
171	Maldives	293
172	Iceland	286
173	Barbados	271
174	Belize	259
175	French Polynesia	243

Ranking	Economy	(thousands)
176	New Caledonia	225
177	Netherlands Antilles	220
178	Vanuatu	210
179	Samoa	178
180	Mayotte	166
181	Guam	162
182	St. Lucia	161
183	São Tomé and Principe	157
184	Channel Islands	149
185	Micronesia, Fed. Sts.	125
186	Virgin Islands (U.S.)	112
187	St.Vincent and the Grenadines	109
188	Grenada	105
189	Tonga	102
190	Aruba	97
191	Kiribati	96
192	Seychelles	84
193	Northern Mariana Islands	80
194	Antigua and Barbuda	79
195	Isle of Man	74
196	Dominica	71
197	American Samoa	70
198	Andorra	69
199	Bermuda	64
200	Greenland	56
201	Marshall Islands	53
202	St.Kitts and Nevis	47
203	Faeroe Islands	46
204	Cayman Islands	39
205	Liechtenstein	33
206	Monaco	32
207	San Marino	28
208	Palau	20

World	6,271,698
Low income	2,310,259
Middle income	2,990,074
Lower middle income	2,655,152
Upper middle income	334,922
Low & middle income	5,300,333
East Asia & Pacific	1,854,532
Europe & Central Asia	472,724
Latin America & Caribbean	534,186
Middle East & North Africa	311,613
South Asia	1,424,690
Sub-Saharan Africa	702,588
High income	971,365
European Monetary Union	306,121

World birth rate

Table 2. World birth rate 2003

Country	Birth rate
Afghanistan	40.63 births/1,000 population (2003 est.)
Albania	18.2 births/1,000 population (2003 est.)
Algeria	21.94 births/1,000 population (2003 est.)
American Samoa	23.26 births/1,000 population (2003 est.)
Andorra	9.65 births/1,000 population (2003 est.)
Angola	45.57 births/1,000 population (2003 est.)
Anguilla	14.68 births/1,000 population (2003 est.)
Antigua and Barbuda	18.23 births/1,000 population (2003 est.)
Argentina	17.47 births/1,000 population (2003 est.)
Armenia	12.57 births/1,000 population (2003 est.)
Aruba	11.86 births/1,000 population (2003 est.)
Australia	12.55 births/1,000 population (2003 est.)
Austria	9.43 births/1,000 population (2003 est.)
Azerbaijan	19.28 births/1,000 population (2003 est.)

Country	Birth rate
Bahamas, The	18.57 births/1,000 population (2003 est.)
Bahrain	19.02 births/1,000 population (2003 est.)
Bangladesh	29.9 births/1,000 population (2003 est.)
Barbados	13.15 births/1,000 population (2003 est.)
Belarus	10.18 births/1,000 population (2003 est.)
Belgium	10.45 births/1,000 population (2003 est.)
Belize	30.46 births/1,000 population (2003 est.)
Benin	43.15 births/1,000 population (2003 est.)
Bermuda	12.13 births/1,000 population (2003 est.)
Bhutan	34.82 births/1,000 population (2003 est.)
Bolivia	25.53 births/1,000 population (2003 est.)
Bosnia and Herzegovina	12.65 births/1,000 population (2003 est.)
Botswana	25.5 births/1,000 population (2003 est.)
Brazil	17.67 births/1,000 population (2003 est.)
British Virgin Islands	15 births/1,000 population (2003 est.)
Brunei	19.68 births/1,000 population (2003 est.)
Bulgaria	8.02 births/1,000 population (2003 est.)
Burkina Faso	44.78 births/1,000 population (2003 est.)
Burma	19.15 births/1,000 population (2003 est.)
Burundi	39.72 births/1,000 population (2003 est.)
Cambodia	27.28 births/1,000 population (2003 est.)
Cameroon	35.49 births/1,000 population (2003 est.)
Canada	10.99 births/1,000 population (2003 est.)
Cape Verde	26.95 births/1,000 population (2003 est.)
Cayman Islands	13.33 births/1,000 population (2003 est.)
Central African Republic	35.93 births/1,000 population (2003 est.)
Chad	47.06 births/1,000 population (2003 est.)
Chile	16.1 births/1,000 population (2003 est.)
China	12.96 births/1,000 population (2003 est.)
Christmas Island	NA births/1,000 population (2003 est.)
Cocos (Keeling) Islands	NA births/1,000 population (2003 est.)

Country	Birth rate
Colombia	21.59 births/1,000 population (2003 est.)
Comoros	38.5 births/1,000 population (2003 est.)
Congo, Dem,Rep.of the	45.12 births/1,000 population (2003 est.)
Congo, Republic of the	29.46 births/1,000 population (2003 est.)
Cook Islands	NA births/1,000 population (2003 est.)
Costa Rica	19.4 births/1,000 population (2003 est.)
Cote d'Ivoire	40.01 births/1,000 population (2003 est.)
Croatia	12.76 births/1,000 population (2003 est.)
Cuba	11.87 births/1,000 population (2003 est.)
Cyprus	12.77 births/1,000 population (2003 est.)
Czech Republic	9.01 births/1,000 population (2003 est.)
Denmark	11.52 births/1,000 population (2003 est.)
Djibouti	40.78 births/1,000 population (2003 est.)
Dominica	16.78 births/1,000 population (2003 est.)
Dominican Republic	23.94 births/1,000 population (2003 est.)
East Timor	27.75 births/1,000 population (2003 est.)
Ecuador	24.94 births/1,000 population (2003 est.)
Egypt	24.36 births/1,000 population (2003 est.)
El Salvador	27.9 births/1,000 population (2003 est.)
Equatorial Guinea	36.94 births/1,000 population (2003 est.)
Eritrea	39.44 births/1,000 population (2003 est.)
Estonia	9.24 births/1,000 population (2003 est.)
Ethiopia	39.81 births/1,000 population (2003 est.)
Falkland Islands	NA births/1,000 population
Faroe Islands	13.81 births/1,000 population (2003 est.)
Fiji	23.06 births/1,000 population (2003 est.)
Finland	10.54 births/1,000 population (2003 est.)
France	12.54 births/1,000 population (2003 est.)
French Guiana	21.33 births/1,000 population (2003 est.)
French Polynesia	17.74 births/1,000 population (2003 est.)
Gabon	36.54 births/1,000 population (2003 est.)

Country	Birth rate
Gambia, The	40.77 births/1,000 population (2003 est.)
Gaza Strip	41.23 births/1,000 population (2003 est.)
Georgia	11.79 births/1,000 population (2003 est.)
Germany	8.6 births/1,000 population (2003 est.)
Ghana	25.84 births/1,000 population (2003 est.)
Gibraltar	11.09 births/1,000 population (2003 est.)
Greece	9.79 births/1,000 population (2003 est.)
Greenland	16.09 births/1,000 population (2003 est.)
Grenada	22.87 births/1,000 population (2003 est.)
Guadeloupe	16.16 births/1,000 population (2003 est.)
Guam	23.19 births/1,000 population (2003 est.)
Guatemala	35.05 births/1,000 population (2003 est.)
Guernsey	9.43 births/1,000 population (2003 est.)
Guinea	42.5 births/1,000 population (2003 est.)
Guinea-Bissau	38.41 births/1,000 population (2003 est.)
Guyana	17.87 births/1,000 population (2003 est.)
Haiti	34.06 births/1,000 population (2003 est.)
Honduras	31.67 births/1,000 population (2003 est.)
Hong Kong	10.71 births/1,000 population (2003 est.)
Hungary	9.32 births/1,000 population (2003 est.)
Iceland	14.13 births/1,000 population (2003 est.)
India	23.28 births/1,000 population (2003 est.)
Indonesia	21.49 births/1,000 population (2003 est.)
Iran	17.23 births/1,000 population (2003 est.)
Iraq	33.66 births/1,000 population (2003 est.)
Ireland	14.63 births/1,000 population (2003 est.)
Israel	18.67 births/1,000 population (2003 est.)
Italy	9.18 births/1,000 population (2003 est.)
Jamaica	17.35 births/1,000 population (2003 est.)
Japan	9.61 births/1,000 population (2003 est.)
Jersey	10.44 births/1,000 population (2003 est.)

Country	Birth rate
Jordan	23.68 births/1,000 population (2003 est.)
Kazakhstan	18.36 births/1,000 population (2003 est.)
Kenya	28.81 births/1,000 population (2003 est.)
Kiribati	31.24 births/1,000 population (2003 est.)
Korea, North	17.61 births/1,000 population (2003 est.)
Korea, South	12.6 births/1,000 population (2003 est.)
Kuwait	21.83 births/1,000 population (2003 est.)
Kyrgyzstan	26.06 births/1,000 population (2003 est.)
Laos	36.93 births/1,000 population (2003 est.)
Latvia	8.55 births/1,000 population (2003 est.)
Lebanon	19.68 births/1,000 population (2003 est.)
Lesotho	27.26 births/1,000 population (2003 est.)
Liberia	45.28 births/1,000 population (2003 est.)
Libya	27.43 births/1,000 population (2003 est.)
Liechtenstein	10.92 births/1,000 population (2003 est.)
Lithuania	10.48 births/1,000 population (2003 est.)
Luxembourg	11.92 births/1,000 population (2003 est.)
Macau	12.07 births/1,000 population (2003 est.)
Macedonia, FYR	13.2 births/1,000 population (2003 est.)
Madagascar	42.16 births/1,000 population (2003 est.)
Malawi	44.7 births/1,000 population (2003 est.)
Malaysia	23.7 births/1,000 population (2003 est.)
Maldives	36.71 births/1,000 population (2003 est.)
Mali	47.79 births/1,000 population (2003 est.)
Malta	12.75 births/1,000 population (2003 est.)
Man, Isle of	11.38 births/1,000 population (2003 est.)
Marshall Islands	34.18 births/1,000 population (2003 est.)
Martinique	14.96 births/1,000 population (2003 est.)
Mauritania	42.16 births/1,000 population (2003 est.)
Mauritius	16.1 births/1,000 population (2003 est.)
Mayotte	42.86 births/1,000 population (2003 est.)

Country	Birth rate
Mexico	21.92 births/1,000 population (2003 est.)
Micronesia, Fed.States of	26.47 births/1,000 population (2003 est.)
Moldova	14.31 births/1,000 population (2003 est.)
Monaco	9.46 births/1,000 population (2003 est.)
Mongolia	21.39 births/1,000 population (2003 est.)
Montserrat	17.57 births/1,000 population (2003 est.)
Morocco	23.26 births/1,000 population (2003 est.)
Mozambique	38.2 births/1,000 population (2003 est.)
Namibia	34.1 births/1,000 population (2003 est.)
Nauru	26.09 births/1,000 population (2003 est.)
Nepal	32.46 births/1,000 population (2003 est.)
Netherlands	11.31 births/1,000 population (2003 est.)
Netherlands Antilles	15.76 births/1,000 population (2003 est.)
New Caledonia	19.45 births/1,000 population (2003 est.)
New Zealand	14.14 births/1,000 population (2003 est.)
Nicaragua	26.29 births/1,000 population (2003 est.)
Niger	49.54 births/1,000 population (2003 est.)
Nigeria	38.75 births/1,000 population (2003 est.)
Niue	NA births/1,000 population (2003 est.)
Norfolk Island	NA births/1,000 population (2003 est.)
Northern Mariana Islands	19.97 births/1,000 population (2003 est.)
Norway	12.17 births/1,000 population (2003 est.)
Oman	37.47 births/1,000 population (2003 est.)
Pakistan	29.59 births/1,000 population (2003 est.)
Palau	19.02 births/1,000 population (2003 est.)
Panama	20.78 births/1,000 population (2003 est.)
Papua New Guinea	31.07 births/1,000 population (2003 est.)
Paraguay	30.14 births/1,000 population (2003 est.)
Peru	22.81 births/1,000 population (2003 est.)
Philippines	26.3 births/1,000 population (2003 est.)
Pitcairn Islands	NA births/1,000 population (2003 est.)

Country	Birth rate
Poland	10.47 births/1,000 population (2003 est.)
Portugal	11.45 births/1,000 population (2003 est.)
Puerto Rico	15 births/1,000 population (2003 est.)
Qatar	15.68 births/1,000 population (2003 est.)
Reunion	20.17 births/1,000 population (2003 est.)
Romania	10.79 births/1,000 population (2003 est.)
Russia	10.09 births/1,000 population (2003 est.)
Rwanda	40.1 births/1,000 population (2003 est.)
Saint Helena	12.9 births/1,000 population (2003 est.)
Saint Kitts and Nevis	18.45 births/1,000 population (2003 est.)
Saint Lucia	20.93 births/1,000 population (2003 est.)
Saint Pierre and Miquelon	14.62 births/1,000 population (2003 est.)
Saint. Vincent and Grenadines	17.16 births/1,000 population (2003 est.)
Samoa	15.41 births/1,000 population (2003 est.)
San Marino	10.49 births/1,000 population (2003 est.)
Sao Tome and Principe	41.87 births/1,000 population (2003 est.)
Saudi Arabia	37.2 births/1,000 population (2003 est.)
Senegal	36.23 births/1,000 population (2003 est.)
Serbia and Montenegro	12.74 births/1,000 population (2003 est.)
Seychelles	16.89 births/1,000 population (2003 est.)
Sierra Leone	43.89 births/1,000 population (2003 est.)
Singapore	12.75 births/1,000 population (2003 est.)
Slovakia	10.1 births/1,000 population (2003 est.)
Slovenia	9.23 births/1,000 population (2003 est.)
Solomon Islands	32.45 births/1,000 population (2003 est.)
Somalia	46.42 births/1,000 population (2003 est.)
South Africa	18.87 births/1,000 population (2003 est.)
Spain	10.08 births/1,000 population (2003 est.)
Sri Lanka	16.12 births/1,000 population (2003 est.)
Sudan	36.48 births/1,000 population (2003 est.)
Suriname	19.4 births/1,000 population (2003 est.)

Country	Birth rate
Svalbard	NA births/1,000 population (2003 est.)
Swaziland	29.37 births/1,000 population (2003 est.)
Sweden	9.71 births/1,000 population (2003 est.)
Switzerland	9.59 births/1,000 population (2003 est.)
Syria	29.54 births/1,000 population (2003 est.)
Taiwan	12.74 births/1,000 population (2003 est.)
Tajikistan	32.78 births/1,000 population (2003 est.)
Tanzania	39.5 births/1,000 population (2003 est.)
Thailand	16.37 births/1,000 population (2003 est.)
Togo	35.23 births/1,000 population (2003 est.)
Tokelau	NA births/1,000 population (2003 est.)
Tonga	24.51 births/1,000 population (2003 est.)
Trinidad and Tobago	12.74 births/1,000 population (2003 est.)
Tunisia	16.53 births/1,000 population (2003 est.)
Turkey	17.59 births/1,000 population (2003 est.)
Turkmenistan	28.02 births/1,000 population (2003 est.)
Turks and Caicos Islands	23.51 births/1,000 population (2003 est.)
Tuvalu	21.58 births/1,000 population (2003 est.)
Uganda	46.57 births/1,000 population (2003 est.)
Ukraine	9.89 births/1,000 population (2003 est.)
United Arab Emirates	18.48 births/1,000 population (2003 est.)
United Kingdom	10.99 births/1,000 population (2003 est.)
United States	14.14 births/1,000 population (2003 est.)
Uruguay	17.19 births/1,000 population (2003 est.)
Uzbekistan	26.09 births/1,000 population (2003 est.)
Vanuatu	24.26 births/1,000 population (2003 est.)
Venezuela	19.78 births/1,000 population (2003 est.)
Vietnam	19.58 births/1,000 population (2003 est.)
Virgin Islands	15.8 births/1,000 population (2003 est.)
Wallis and Futuna	NA births/1,000 population (2003 est.)
West Bank	34.07 births/1,000 population (2003 est.)

Country	Birth rate
Western Sahara	NA births/1,000 population (2003 est.)
World	20.43 births/1,000 population (2003 est.)
Yemen	43.23 births/1,000 population (2003 est.)
Zambia	39.53 births/1,000 population (2003 est.)
Zimbabwe	30.34 births/1,000 population (2003 est.)

Infant mortality rate

Table 3. Infant mortality rate(deaths/1,000 live births) 2003

Ranking	Country	(thousands)
4	Afghanistan	142.48
85	Albania	37.28
83	Algeria	37.74
163	American Samoa	9.82
219	Andorra	4.06
2	Angola	193.82
114	Anguilla	22.80
121	Antigua and Barbuda	20.90
136	Argentina	16.16
80	Armenia	40.86
190	Aruba	6.14
208	Australia	4.83
216	Austria	4.33
30	Azerbaijan	82.41
104	Bahamas, The	26.21
130	Bahrain	18.59
52	Bangladesh	66.08
156	Barbados	12.72
148	Belarus	13.87
210	Belgium	4.57
99	Belize	27.07
28	Benin	86.76

Ranking	Country	(thousands)
166	Bermuda	9.05
13	Bhutan	104.68
64	Bolivia	56.05
115	Bosnia and Herzegovina	22.70
50	Botswana	67.34
91	Brazil	31.74
129	British Virgin Islands	18.80
151	Brunei	13.50
150	Bulgaria	13.70
17	Burkina Faso	99.78
45	Burma	70.35
41	Burundi	71.54
36	Cambodia	75.94
46	Cameroon	70.12
205	Canada	4.88
72	Cape Verde	50.50
171	Cayman Islands	8.64
23	Central African Republic	93.30
21	Chad	95.74
169	Chile	8.88
106	China	25.26
116	Colombia	22.47
32	Comoros	79.51
20	Congo, Democratic Republic of the	96.56
22	Congo, Republic of the	95.34
161	Costa Rica	10.56
19	Cote d'Ivoire	98.33
183	Croatia	6.92
182	Cuba	7.15
178	Cyprus	7.54
200	Czech Republic	5.37

Ranking	Country	(thousands)
204	Denmark	4.90
11	Djibouti	106.96
142	Dominica	15.34
88	Dominican Republic	34.19
73	East Timor	50.47
90	Ecuador	31.97
87	Egypt	35.26
102	El Salvador	26.75
25	Equatorial Guinea	89.02
34	Eritrea	76.32
158	Estonia	12.03
15	Ethiopia	103.22
186	Faroe Islands	6.52
152	Fiji	13.35
221	Finland	3.73
214	France	4.37
155	French Guiana	12.84
170	French Polynesia	8.78
66	Gabon	55.05
38	Gambia, The	74.93
110	Gaza Strip	24.15
71	Georgia	51.24
218	Germany	4.23
68	Ghana	53.02
202	Gibraltar	5.31
191	Greece	6.12
134	Greenland	16.80
144	Grenada	14.63
165	Guadeloupe	9.07
187	Guam	6.46
82	Guatemala	37.92

Ranking	Country	(thousands)
206	Guernsey	4.85
24	Guinea	93.30
10	Guinea-Bissau	110.29
84	Guyana	37.55
35	Haiti	76.01
96	Honduras	29.96
195	Hong Kong	5.63
172	Hungary	8.58
223	Iceland	3.50
59	India	59.59
81	Indonesia	38.09
78	Iran	44.17
65	Iraq	55.16
201	Ireland	5.34
180	Israel	7.37
188	Italy	6.19
154	Jamaica	13.26
225	Japan	3.30
199	Jersey	5.43
128	Jordan	18.86
60	Kazakhstan	58.73
56	Kenya	63.36
70	Kiribati	51.26
105	Korea, North	25.66
181	Korea, South	7.31
160	Kuwait	10.57
37	Kyrgyzstan	75.34
26	Laos	88.94
145	Latvia	14.59
103	Lebanon	26.43
29	Lesotho	86.21

Ranking	Country	(thousands)
5	Liberia	132.18
101	Libya	26.80
207	Liechtenstein	4.85
147	Lithuania	14.17
209	Luxembourg	4.65
212	Macau	4.42
157	Macedonia, FYR	12.14
31	Madagascar	80.21
12	Malawi	105.15
127	Malaysia	19.00
58	Maldives	60.13
8	Mali	119.20
197	Malta	5.62
189	Man, Isle of	6.17
93	Marshall Islands	31.58
179	Martinique	7.44
39	Mauritania	73.80
137	Mauritius	16.11
53	Mayotte	65.98
112	Mexico	23.68
89	Micronesia, Federated States of	32.39
79	Moldova	41.58
196	Monaco	5.63
63	Mongolia	57.16
177	Montserrat	7.77
76	Morocco	44.87
1	Mozambique	199.00
48	Namibia	68.44
162	Nauru	10.33
44	Nepal	70.57
217	Netherlands	4.26

Ranking	Country	(thousands)
159	Netherlands Antilles	10.71
175	New Caledonia	8.06
192	New Zealand	6.07
94	Nicaragua	31.39
6	Niger	123.64
43	Nigeria	71.35
198	Northern Mariana Islands	5.52
220	Norway	3.87
120	Oman	21.01
33	Pakistan	76.53
138	Palau	15.76
118	Panama	21.44
67	Papua New Guinea	54.84
98	Paraguay	27.71
86	Peru	36.97
107	Philippines	24.98
168	Poland	8.95
194	Portugal	5.73
164	Puerto Rico	9.38
125	Qatar	20.03
174	Reunion	8.13
131	Romania	18.40
126	Russia	19.51
16	Rwanda	102.61
123	Saint Helena	20.70
141	Saint Kitts and Nevis	15.39
146	Saint Lucia	14.37
176	Saint Pierre and Miquelon	7.97
139	Saint Vincent and the Grenadines	15.70
97	Samoa	29.73
193	San Marino	5.97

Ranking	Country	(thousands)
75	Sao Tome and Principe	46.04
74	Saudi Arabia	47.94
62	Senegal	57.57
132	Serbia and Montenegro	16.90
135	Seychelles	16.41
3	Sierra Leone	146.86
222	Singapore	3.57
173	Slovakia	8.55
213	Slovenia	4.42
113	Solomon Islands	22.88
7	Somalia	120.34
57	South Africa	60.84
211	Spain	4.54
143	Sri Lanka	15.22
54	Sudan	65.59
109	Suriname	24.74
49	Swaziland	67.44
224	Sweden	3.42
215	Switzerland	4.36
92	Syria	31.67
185	Taiwan	6.65
9	Tajikistan	113.43
14	Tanzania	103.68
117	Thailand	21.83
47	Togo	68.73
153	Tonga	13.35
108	Trinidad and Tobago	24.97
100	Tunisia	26.91
77	Turkey	44.20
40	Turkmenistan	73.17
133	Turks and Caicos Islands	16.87

Ranking	Country	(thousands)
119	Tuvalu	21.34
27	Uganda	87.90
122	Ukraine	20.87
140	United Arab Emirates	15.58
203	United Kingdom	5.28
184	United States	6.75
149	Uruguay	13.80
42	Uzbekistan	71.51
61	Vanuatu	58.11
111	Venezuela	23.79
95	Vietnam	30.83
167	Virgin Islands	9.00
124	West Bank	20.68
69	World	51.38
55	Yemen	65.02
18	Zambia	99.29
51	Zimbabwe	66.47

Table 4. World Fertility 2003

Country	Fertility rate (children born/woman)
Afghanistan	5.64 children born/woman (2003 est.)
Albania	2.22 children born/woman (2003 est.)
Algeria	2.55 children born/woman (2003 est.)
American Samoa	3.3 children born/woman (2003 est.)
Andorra	1.27 children born/woman (2003 est.)
Angola	6.38 children born/woman (2003 est.)
Anguilla	1.76 children born/woman (2003 est.)
Antigua and Barbuda	2.28 children born/woman (2003 est.)
Argentina	2.28 children born/woman (2003 est.)
Armenia	1.56 children born/woman (2003 est.)

Country	Fertility rate (children born/woman)
Australia	1.76 children born/woman (2003 est.)
Austria	1.41 children born/woman (2003 est.)
Azerbaijan	2.34 children born/woman (2003 est.)
Bahamas, The	2.25 children born/woman (2003 est.)
Bahrain	2.71 children born/woman (2003 est.)
Bangladesh	3.17 children born/woman (2003 est.)
Barbados	1.65 children born/woman (2003 est.)
Belarus	1.34 children born/woman (2003 est.)
Belgium	1.62 children born/woman (2003 est.)
Belize	3.86 children born/woman (2003 est.)
Benin	6.04 children born/woman (2003 est.)
Bermuda	1.9 children born/woman (2003 est.)
Bhutan	4.94 children born/woman (2003 est.)
Bolivia	3.23 children born/woman (2003 est.)
Bosnia and Herzegovina	1.71 children born/woman (2003 est.)
Botswana	3.27 children born/woman (2003 est.)
Brazil	2.01 children born/woman (2003 est.)
British Virgin Islands	1.72 children born/woman (2003 est.)
Brunei	2.37 children born/woman (2003 est.)
Bulgaria	1.13 children born/woman (2003 est.)
Burkina Faso	6.34 children born/woman (2003 est.)
Burma	2.15 children born/woman (2003 est.)
Burundi	5.99 children born/woman (2003 est.)
Cambodia	3.58 children born/woman (2003 est.)
Cameroon	4.63 children born/woman (2003 est.)
Canada	1.61 children born/woman (2003 est.)
Cape Verde	3.77 children born/woman (2003 est.)
Cayman Islands	1.91 children born/woman (2003 est.)
Central African Republic	4.68 children born/woman (2003 est.)
Chad	6.44 children born/woman (2003 est.)
Chile	2.09 children born/woman (2003 est.)

Country	Fertility rate (children born/woman)
China	1.7 children born/woman (2003 est.)
Christmas Island	NA children born/woman (2003 est.)
Cocos (Keeling) Islands	NA children born/woman (2003 est.)
Colombia	2.61 children born/woman (2003 est.)
Comoros	5.21 children born/woman (2003 est.)
Congo, Dem. Rep.of the	6.69 children born/woman (2003 est.)
Congo, Republic of the	3.65 children born/woman (2003 est.)
Cook Islands	NA children born/woman (2003 est.)
Costa Rica	2.38 children born/woman (2003 est.)
Cote d'Ivoire	5.51 children born/woman (2003 est.)
Croatia	1.93 children born/woman (2003 est.)
Cuba	1.61 children born/woman (2003 est.)
Cyprus	1.88 children born/woman (2003 est.)
Czech Republic	1.18 children born/woman (2003 est.)
Denmark	1.73 children born/woman (2003 est.)
Djibouti	5.56 children born/woman (2003 est.)
Dominica	1.99 children born/woman (2003 est.)
Dominican Republic	2.92 children born/woman (2003 est.)
East Timor	3.79 children born/woman (2003 est.)
Ecuador	2.99 children born/woman (2003 est.)
Egypt	3.02 children born/woman (2003 est.)
El Salvador	3.25 children born/woman (2003 est.)
Equatorial Guinea	4.75 children born/woman (2003 est.)
Eritrea	5.74 children born/woman (2003 est.)
Estonia	1.27 children born/woman (2003 est.)
Ethiopia	5.55 children born/woman (2003 est.)
Falkland Islands	NA children born/woman
Faroe Islands	2.24 children born/woman (2003 est.)
Fiji	2.81 children born/woman (2003 est.)
Finland	1.7 children born/woman (2003 est.)
France	1.85 children born/woman (2003 est.)

Country	Fertility rate (children born/woman)
French Guiana	3.09 children born/woman (2003 est.)
French Polynesia	2.14 children born/woman (2003 est.)
Gabon	4.83 children born/woman (2003 est.)
Gambia, The	5.53 children born/woman (2003 est.)
Gaza Strip	6.17 children born/woman (2003 est.)
Georgia	1.51 children born/woman (2003 est.)
Germany	1.37 children born/woman (2003 est.)
Ghana	3.32 children born/woman (2003 est.)
Gibraltar	1.65 children born/woman (2003 est.)
Greece	1.35 children born/woman (2003 est.)
Greenland	2.43 children born/woman (2003 est.)
Grenada	2.45 children born/woman (2003 est.)
Guadeloupe	1.92 children born/woman (2003 est.)
Guam	3.62 children born/woman (2003 est.)
Guatemala	4.67 children born/woman (2003 est.)
Guernsey	1.37 children born/woman (2003 est.)
Guinea	5.9 children born/woman (2003 est.)
Guinea-Bissau	5.07 children born/woman (2003 est.)
Guyana	2.07 children born/woman (2003 est.)
Haiti	4.86 children born/woman (2003 est.)
Honduras	4.07 children born/woman (2003 est.)
Hong Kong	1.32 children born/woman (2003 est.)
Hungary	1.25 children born/woman (2003 est.)
Iceland	1.98 children born/woman (2003 est.)
India	2.91 children born/woman (2003 est.)
Indonesia	2.5 children born/woman (2003 est.)
Iran	1.99 children born/woman (2003 est.)
Iraq	4.52 children born/woman (2003 est.)
Ireland	1.89 children born/woman (2003 est.)
Israel	2.5 children born/woman (2003 est.)
Italy	1.26 children born/woman (2003 est.)

Country	Fertility rate (children born/woman)
Jamaica	2.01 children born/woman (2003 est.)
Japan	1.38 children born/woman (2003 est.)
Jersey	1.57 children born/woman (2003 est.)
Jordan	3 children born/woman (2003 est.)
Kazakhstan	2.16 children born/woman (2003 est.)
Kenya	3.47 children born/woman (2003 est.)
Kiribati	4.28 children born/woman (2003 est.)
Korea, North	2.25 children born/woman (2003 est.)
Korea, South	1.56 children born/woman (2003 est.)
Kuwait	3.08 children born/woman (2003 est.)
Kyrgyzstan	3.12 children born/woman (2003 est.)
Laos	4.94 children born/woman (2003 est.)
Latvia	1.2 children born/woman (2003 est.)
Lebanon	1.98 children born/woman (2003 est.)
Lesotho	3.52 children born/woman (2003 est.)
Liberia	6.23 children born/woman (2003 est.)
Libya	3.49 children born/woman (2003 est.)
Liechtenstein	1.5 children born/woman (2003 est.)
Lithuania	1.43 children born/woman (2003 est.)
Luxembourg	1.7 children born/woman (2003 est.)
Macau	1.32 children born/woman (2003 est.)
Macedonia	1.75 children born/woman (2003 est.)
Madagascar	5.73 children born/woman (2003 est.)
Malawi	6.1 children born/woman (2003 est.)
Malaysia	3.13 children born/woman (2003 est.)
Maldives	5.26 children born/woman (2003 est.)
Mali	6.66 children born/woman (2003 est.)
Malta	1.91 children born/woman (2003 est.)
Man, Isle of	1.65 children born/woman (2003 est.)
Marshall Islands	4.12 children born/woman (2003 est.)
Martinique	1.79 children born/woman (2003 est.)

Country	Fertility rate (children born/woman)
Mauritania	6.08 children born/woman (2003 est.)
Mauritius	1.98 children born/woman (2003 est.)
Mayotte	6.07 children born/woman (2003 est.)
Mexico	2.53 children born/woman (2003 est.)
Micronesia, Fed. States of	3.5 children born/woman (2003 est.)
Moldova	1.74 children born/woman (2003 est.)
Monaco	1.76 children born/woman (2003 est.)
Mongolia	2.28 children born/woman (2003 est.)
Montserrat	1.8 children born/woman (2003 est.)
Morocco	2.89 children born/woman (2003 est.)
Mozambique	4.87 children born/woman (2003 est.)
Namibia	4.71 children born/woman (2003 est.)
Nauru	3.4 children born/woman (2003 est.)
Nepal	4.39 children born/woman (2003 est.)
Netherlands	1.65 children born/woman (2003 est.)
Netherlands Antilles	2.04 children born/woman (2003 est.)
New Caledonia	2.39 children born/woman (2003 est.)
New Zealand	1.79 children born/woman (2003 est.)
Nicaragua	3 children born/woman (2003 est.)
Niger	6.91 children born/woman (2003 est.)
Nigeria	5.4 children born/woman (2003 est.)
Niue	NA children born/woman (2003 est.)
Norfolk Island	NA children born/woman (2003 est.)
Northern Mariana Islands	1.75 children born/woman (2003 est.)
Norway	1.8 children born/woman (2003 est.)
Oman	5.94 children born/woman (2003 est.)
Pakistan	4.1 children born/woman (2003 est.)
Palau	2.47 children born/woman (2003 est.)
Panama	2.53 children born/woman (2003 est.)
Papua New Guinea	4.13 children born/woman (2003 est.)
Paraguay	4.02 children born/woman (2003 est.)

Country	Fertility rate (children born/woman)
Peru	2.81 children born/woman (2003 est.)
Philippines	3.29 children born/woman (2003 est.)
Pitcairn Islands	NA children born/woman (2003 est.)
Poland	1.37 children born/woman (2003 est.)
Portugal	1.49 children born/woman (2003 est.)
Puerto Rico	2.02 children born/woman (2003 est.)
Qatar	3.02 children born/woman (2003 est.)
Reunion	2.53 children born/woman (2003 est.)
Romania	1.36 children born/woman (2003 est.)
Russia	1.33 children born/woman (2003 est.)
Rwanda	5.6 children born/woman (2003 est.)
Saint Helena	1.54 children born/woman (2003 est.)
Saint Kitts and Nevis	2.37 children born/woman (2003 est.)
Saint Lucia	2.29 children born/woman (2003 est.)
Saint Pierre and Miquelon	2.07 children born/woman (2003 est.)
Saint Vincent and Grenadines	1.95 children born/woman (2003 est.)
Samoa	3.21 children born/woman (2003 est.)
San Marino	1.31 children born/woman (2003 est.)
Sao Tome and Principe	5.88 children born/woman (2003 est.)
Saudi Arabia	6.15 children born/woman (2003 est.)
Senegal	4.93 children born/woman (2003 est.)
Serbia and Montenegro	1.77 children born/woman (2003 est.)
Seychelles	1.79 children born/woman (2003 est.)
Sierra Leone	5.86 children born/woman (2003 est.)
Singapore	1.24 children born/woman (2003 est.)
Slovakia	1.25 children born/woman (2003 est.)
Slovenia	1.27 children born/woman (2003 est.)
Solomon Islands	4.34 children born/woman (2003 est.)
Somalia	6.98 children born/woman (2003 est.)
South Africa	2.24 children born/woman (2003 est.)
Spain	1.26 children born/woman (2003 est.)

Country	Fertility rate (children born/woman)
Sri Lanka	1.9 children born/woman (2003 est.)
Sudan	5.1 children born/woman (2003 est.)
Suriname	2.4 children born/woman (2003 est.)
Svalbard	NA children born/woman (2003 est.)
Swaziland	3.92 children born/woman (2003 est.)
Sweden	1.54 children born/woman (2003 est.)
Switzerland	1.48 children born/woman (2003 est.)
Syria	3.72 children born/woman (2003 est.)
Taiwan	1.57 children born/woman (2003 est.)
Tajikistan	4.17 children born/woman (2003 est.)
Tanzania	5.24 children born/woman (2003 est.)
Thailand	1.91 children born/woman (2003 est.)
Togo	4.97 children born/woman (2003 est.)
Tokelau	NA children born/woman (2003 est.)
Tonga	3 children born/woman (2003 est.)
Trinidad and Tobago	1.78 children born/woman (2003 est.)
Tunisia	1.9 children born/woman (2003 est.)
Turkey	2.03 children born/woman (2003 est.)
Turkmenistan	3.5 children born/woman (2003 est.)
Turks and Caicos Islands	3.15 children born/woman (2003 est.)
Tuvalu	3.05 children born/woman (2003 est.)
Uganda	6.72 children born/woman (2003 est.)
Ukraine	1.34 children born/woman (2003 est.)
United Arab Emirates	3.09 children born/woman (2003 est.)
United Kingdom	1.66 children born/woman (2003 est.)
United States	2.07 children born/woman (2003 est.)
Uruguay	2.35 children born/woman (2003 est.)
Uzbekistan	3 children born/woman (2003 est.)
Vanuatu	2.98 children born/woman (2003 est.)
Venezuela	2.36 children born/woman (2003 est.)
Vietnam	2.24 children born/woman (2003 est.)

Country	Fertility rate (children born/woman)
Virgin Islands	2.22 children born/woman (2003 est.)
Wallis and Futuna	NA children born/woman (2003 est.)
West Bank	4.65 children born/woman (2003 est.)
Western Sahara	NA children born/woman (2003 est.)
World	2.65 children born/woman (2003 est.)
Yemen	6.82 children born/woman (2003 est.)
Zambia	5.25 children born/woman (2003 est.)
Zimbabwe	3.66 children born/woman (2003 est.)

Demographic Changes in Transition Countries

The formerly socialist countries of Central and Eastern Europe present a major exception to the broad similarity of demographic trends in developed and developing countries. The rapid decline in death rates that occurred in the 1950s and 1960s slowed down in the 1970s and 1980s. In the 1990s death rates actually increased in Russia and some other transition countries, including Belarus, Bulgaria, Estonia, Latvia, Lithuania, Moldova, Romania, and Ukraine. In 1995 the death rate in Russia equaled the average for Sub-Saharan Africa—15 deaths per 1,000 people—while the average death rate for developing countries was 9 per 1,000 and for developed countries was 8 per 1,000.

This dramatic and historically unprecedented reversal in mortality trends is primarily explained by higher adult male mortality: among older men mainly because of the increase in cardiovascular disease, among younger men because of more accidents, suicides, and murders. Many of these factors can be related to substance abuse—heavy drinking and smoking, which in turn can be linked to worsening living conditions and the greater uncertainty and stress that have accompanied the transition.

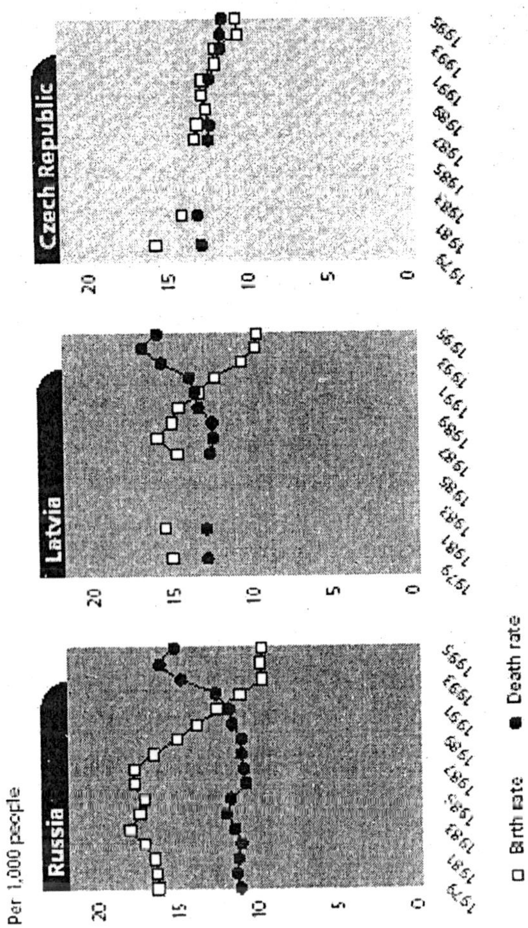

Figure 3. Demographic changes in three countries with transition economies, 1979–95

But rapid economic reforms have not necessarily been detrimental to people's health in all transition countries. For example, in the Czech Republic the death rate has continued to decline, while in Hungary and Poland it has held steady.

Birth rates in the transition countries of Europe have dropped sharply in the past 5–10 years. The reasons for that drop are different from those in most developing countries: they are believed to be closely associated with a lower quality of life caused by the social and economic crisis of transition. As a result fertility rates in these countries are now far below the "replacement level" (equaling slightly more than two children per family) and lower than those in most developed countries.

Because of these unusual demographic trends—increasing death rates combined with dropping birth rates—many of the transition countries of Europe (for example, Russia and Latvia have experienced natural decreases in population.

Population Projections

The 1994 International Conference on Population and Development (ICPD) in Cairo focused the world's attention on the challenge facing all nations as they seek to integrate population and development policies and programs. This section describes trends in population growth and other key demographic indicators over the next quarter century. It summarizes the U.S. Census Bureau's latest estimates and projections of worldwide population, population growth, fertility, life expectancy, and infant mortality. The impact of AIDS mortality, trends in family planning, and the special problem of adolescent fertility also are discussed.

According to Census Bureau projections, world population will increase from its present level of 5.8 billion persons to almost 6.1 billion in 2000 and 7.6 billion persons by 2020. This increase will occur despite a slowdown in the rate of growth— from the current annual rate of 1.5 percent to less than 1 percent over the next quarter century.

Developing Countries Account for Nearly All of Population Growth

About 95 percent of the world population increase will occur in today's less developed countries (LDC's), although they comprise about 80 percent of current population. Because of the more rapid growth in LDC's, the share of world population living in the more developed countries (MDC's) of today will fall from 20 percent today to 16 percent in 2020. Sub-Saharan Africa and the Near East and North Africa are the fastest growing regions—their combined share of world population will increase, rising from 15 percent today to 20 percent in 2020.

Half the World's Population Lives in Six Countries

China, India, the United States, Indonesia, Brazil, and Russia are the most populous countries in the world today, but shifts in ranks will occur over the coming 25 years as some of today's smaller high-fertility countries overtake currently larger ones. By 2020, Nigeria and Pakistan will have joined the six biggest list while Brazil and Russia will have dropped off. Although India will not overtake China in the next quarter century, it will add more people—337 million compared to China's increase of 207 million.

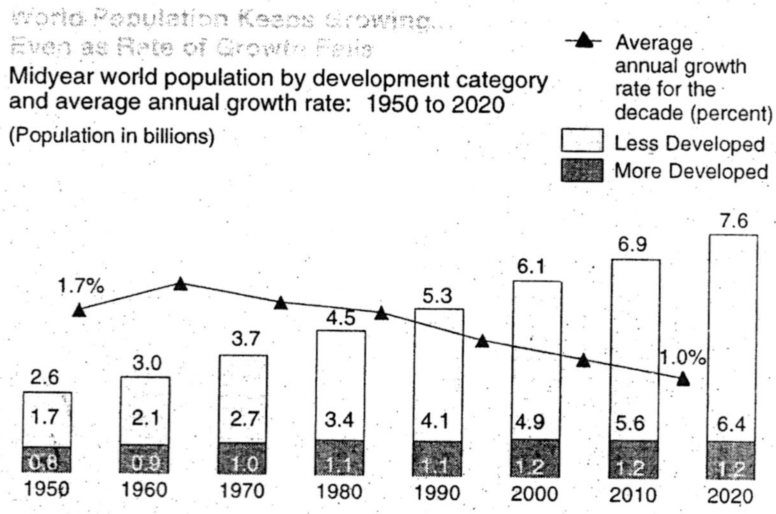

Note: Figures for components may not add to total because of rounding.

Source: U.S. Bureau of the Census, 1996, *World Population Profile: 1996*, tables A-1 and A-2.

Figure 4. World Population Keeps Growing Even as Rate of Growth Falls

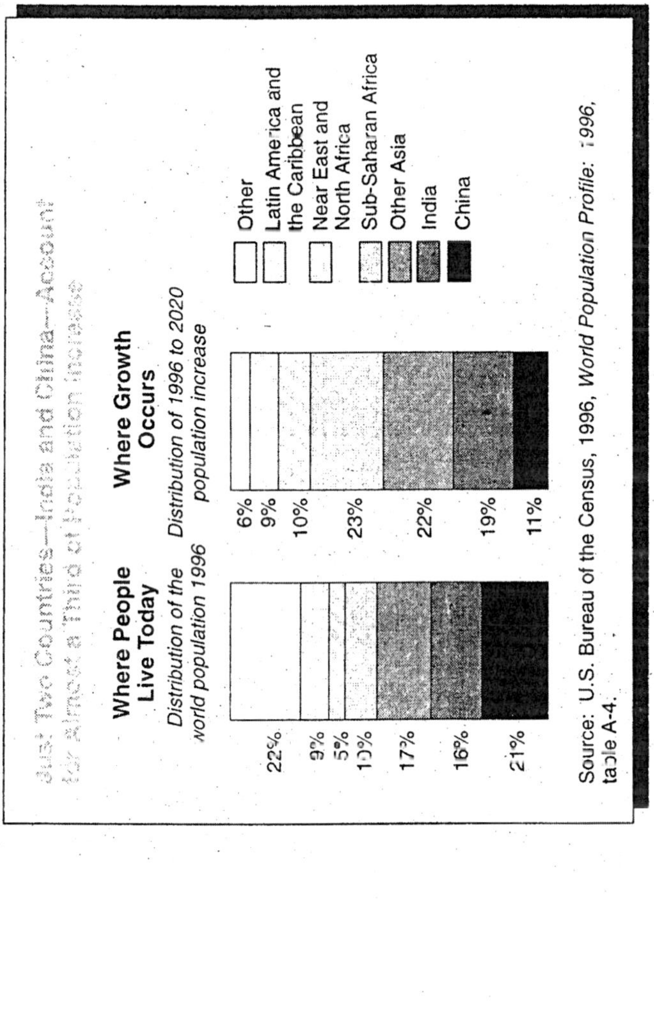

Figure 5.Just Two Countries—India and China—Account for Almost a Third of Population Increase

World Population Grows Even as Births Plateau

The equation of world population growth—births minus deaths equals increase—will result in almost 80 million more people in 1996. While annual births (133 million in 1996) remain at about the same level over the next 25 years, deaths will continue to rise (54 million in 1996 to 64 million in 2020) as populations age. But total population will continue to increase.

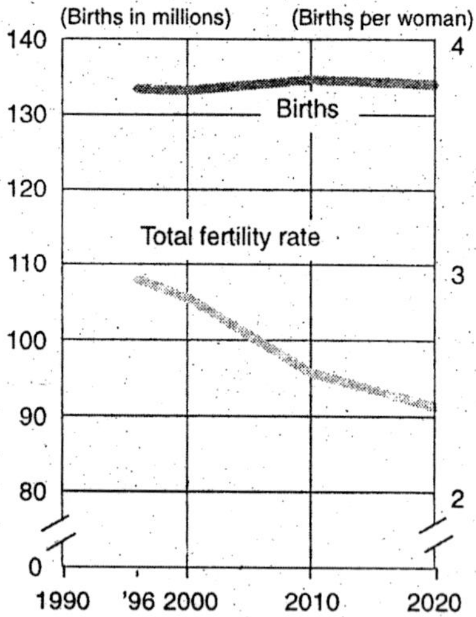

Source: U.S. Bureau of the Census, 1996, *World Population Profile: 1996*, figure 18.

Figure 6. Births Study Despite Falling Fertility

Over 130 Million Births Annually Despite Falling Fertility

For at least the next quarter century, some 132 to 135 million births will occur annually—even though, on average, women will be having fewer children. The steady number of births despite lower fertility reflects the growing number of women of childbearing age (15-49 years), particularly in the developing world.

Percent change from 1996 to 2020 in number of women ages 15 to 49

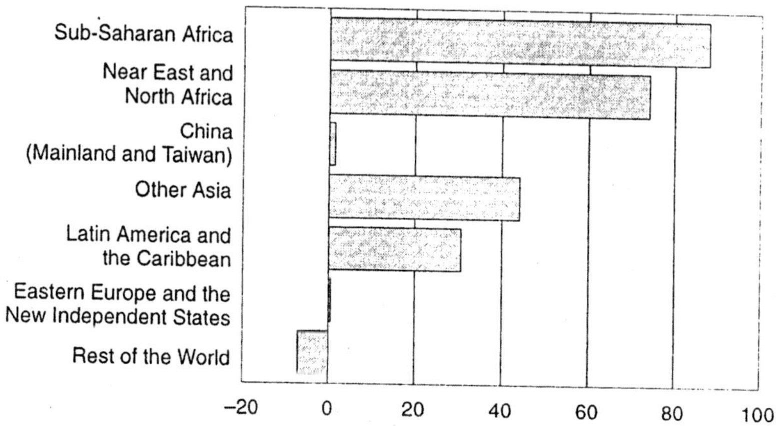

Source: U.S. Bureau of the Census, 1996, *World Population Profile: 1996*, figure 11.

Figure 7. Large Increase in Numbers of Women of Childbearing Age in Most Regions

Just the increase (119 million) in the number of women ages 15-49 in Sub-Saharan Africa is almost as large as the total number of women in these ages in the Near East and North Africa in 2020 (123 million). As a result, the number of births in Sub-Saharan Africa will rise from 25 million in 1996 to 33 million in 2020.

The Gap in Life Expectancy Between More and Less Developed Countries Continues

Life expectancy at birth is increasing in almost all countries. However, the gap between the more and less developed countries will probably narrow only slightly by 2020. Life expectancy in LDC's increases by 6 years to 67, while in MDC's it rises by 5 years to 79.

Table 5. Life Expectancy and Infant Mortality

	Life expectancy at birth (years)		Infant deaths per 1,000 live births	
	2020	1996	2020	1996
World	62	69	60	34
Less Developed Countries	61	67	66	37
More Developed Countries	74	79	11	6
Sub-Saharan Africa	50	55	95	62
Near East and North Africa	67	75	52	20
China (Mainland and Taiwan)	70	77	39	13
Other Asia	60	69	71	35
Latin America and the Caribbean	68	74	40	19
Eastern Europe and the New Independent States	66	73	39	22
Rest of the World	77	80	7	5

Fifty Million Persons Will Die From AIDS From 1996 to 2010.

Population projections of the U.S. Bureau of the Census incorporate the mortality impact of AIDS in 23 less developed countries particularly hard hit by the AIDS pandemic— nearly 2 million additional deaths in 1996, rising to about 4.5 million in 2010. AIDS-related deaths account for about 22 percent of all deaths in these countries in 1996; 38 percent in 2010.

Slowing but Not Halting Population Growth

Even for the 23 countries most affected by the HIV/AIDS pandemic, the total population will continue to grow, increasing at an average annual rate of 1.8 percent (between 1996 and 2010) rather than 2.3 percent. Even at the slower rate of increase, this is still faster than the rest of the developing world.

The World is Getting Older

Between now and 2020, the median age—the midpoint that separates the younger half from the older half of the population—of world population will rise 5 years, from 26 to 31.

The elderly (65 and over) are the fastest growing segment of the population—increasing 88 percent by 2020 compared with a 28 percent increase for the rest of the population. Even in the LDC's, the elderly are the fastest growing age group and will increase from less than 5 percent of the population today to 7.5 percent in 2020.

Table 6. Age Structure of World Population (In percent)

	Children	Working age	Elderly
	0-14	15-64	65+
1996	31	62	7
2020	25	66	9

Urban Population

Urban population is expected to rise from 46 to 58 percent of total population between 1996 and 2020. The most urbanized major region in the developing world is Latin America and the Caribbean (already 75 percent and rising to 83 percent), while Sub-Saharan Africa will increase at the most rapid rate, growing from 31 percent urban today to 48 percent urban by the year 2020.

More Women Everywhere Are Adopting Family Planning

Trends vary considerably around the world, but contraceptive prevalence —the percentage of married women of reproductive age using some method of contraception— has risen virtually everywhere during the past two decades.

Unmet Need for Family Planning is Widespread

Despite growing contraceptive use, surveys suggest that about 20 percent of married women in LDC's are not using family planning despite a desire to limit or space their births. This unmet need for family planning is greatest in Sub-Saharan Africa, where it exceeds 20 percent in almost all surveyed countries and is as high as 40 percent in some (Rwanda, Togo).

From 15 to 48 percent of currently married adolescent women (ages 15 to 19) in each region of the developing world classify themselves as having unmet need for contraception —3 million women in Sub-Saharan Africa, 8 million women in Asia (excluding China and Japan), Near East and North Africa, and 1 million women in Latin America and the Caribbean.

Challenge of Teenage Pregnancy and Childbearing

The need for special attention to adolescents' reproductive health is recognized in the ICPD Program of Action. Pregnancies among adolescents are high risk—these young women are more likely than older women to suffer pregnancy- related complications that endanger both their lives and the lives of their babies.

In some less developed countries, maternal mortality rates for women ages 15-19 are more than double those of women in their 20's and early 30's. Infant mortality rates for teenage births are as much as 80 percent higher than those for births to women in their 20's. And infants born to adolescent mothers face greater risks of low birth weight, prematurity, birth injuries, stillbirth, and mortality than do babies born to older women.

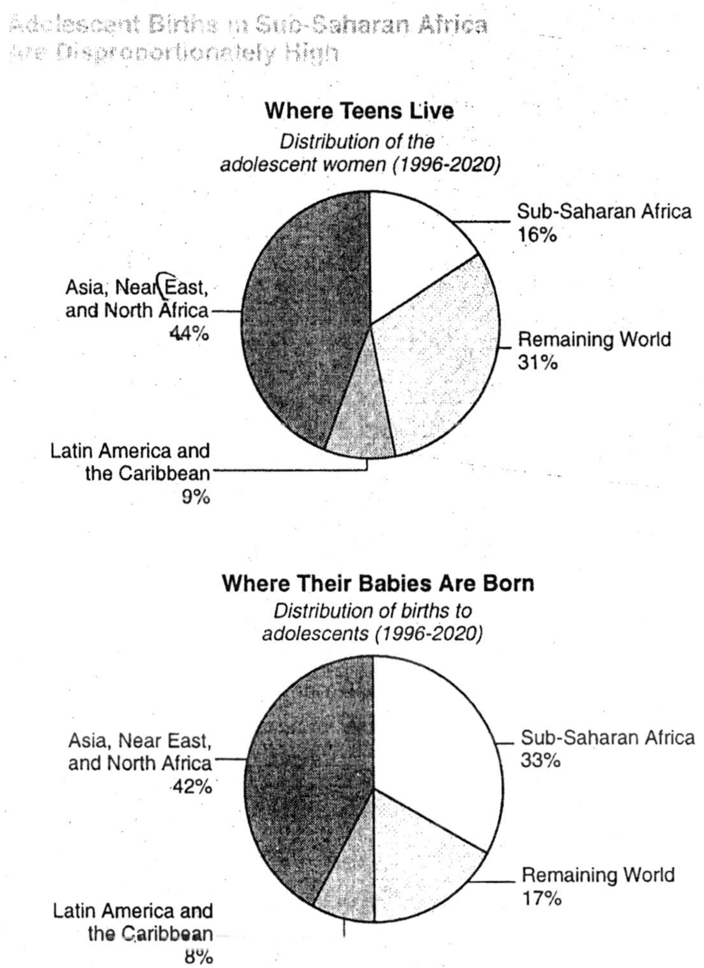

Note: Asia, Near East, and North Africa excludes China and Japan. The Remaining World includes North America, Europe, Japan, Oceania, and China.

Source: U.S. Bureau of the Census, 1996, *World Population Profile: 1996,* figures 49 and 50.

Figure 8. Adolescent Births in Sub-Saharan Africa Are Disproportionately High

Because of their high rates of adolescent fertility, developing countries account for 90 percent of births to teenagers: more than 300 million babies will be born to adolescent women living in Africa, Asia, and Latin America over the next quarter of a century.

Sub-Saharan African adolescent fertility rates are generally higher than those elsewhere. The regional average rate (138 births per 1,000 women ages 15 to 19) is over twice that of the other developing regions. Many European and other more developed countries have rates under 30 births per 1,000 women, although the adolescent fertility rate in the United States (61) is almost equal to the average rate for the developing world (63).

2

Demographic Transition

The 'Demographic Transition' is a model that describes population change over time. It is based on an interpretation begun in 1929 by the American demographer Warren Thompson, of the observed changes, or transitions, in birth and death rates in industrialized societies over the past two hundred years or so. By 'model' which mean that it is an idealized, composite picture of population change in these countries.

The model is a generalization that applies to these countries as a group and may not accurately describe all individual cases. Whether or not it applies to less developed societies today remains to be seen. Before proceeding you should review some demographic terminology or be sure to follow the links given below as the terms arise. The model is illustratedin the next page.

As shown, there are four stages of transition. They will be described first in terms of a typical fully developed country today, such as The United States or Canada, the countries of Europe, or similar societies elsewhere (e.g. Japan, Australia etc.). Stage one is associated with pre Modern times, and is characterized by a balance between birth rates and death rates.

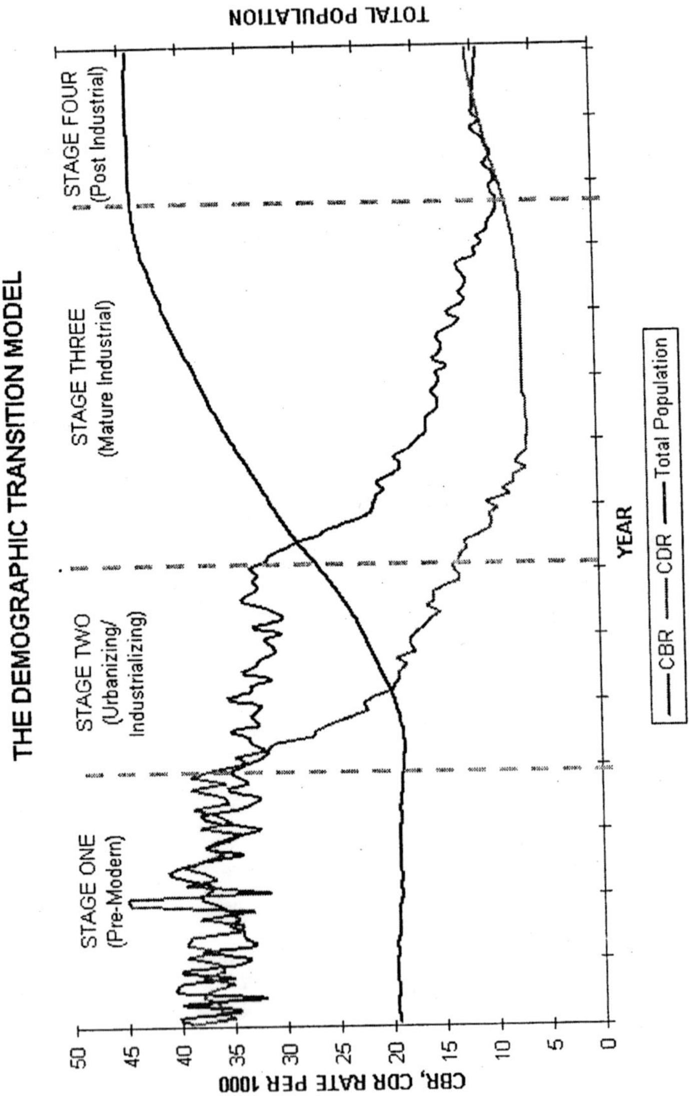
THE DEMOGRAPHIC TRANSITION MODEL
STAGE ONE
(Pre-Modern)
STAGE TWO
(Urbanizing/
Industrializing)
STAGE THREE
(Mature Industrial)
STAGE FOUR
(Post Industrial)
CBR, CDR RATE PER 1000
50
45
40
35
30
25
20
15
10
5
0
TOTAL POPULATION
YEAR
CBR
CDR
Total Population

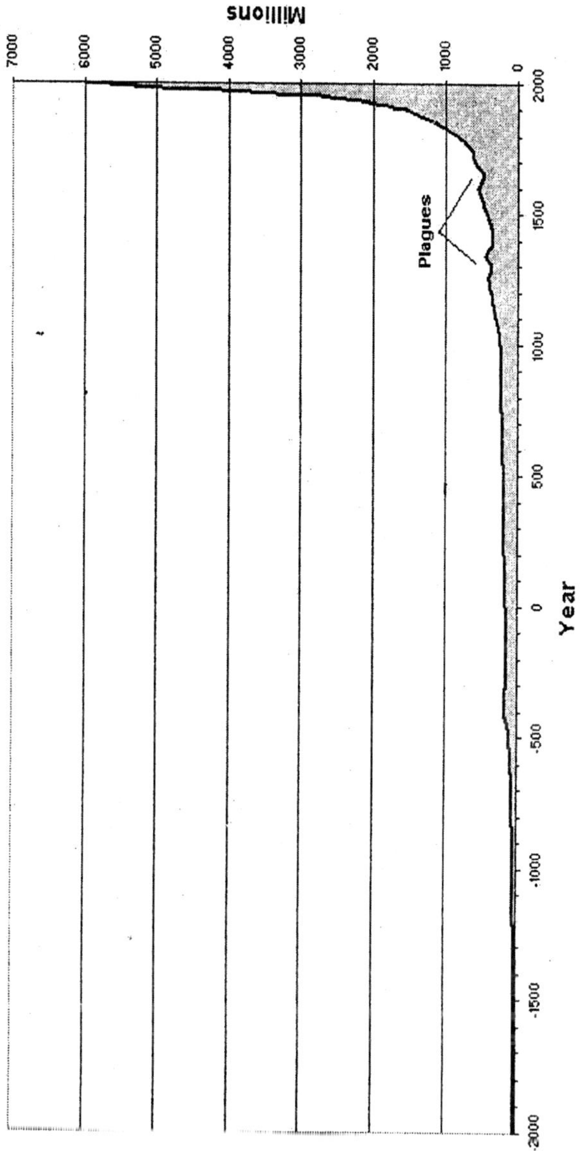
Millions
7000
6000
5000
4000
3000
2000
1000
0
Plagues
2000
1500
1000
500
0
-500
-1000
-1500
-2000
Year

This situation was true of all human populations up until the late 18th.C. when the balance was broken in western Europe. Note that, in this stage, birth and death rates are both very high (30-50 per thousand). Their approximate balance results in only very slow population growth. Over much of pre-history, at least since the "Agricultural Revolution" 10,000 years ago, population growth was extremely slow. Growth rates would have been less than 0.05%, resulting in long doubling times of the order of 1-5,000 yrs.

Given its characteristics, Stage One is sometimes referred to as the "High Stationary Stage" of population growth ("high" birth and death rates; "stationary" rates and "stationary" total population numbers). Death rates were very high at all times in this stage for a number of reasons, including:

— Lack of knowledge of disease prevention and cure;

— occasional food shortages.

Spikes in the rate of death were caused by outbreaks of infectious diseases such as influenza, scarlet fever, or plague. However, on a daily basis, it was primarily the lack of clean drinking water and efficient sewage disposal, and poor food hygiene that created an environment in which only a minority of children survived childhood. Water and food borne diseases such as cholera, typhoid, typhus, dysentery, and diarrhea were common killers, as were TB, measles, diphtheria, and whooping cough.

Today in the developed world, at least, these are now minority causes of death. The high rate of birth (even higher if one were to adjust it for women of childbearing age) could be due any or all of the factors that are associated with high fertility even today in many less developed countries.

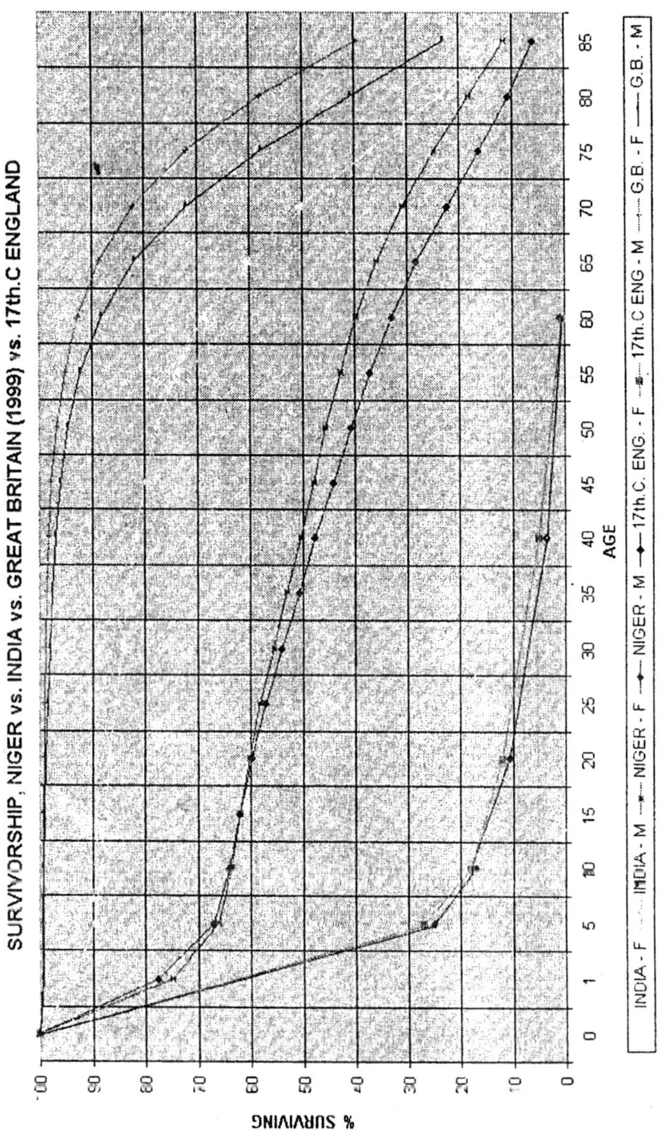
SURVIVORSHIP, NIGER vs. INDIA vs. GREAT BRITAIN (1999) vs. 17th.C ENGLAND
% SURVIVING
AGE
INDIA - F
INDIA - M
NIGER - F
NIGER - M
17th.C. ENG. - F
17th.C ENG - M
G.B. - F
G.B. - M

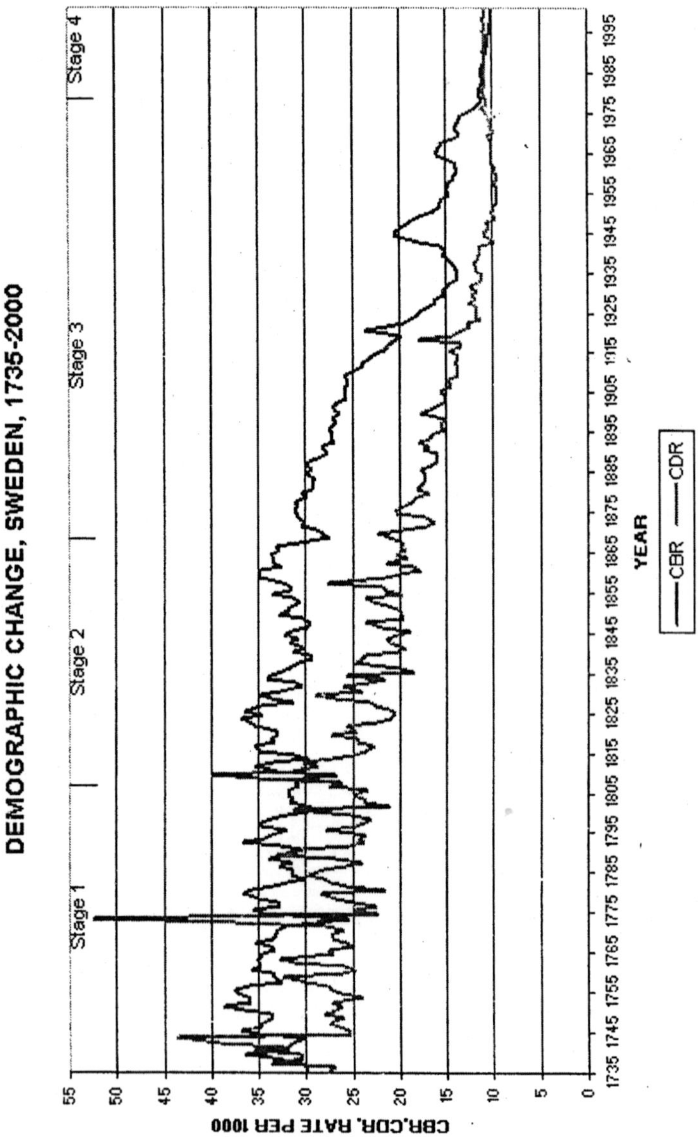
DEMOGRAPHIC CHANGE, SWEDEN, 1735-2000
Stage 1
Stage 2
Stage 3
Stage 4
CBR,CDR, RATE PER 1000
55 50 45 40 35 30 25 20 15 10 5 0
1735 1745 1755 1765 1775 1785 1795 1805 1815 1825 1835 1845 1855 1865 1875 1885 1895 1905 1915 1925 1935 1945 1955 1965 1975 1985 1995
YEAR
CBR
CDR

With a high death rate among children, there would be little incentive in rural societies to control fertility except in the most unbearable of circumstances. Stage One, then, characterizes all world regions up until the 17th.C. Some demographers sum up its character as a "Malthusian stalemate".

Stage two sees a rise in population caused by a decline in the death rate while the birth rate remains high, or perhaps even rises slightly. The decline in the death rate in Europe began in the late 18th.C. in northwestern Europe and spread over the next 100 years to the south end east. Data from Sweden clearly show this stage.

The decline in the death rate is due initially to two factors:

1. Improvements in food supply brought about by higher yields as agricultural practices were improved in the Agricultural Revolution of the 18th.C. These improvements included crop rotation, selective breeding, and seed drill technology. In England, the greater wealth this brought about enabled people to marry earlier, thus raising the birth rate slightly at the same time. Another food related factor was the introduction of the potato and maïze (corn) from the Americas. These new crops increased the quantity of foodstuffs in the European diet, especially in northern Europe.

2. There were significant improvements in public health that reduced mortality, particularly in childhood. These are not so much medical breakthroughs (which did not come until the mid 20th.C.) as they are improvements in water supply, sewage, food handling, and general personal hygiene following on from growing scientific knowledge of the causes of disease.

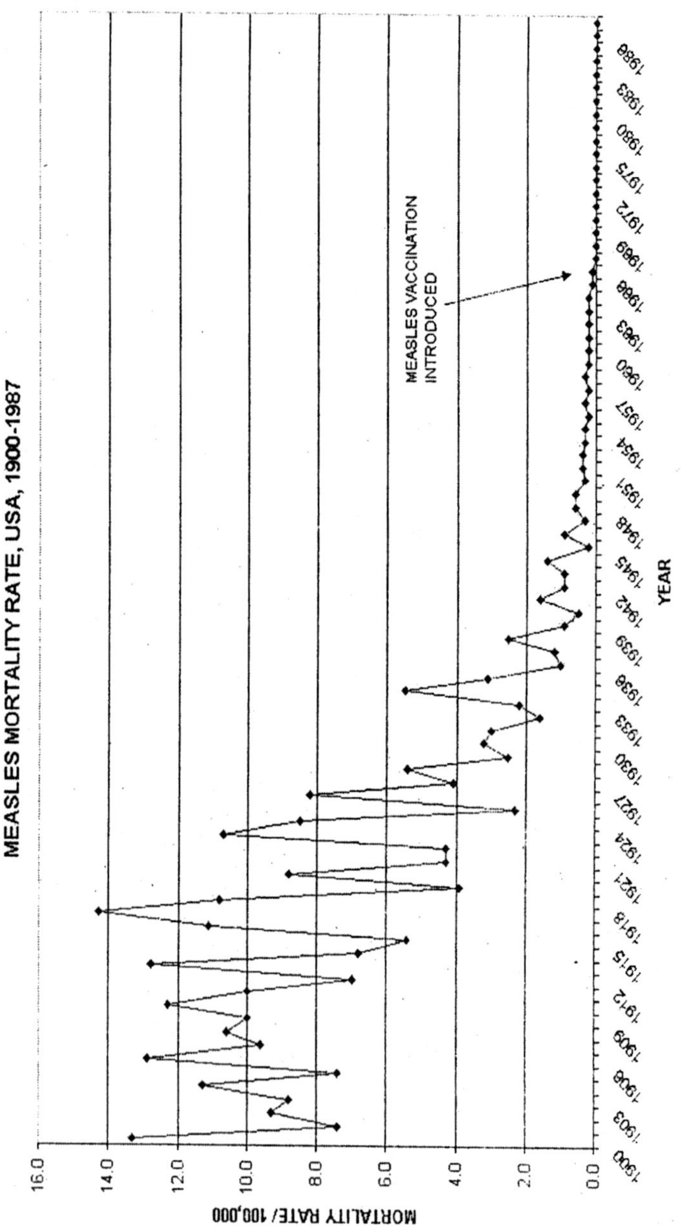
MEASLES MORTALITY RATE, USA, 1900-1987
MORTALITY RATE/ 100,000
16.0
14.0
12.0
10.0
8.0
6.0
4.0
2.0
0.0
MEASLES VACCINATION INTRODUCED
YEAR

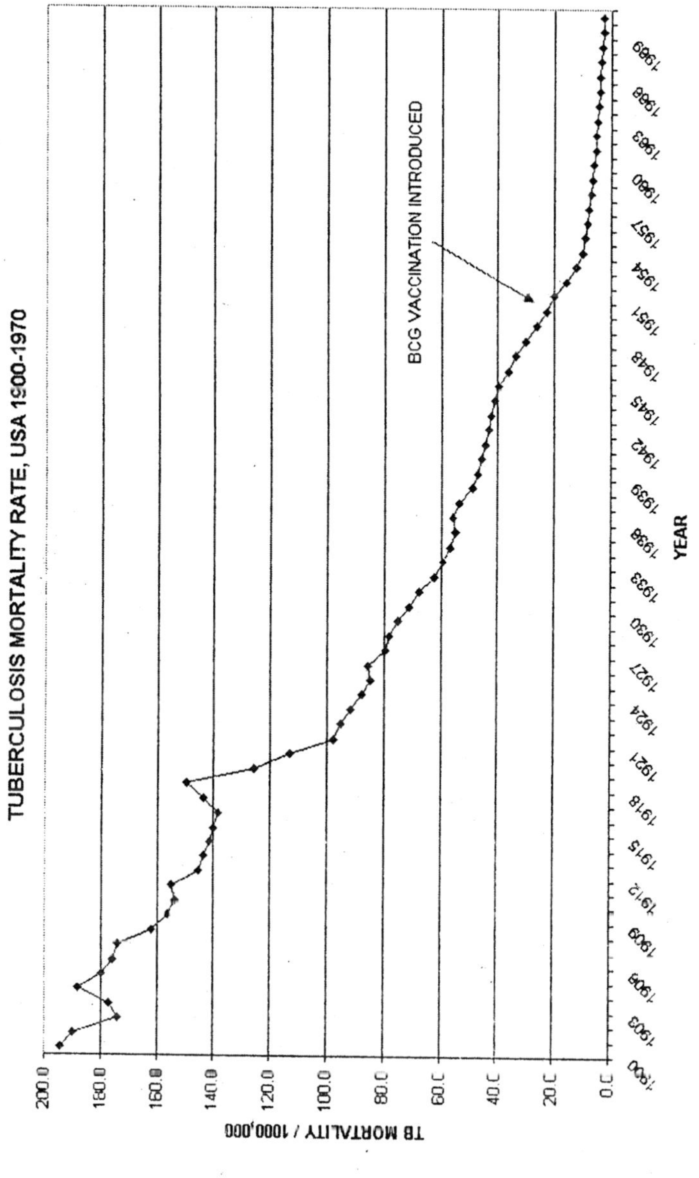
TUBERCULOSIS MORTALITY RATE, USA 1900-1970
BCG VACCINATION INTRODUCED
TB MORTALITY / 1000,000
YEAR
200.0
180.0
160.0
140.0
120.0
100.0
80.0
60.0
40.0
20.0
0.0
1900
1903
1906
1909
1912
1915
1918
1921
1924
1927
1930
1933
1936
1939
1942
1945
1948
1951
1954
1957
1960
1963
1966
1969

> This is illustrated in the previouse page for the case of measles and TB in the USA over the past 100 years. However, bear in mind that killer infectious diseases such as TB are airborne and not water borne, so public engineering works such as sewer and water supply cannot take all the credit. In fact, perhaps the most important factor here was increased female literacy allied with public health education programs in the late 19th. and early 20th. Centuries.

From the relationship between scurvy and measles in England and Wales (scurvy is caused by a dietary deficiency in vitamin C), one could surmise that general improvements in human well-being, an increase in public health awareness, and a decline in poverty was most at work in the decline of infectious diseases. A consequence of the decline in mortality in Stage Two is an increasingly rapid rise in population growth (a "population explosion") as the gap between deaths and births grows wider.

Note that this growth is not due to an increase in fertility (or birth rates) but to a decline in deaths. This change in population growth in north western Europe begins the population rise that has characterized the last two centuries, climaxing in the second half of the 20th.C. as less developed countries entered Stage Two.

Another characteristic of Stage Two of the demographic transition is a change in the age structure of the population. In Stage One the majority of death is concentrated in the first 5-10 years of life. Therefore, more than anything else, the decline in death rates in Stage Two entails the increasing survival of children. Hence, the age structure of the population becomes increasingly youthful. This trend is intensified as this increasing number of children enter into reproduction while maintaining the high fertility rate of their parents.

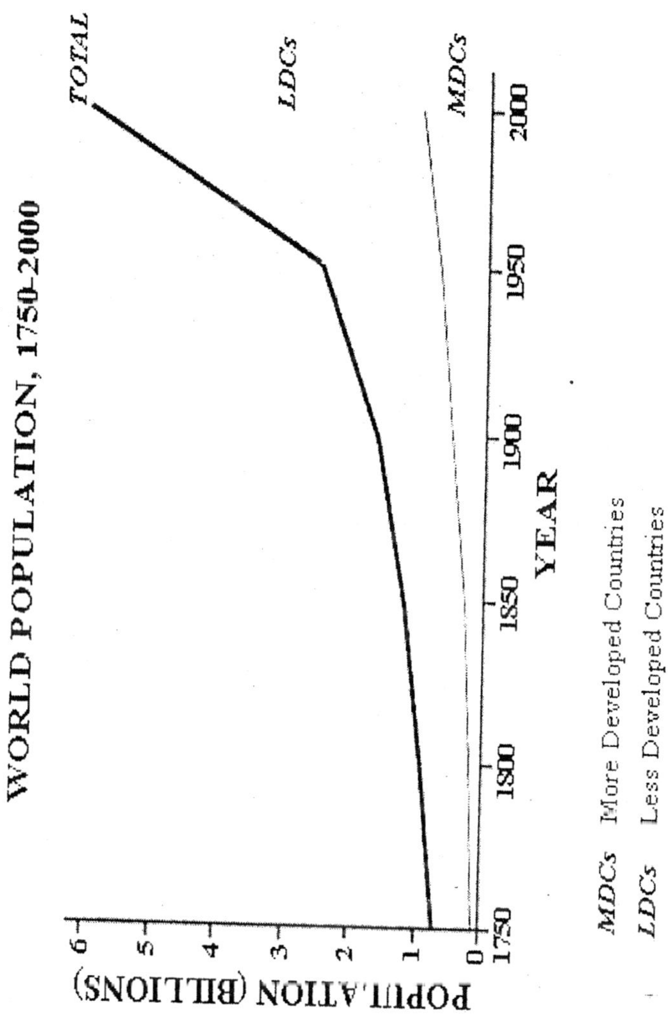
WORLD POPULATION, 1750-2000
POPULATION (BILLIONS)
0
1
2
3
4
5
6
1750
1800
1850
1900
1950
2000
YEAR
TOTAL
LDCs
MDCs
MDCs More Developed Countries
LDCs Less Developed Countries

The age structure of such a population is illustrated below by using an example from the Third World today:

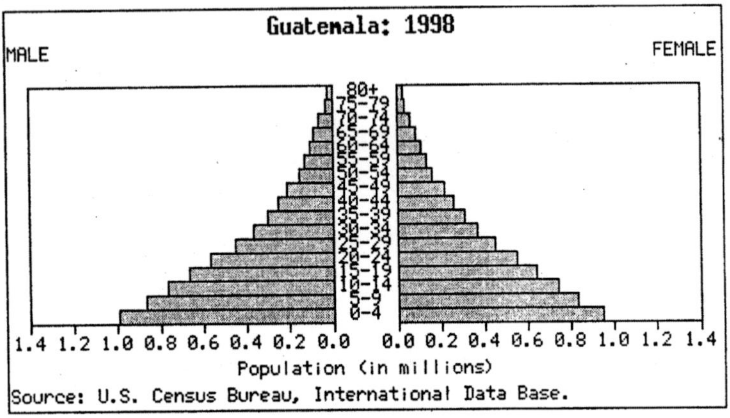

Stage three moves the population towards stability through a decline in the birth rate. This shift belies Malthus's belief that changes in the death rates were the primary cause of population change. In general the decline in birth rates in developed countries began towards the end of the 19th.C. in northern Europe and followed the decline in death rates by several decades (see example of Sweden, in Stage Two above).

There are several factors contributing to this eventual decline, although some of them remain speculative:

— In rural areas continued decline in childhood death means that at some point parents realize they need not require so many children to be born to ensure a comfortable old age. As childhood death continues to fall parents can become increasingly confident that even fewer children will suffice.

— Increasing urbanization changes the traditional values placed upon fertility and the value of children in rural society.

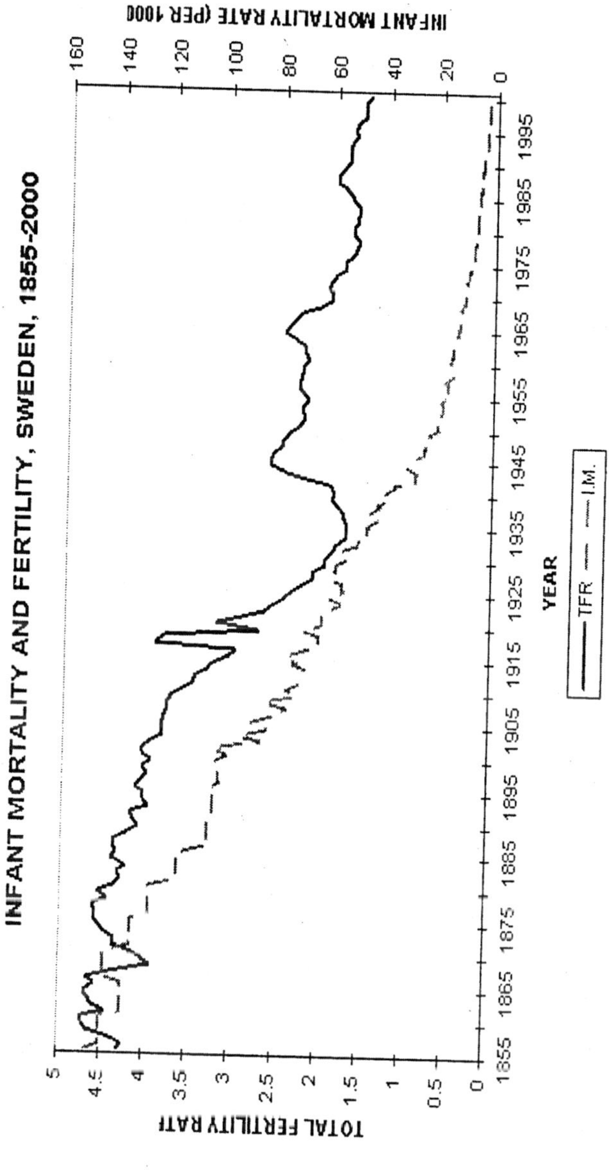
INFANT MORTALITY AND FERTILITY, SWEDEN, 1855-2000
TOTAL FERTILITY RATE
0 0.5 1 1.5 2 2.5 3 3.5 4 4.5 5
INFANT MORTALITY RATE (PER 1000
0 20 40 60 80 100 120 140 160
YEAR
1855 1865 1875 1885 1895 1905 1915 1925 1935 1945 1955 1965 1975 1985 1995
TFR
I.M.

Urban living also raises the cost of dependent children to a nuclear family (education acts and child labor acts increased dependency through the late 1800s). People begin to assess more rationally just how many children they desire or need. Once traditional patterns of thinking are broken the decline is likely to accelerate.

— Increasing female literacy and employment lower the uncritical acceptance of childbearing and motherhood as measures of the status of women. Valuation of women beyond childbearing and motherhood becomes important. In addition, as women enter the work force their life extends beyond the family and the connections they make with other women serve to break their isolation and change their attitudes towards the burdens of childbearing. Within the family they become increasingly influential in childbearing decisions.

— Improvements in contraceptive technology help in the second half of the 20th.C. However, contraceptives were not widely available in the 19th.C. and likely contributed little to the decline. Fertility decline is caused by a change in values than by simply the availability of contraceptives and knowledge of how to use them. Today in the world there exists a close correspondence between fertility and contraceptive use, but this likely means that those families that have chosen to limit family size find contraceptives the easiest and most effective way to do so.

In the following figure, note that once infant mortality had fallen to around 70 (which occurred around 1910 in Sweden -- see figure above), then the fertility rate declines rapidly.

In a similar way, there is a close correspondence between fertility and infant mortality across the world

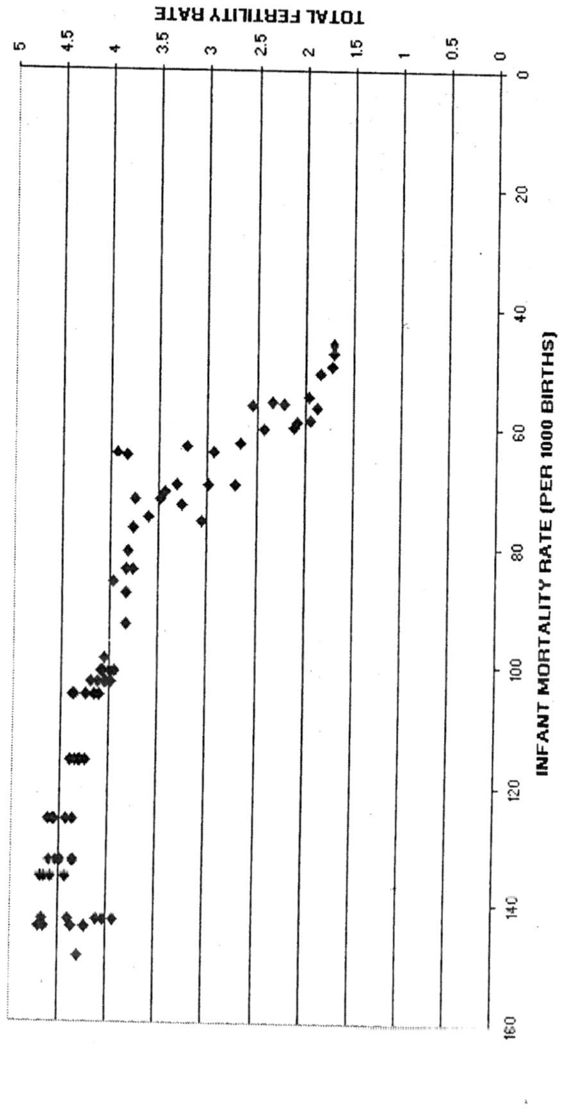

INFANT MORTALITY AND TOTAL FERTILITY, SWEDEN, 1855-1935

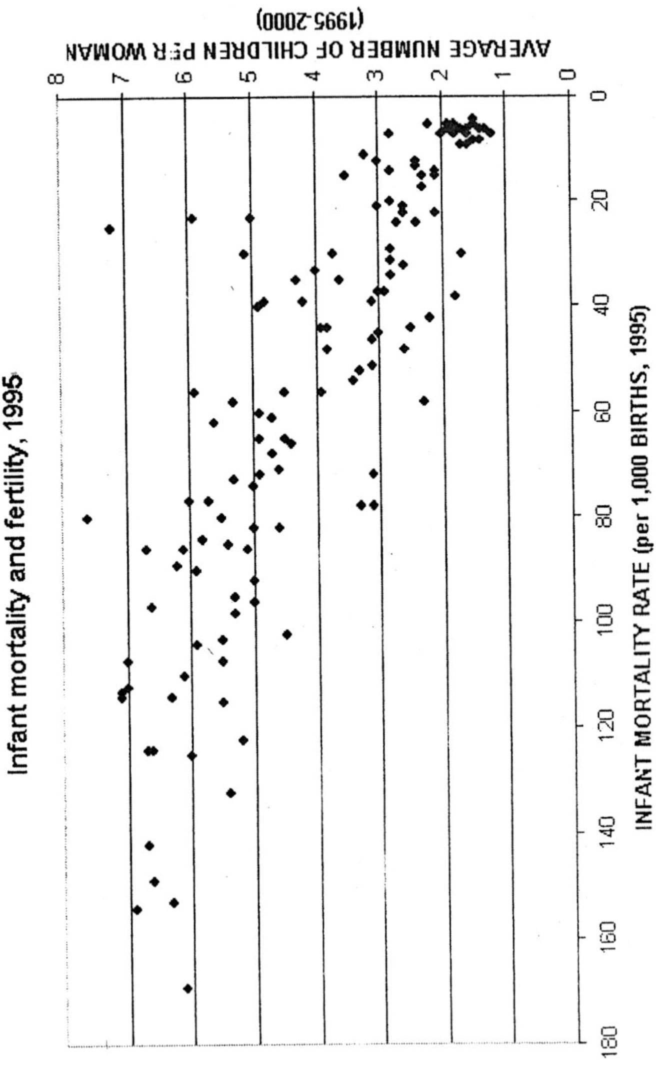
Infant mortality and fertility, 1995
AVERAGE NUMBER OF CHILDREN PER WOMAN (1995-2000)
0
1
2
3
4
5
6
7
8
INFANT MORTALITY RATE (per 1,000 BIRTHS, 1995)
0
20
40
60
80
100
120
140
160
180

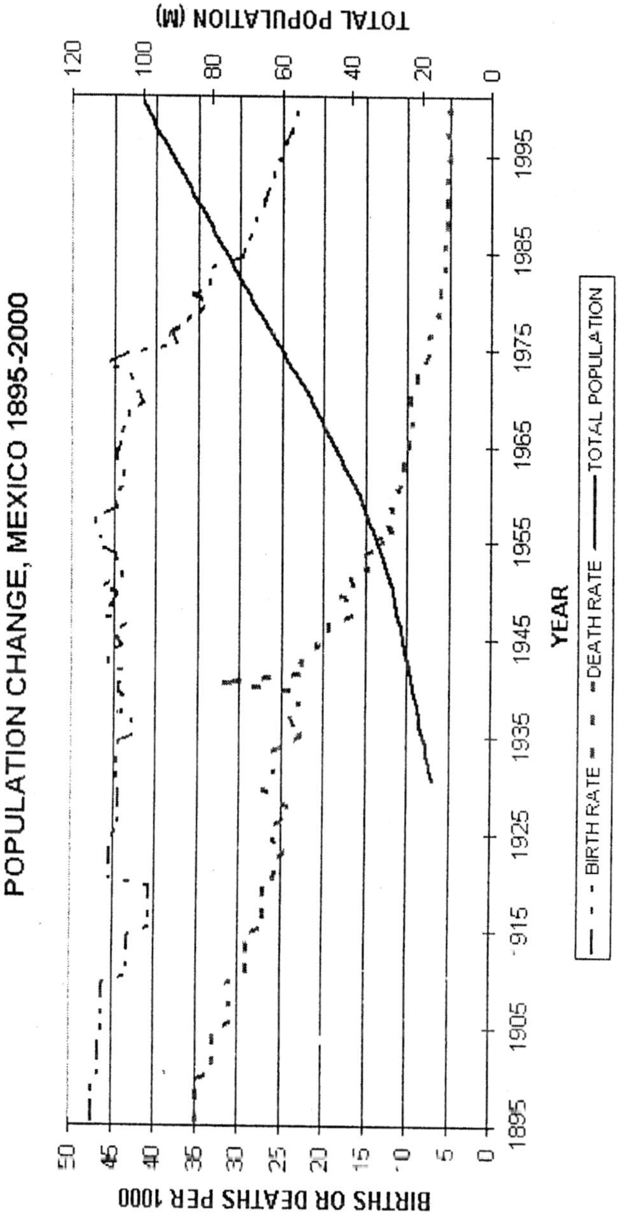
POPULATION CHANGE, MEXICO 1895-2000
TOTAL POPULATION (M)
0
20
40
60
80
100
120
BIRTHS OR DEATHS PER 1000
0
5
10
15
20
25
30
35
40
45
50
YEAR
1895
1905
1915
1925
1935
1945
1955
1965
1975
1985
1995
BIRTH RATE
DEATH RATE
TOTAL POPULATION

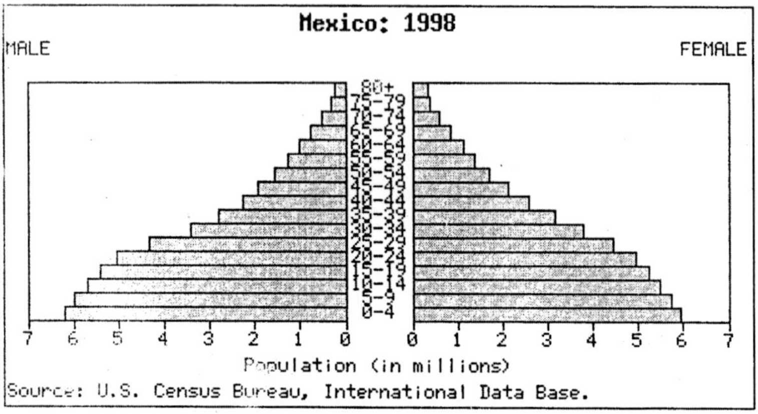

The age structure of a population entering Stage Three is illustrated in previous page by using an example from the Third World today.

In Mexico one can see the decline in growth by means of its increasing impact on the age structure. The youngest base of the population is no longer expanding. At some point towards the end of Stage Three the fertility rate falls to replacement levels.

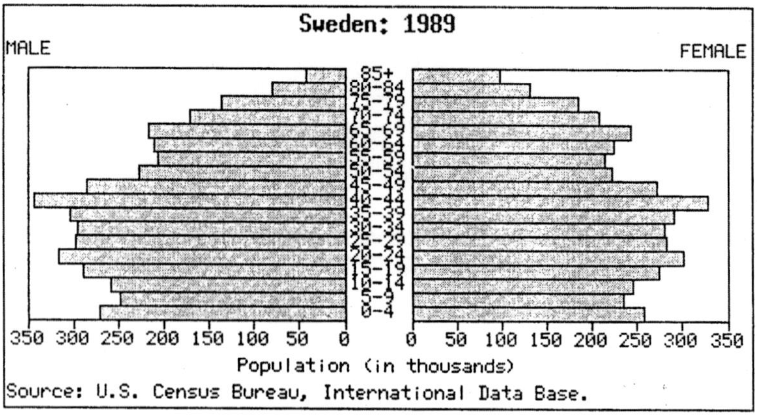

However population growth continues on account of population momentum. This can be seen in the Mexico example, and it is responsible for the continued growth in the population of Sweden in the 1980s. Stage four is characterized by stability. In this stage the population age structure has become older:

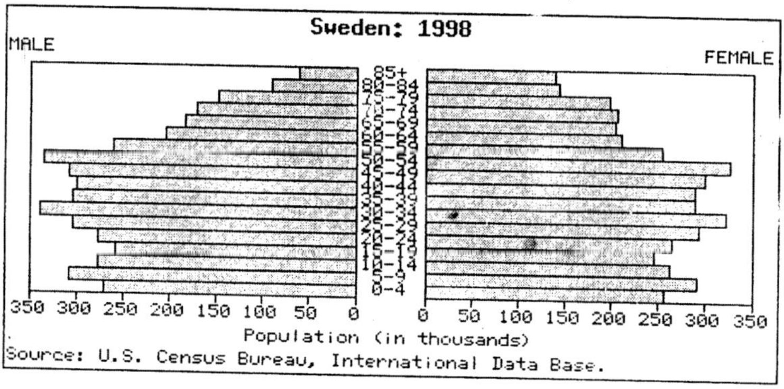

In some cases the fertility rate falls well below replacement and population decline sets in rapidly:

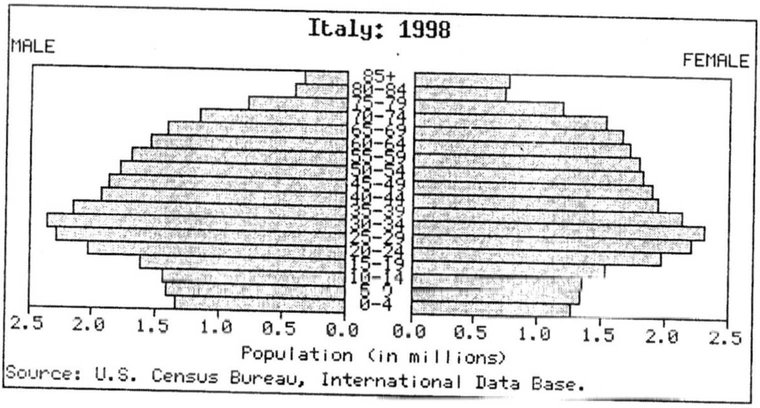

Transitin in LessWell Developed Countries

Mexico and Sweden illustrate the salient differences and similarities between less and more developed countries.

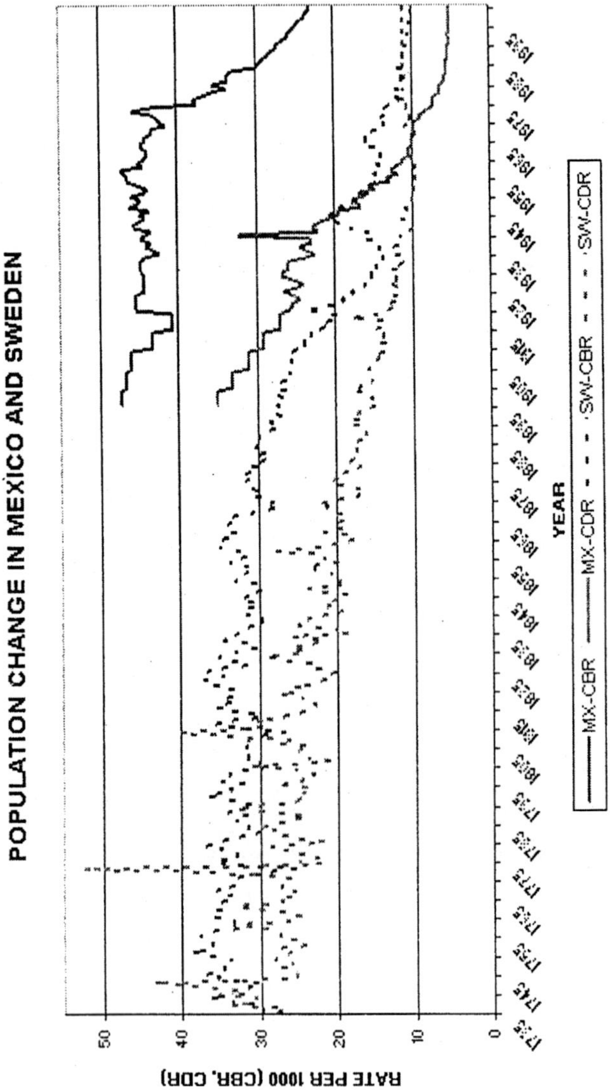
POPULATION CHANGE IN MEXICO AND SWEDEN
RATE PER 1000 (CBR, CDR)
0
10
20
30
40
50
YEAR
MX-CBR
MX-CDR
SW-CBR
SW-CDR

As do Sweden and Mauritius:

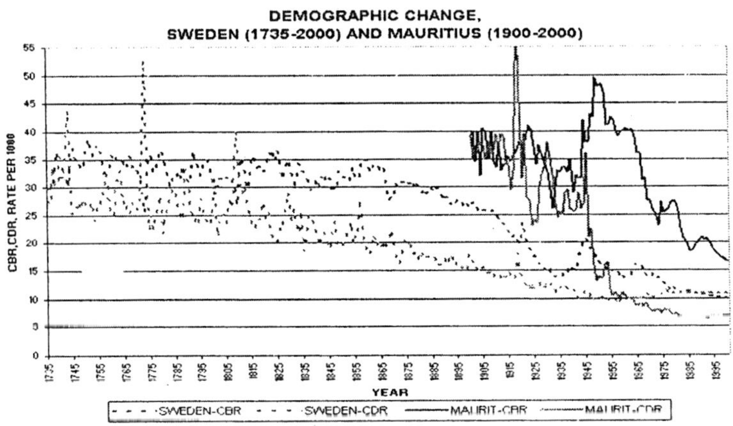

These differences include:

— A later (20th.C.) transition in LDCs.

— A faster decline in death rates (50 yrs. vs. 150 yrs.). Death control has been imported from MDCs and applied rapidly. In most LDCs childhood mortality remains high, but 1/3 to 1/2 what it was 50 years ago. However the most rapid improvements have occurred in places in which female literacy has increased the most. Therefore, it is not simply the application of modern drugs that is responsible but, rather, behavioral changes that have improved survival (e.g. changes related to hygiene). These types of behavioral change are readily adopted because, in so far as they improve survival, they act to support traditional values that favor life over death in almost all societies.

— A relatively longer lag between the decline in death rates and the decline in birth rates (death rates are lower before decline in birth rate starts). Fertility change requires a more conscious effort than mortality change and requires social and behavioral changes that conflict more with traditional values. This has been slower coming in LDCs because economic change has been delayed in many cases. The same economic pressures that existed in urban areas 100 years ago in MDCs have been slower to develop in LDCs because many, particularly in Africa, remain very rural. Hence, attitudes and values have been slower to change.

— Higher maximum rates of growth in LDCs: over 3.5% growth per year at the height of Stage 2 in Mauritius and Mexico, compared to 1.3% in the same stage in Sweden. Also, therefore, age structures are far younger in LDCs. These data yield doubling times of 20 years versus 55 years.

But the greatest similarity concerns the fertility behavior of both populations (at different times) with respect to infant mortality here shown for Brazil, Chile and Sweden:

INFANT MORTALITY AND TOTAL FERTILITY, SWEDEN (1855-2000), BRAZIL (1950-2000), AND CHILE (1960-2000)

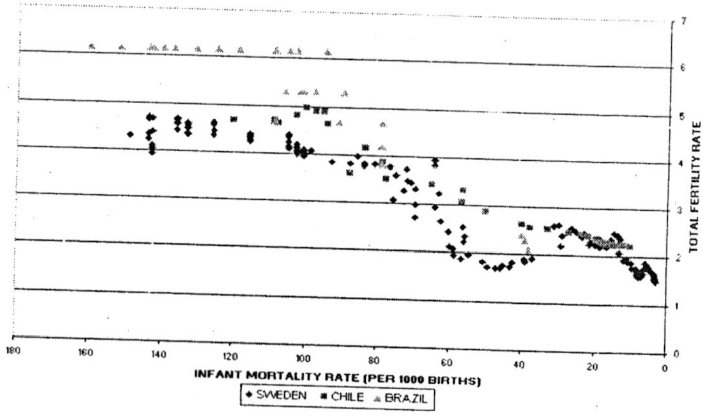

Another Form of Transition

The demographic transition model summarizes change in

population growth over time. Another form of transition exists in the world today and is associated with the differences in growth rates across countries of differing wealth. This is implied by the alternative labels on the traditional transition model (pre Modern, Urbanizing/ Industrializing, etc.).

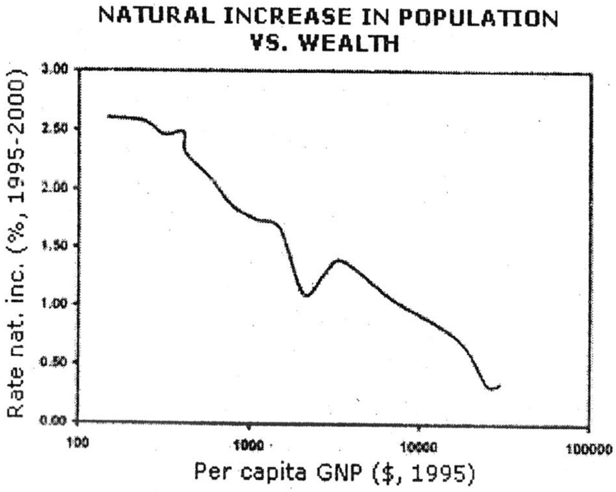

By using these concepts we can then explain the differences we see in population growth rates across the world today.

3

World Urbanisation Prospects

Since 1988 the Population Division of the United Nations has been issuing every two years revised and updated estimates and projections of the urban and rural populations of all countries in the world and of their major urban agglomerations. Each revision of the urban, rural and city projections is consistent with the most recent revision of the estimates and projections of the total population, also prepared biennially by the Population Division. The previous set of urban, rural and city projections was entitled World Urbanization Prospects: The 1996 Revision, to indicate that its results were consistent with the 1996 Revision of World Population Prospects.

However, because the preparation of World Urbanization Prospects can only be carried out once the corresponding revision of World Population Prospects is completed, there is usually a delay of at least a year between the release of the latter and that of the former. That delay allows the preparation of urban, rural and city estimates on the basis of more recent data than that incorporated in World Population Prospects. To reflect this point, this revision of World Urbanization Prospects has been renamed the 1999 Revision. Its results, although based on data on urban and city population growth available up to 1999, are consistent with the size of the total population of each country as estimated or projected in the 1998 Revision of World Population Prospects. The 1999 Revision presents estimates and projections for the period 1950-2030 of the total, urban and rural populations of the world, its 21 regions and five major areas, as well as for the 228 countries or areas of the world. It also provides estimates and projections of the population of urban agglomerations with 750,000 inhabitants or more in 1995 for the period 1950-2015.

To estimate and project the urban population of each country, the basic information needed consists of a time series of the total population and the corresponding proportion of the population living in urban areas. The total population is obtained from the estimates and the medium-fertility variant of the 1998 Revision of World Population Prospects. Estimates for the proportion of the population living in urban areas are obtained from national data sources. The most common source of such information is the population census.

In some countries, population registers or administrative statistics are used by national authorities to produce estimates of the proportion urban. For each country, a time series of estimates of the proportion urban is available. However, reference dates for the estimates available from national sources do not necessarily coincide from one country to another. Furthermore, the series available for each country does not necessarily cover the period 1950-1995. Hence, to obtain comparable estimates for all countries over the period 1950-1995 at intervals of five years, interpolation or extrapolation among the available national estimates is required.

Beyond 1995 projections are carried out using a particular which derives projections of the pro-portion urban on the basis of changes occurring between the two most recent national estimates available by assuming that the pace of growth of the proportion urban declines as that proportion increases. Consequently, the projected values are highly dependent on the most recent recorded ex-perience for each country.

The projections for city populations are carried out in a similar fashion, although more information is required as input. Specifically, the population of a city should be available for at least two points in time together with estimates of the total urban and the total population of a country. The data required are normally obtained from the results of population censuses, although for some countries population registers, other types of administrative registers for the population of cities or the results of suitably expanded population surveys can be used by national statistical offices to provide the required information. Because censuses are normally carried out once every decade, countries requiring updated information on the population of the major cities often produce official estimates of city populations with more recent reference dates.

As in the case of projections of the urban population, projections of city populations tend to be heavily influenced by the most recent recorded change in the size of a city's population. Because city growth is more volatile than that of the urban population as a whole, the projected city populations are less robust than the projected total urban population, especially when long projection periods are involved. For that reason, city projections are only made over a twenty-year horizon (from 1995 to 2015).

The 1999 Revision presents estimates and projections for 488 urban agglomerations that were estimated to have at least 750,000 inhabitants in 1995. This number is 13 per cent higher than the 431 urban agglomerations covered by the 1996 Revision. The difference stems largely from a revision of the number of populous cities in China, which increased from 64 in the 1996 Revision to 114 in the 1999 Revision. The availability of official estimates of the population of Chinese cities referring to 31 December 1996 coupled with the results of the 1990 census of China permitted the inclusion of the additional number of cities.

However, owing to the changes of definition of the urban population that have taken place in China since 1950 and to the rapid growth of certain Chinese cities, especially after the economic reforms that began in 1979, the preparation of consistent time-series of estimates and projections for all major cities of China is fraught with difficulty and, for some cities, the data presented in this volume may require substantive revision as more information becomes available.

The 1999 Revision uses data on urban areas and on cities or urban agglomerations that reflect national definitions. Some countries report both data referring to "city proper", that is, the population living within the administrative boundaries of a city, and to the "urban agglomeration" associated with each city. Because the urban agglomeration refers to the population contained within the contours of contiguous territory inhabited at urban levels of residential density irrespective of whether that population lives within or outside the administrative boundaries of the city, the data referring to the urban agglomeration are preferred as indicators of the population dynamics of urban expansion and of the urban structure.

However, users of the estimates and projections presented in this volume should be aware that the urban agglomerations associated with major cities are often a combination of several cities that are functionally linked but remain distinct from an administrative perspective. For instance, the urban agglomeration of Tokyo, which is today and is expected to remain the most populous of the world, includes the cities of Chiba, Kawasaki and Yokohama.

In the 1999 Revision, data classified in terms of urban agglomeration were used for 106 countries or areas, whereas for 107 countries or areas the only data available were based on the concept of city proper. For an additional 11 countries, the population of the capital city was recorded in terms of the urban agglomeration associated with the capital whereas the population of all other cities was recorded in terms of the concept of city proper.

Key findings of the 1999 Revision are given below:

1. The world's urban population is estimated to have reached 2.9 billion in 2000 and is expected to rise to 4.9 billion by 2030. By mid-2000, 47 per cent of the world's 6.1 billion inhabitants lived in urban areas and that proportion is expected to reach 60 per cent by 2030. The number of urban dwellers is expected to equal that of rural dwellers in 2007 when the proportion urban will cross the 50 per cent mark. In 2000, 4.3 per cent of the world population lived in urban agglomeration of 10 million inhabitants or more (known as megacities). The most populous urban agglomeration is that of Tokyo with 26.4 million inhabitants (table 1), followed by Mexico City (18.1 million), Bombay (18.1 million) and São Paulo (17.8 million). By 2015, the urban agglomeration of Tokyo will remain as the most populous, still with 26.4 million inhabitants, followed by Bombay (26.1 million), Lagos (23.2 million) and Dhaka (21.1 million).

Table 1. Population of cities with 10 million inhabitants or more, 1950, 1975, 2000 and 2015 (in millions)

City	1950	City	1975	City	2000	City	2015
1 New York	12.3	1 Tokyo	19.8	1 Tokyo	26.4	1 Tokyo	26.4
		2 New York	15.9	2 Mexico City	18.1	2 Bombay	26.1
		3 Shanghai	11.4	3 Bombay	18.1	3 Lagos	23.2
		4 Mexico City	11.2	4 Sao Paulo	17.8	4 Dhaka	21.1
		5 Sao Paulo	10.0	5 New York	16.6	5 Sao Paulo	20.4
				6 Lagos	13.4	6 Karachi	19.2
				7 Los Angeles	13.1	7 Mexico City	19.2
				8 Calcutta	12.9	8 New York	17.4
				9 Shanghai	12.9	9 Jakarta	17.3
				10 Buenos Aires	12.6	10 Calcutta	17.3
				11 Dhaka	12.3	11 Delhi	16.8
				12 Karachi	11.8	12 Metro Manila	14.8
				13 Delhi	11.7	13 Shanghai	14.6
				14 Jakarta	11.0	14 Los Angeles	14.1
				15 Osaka	11.0	15 Buenos Aires	14.1
				16 Metro Manila	10.9	16 Cairo	13.8
				17 Beijing	10.8	17 Istanbul	12.5
				18 Rio de Janeiro	10.6	18 Beijing	12.3
				19 Cairo	10.5	19 Rio de Janeiro	11.9
						20 Osaka	11.0
						21 Tianjin	10.7
						22 Hyderabad	10.5
						23 Bangkok	10.1

2. Virtually all the population growth expected during 2000-2030 will be concentrated in the urban areas of the world. During that period the urban population is expected to increase by 2 billion persons (from 2.9 billion to 4.9 billion persons), the same number that will be added to the whole population of the world, which will rise from 6.1 billion inhabitants in 2000 to 8.1 billion in 2030 (table 2).

3. Most of the population increase expected during 2000-2030 will be absorbed by the urban areas of the less developed regions whose population will likely rise from 1.9 billion in 2000 to 3.9 billion in 2030. The urban population of the more developed regions is expected to increase very slowly, passing from 0.9 billion in 2000 to 1 billion in 2030.

4. During 2000-2030, the world's urban population will grow at an average annual rate of 1.8 per cent, nearly double the rate expected for the total population of the world (1 per cent per year). At that rate of growth, the world's urban population will double in 38 years.

5. Population growth in the urban areas of less developed regions will be particularly rapid, averaging 2.3 per cent per year during 2000-2030 and leading to a doubling time of 30 years. In contrast, the rural population of the less developed regions is expected to grow very slowly, at just 0.1 per cent per year during 2000-2030 (table 2).

6. Rural-urban migration and the transformation of rural settlements into cities are important determinants of the high population growth expected in urban areas of the less developed regions over the next thirty years. In combination with the universal reduction of fertility levels that is expected to occur in the future, these

changes will lead to the reduction of the rural population of the less developed regions starting in 2020-2025. That is, as of 2020 the rural population of less developed regions will begin to experience a steady decline similar to that characterizing the rural population of more developed regions since 1950.

7. The rapid increase of the world's urban population coupled with the slowing growth of the rural population has led to a major redistribution of the population. Thus, whereas in 1950, 30 per cent of the world population lived in urban areas, by 2000 the proportion of urban dwellers had risen to 47 per cent and it is expected to reach 60 per cent by 2030.

8. The process of urbanization is already very advanced in the more developed regions, where 76 per cent of the population lives in urban areas. Nevertheless, the concentration of population in cities is expected to continue so that, by 2030, 84 per cent of the inhabitants of more developed countries will be urban dwellers.

9. The level of urbanization is considerably lower in the less developed regions, where 40 per cent of the population lives today in urban areas. This proportion is considerably higher than it was in 1950 (18 per cent) and is expected to rise to 56 per cent by 2030. Consequently by 2030 the less developed regions will reach a level of urbanization similar to that exhibited by the more developed regions in 1950 (table 2).

10. There are marked differences in the level and pace of urbanization among the major areas constituting the less developed regions. Latin America and the Caribbean as a whole is highly urbanized, with 75 per cent of its population living in cities in 2000.

Table 2. Distribution of the world population by urban or rural place of residence, 1950-2030

	Population (in billions)				Growth rate (percentage)		Doubling time (years)	
Major area	1950	1975	2000	2030	1950-2000	2000-2030	1950-2000	2000-2030
A. Population size and growth								
Total population								
World	2.52	4.07	6.06	8.11	1.75	0.97	40	71
More developed regions	0.81	1.05	1.19	1.21	0.76	0.06	91	1 158
Less developed regions	1.71	3.03	4.87	6.90	2.09	1.16	33	60
Urban population								
World	0.75	1.54	2.85	4.89	2.67	1.80	26	38
More developed regions	0.45	0.73	0.90	1.01	1.41	0.37	49	186
Less developed regions	0.30	0.81	1.94	3.88	3.71	2.31	19	30
Rural population								
World	1.77	2.53	3.21	3.22	1.19	0.01	58	5 313
More developed regions	0.37	0.31	0.28	0.20	-0.50	-1.19	—	—
Less developed regions	1.41	2.22	2.93	3.02	1.47	0.11	47	632

B. Urban indicators

	Percentage urban				Urbanization rate (percentage)		Doubling time (years)	
	1950	1975	2000	2030	1950-2000	2000-2030	1950-2000	2000-2030
World	29.7	37.9	47.0	60.3	0.91	0.83	76	83
More developed regions	54.9	70.0	76.0	83.5	0.65	0.31	—	—
Less developed regions	17.8	26.8	39.9	56.2	1.62	1.14	43	61

Asia and Africa are considerably less urbanized, with 37 per cent and 38 per cent, respectively, of their populations living in urban areas. Being less urbanized, Asia and Africa are expected to experience rapid rates of urbanization during 2000-2030. Consequently, by 2030, 53 per cent and 55 per cent, respectively, of their inhabitants are expected to live in urban areas. At that time, 83 per cent of the population of Latin America and the Caribbean will be urban.

11. In Europe and Northern America, the percentage of the population living in urban areas is expected to rise from 75 per cent and 77 per cent, respectively, in 2000 to 83 per cent and 84 per cent in 2030. The increase in Oceania is likely to be smaller, from 70 per cent in 2000 to 74 per cent in 2030.

12. Despite their high levels of urbanization, the combined number of urban dwellers in Europe, Northern America, Latin America and the Carib- bean (1.2 billion) is not as high as that in Asia (1.4 billion), the least urbanized major area of the world today. Furthermore, by 2030, Asia and Africa will both have higher numbers of urban dwellers than any other major area of the world.

13. Asia also has and is expected to have the largest rural population of the world during 2000-2030, amounting to 2.3 billion persons in 2000. Africa, with 487 million rural inhabitants in 2000, is expected to see its rural population rise to 640 million by 2030, remaining the major area with the second largest rural population during the period. Except for Africa and Oceania, all major areas are expected to experience a reduction of the rural population between 2000 and 2030.

14. As a consequence of regional trends, the world rural population will remain nearly stable during 2000-2030, varying between 3.2 billion and 3.3 billion.

15. Although urban areas will encompass an increasing share of the world population, the proportion of people living in very large urban agglomerations is still small. In 2000, 4.3 per cent of the world population is estimated to live in cities of 10 million inhabitants or more and by 2015 that proportion will likely rise to 5.2 per cent. In addition, 2.6 per cent of the world population lives today in cities with populations ranging from 5 to 10 million inhabitants, and the projected figure for 2015 is 3.5 per cent. That is, by 2015, just 8.7 per cent of the world population is expected to live in urban agglomerations with 5 million inhabitants or more (table 3).

16. The proportion of the world population living in smaller cities is considerably larger, though it is increasing at a slower pace. In 2000, 28.5 per cent of the world population is estimated to live in cities of less than a million inhabitants and by 2015 that proportion will likely rise to 30.6 per cent. Consequently, the trend towards concentration of the population in urban settlements with 5 million inhabitants or more has not yet resulted in a marked decline of either the proportion or the number of persons living in urban settlements with less than a million inhabitants.

17. In more developed regions, the concentration of population in urban settlements with less than a million inhabitants is even more marked than at the world level. Thus, in 2000, 48 per cent of the population in developed countries lived in those cities and by 2015 that proportion is expected to be 49 per cent.

Table 3. Distribution of the world population and that of more and less developed regions by size of urban settlement, 1975, 2000 and 2015

Major area	Range of population size	Population (millions) 1975	2000	2015	Percentage 1975	2000	2015
World	5 million or more	195	418	623	4.8	6.9	8.7
	1 to 5 million	327	704	1 006	8.0	11.6	14.1
	Less than 1 million	1 022	1 723	2189	25.1	28.5	30.6
	Rural areas	2 531	3 210	3 337	62.1	53.0	46.6
	Total population	4 075	6 055	7 154	100.0	100.0	100.0
More developed regions	5 million or more	98	112	120	9.3	9.5	9.9
	1 to 5 million	145	219	250	13.9	18.5	20.6
	Less than 1 million	491	571	598	46.8	48.1	49.3
	Rural areas	315	285	246	30.0	24.0	20.3
	Total population	1 048	1 188	1 214	100.0	100.0	100.0
Less developed regions	5 million or more	97	305	503	3.2	6.3	8.5
	1 to 5 million	182	485	756	6.0	10.0	12.7
	Less than 1 million	531	1 152	1 591	17.6	23.7	26.8
	Rural areas	2 217	2 925	3 091	73.2	60.1	52.0
	Total population	3 026	4 867	5 940	100.0	100.0	100.0

Table 4. Distribution of the annual increment of the population among urban settlements of sifferent population size, 1975 to 2015

		Annual population increment (in millions)		Percentage of overall urban increment	
Major area	Type of geographical area	1975-2000	2000-2015	1975-2000	2000-2015
World	Total population	79.2	73.3	—	—
	Urban population	52.1	64.8	100.0	100.0
	Cities of 10 million or more	7.8	7.5	14.9	11.5
	Cities of 5 to 10 million	1.1	6.2	2.2	9.5
	Cities of 1 to 5 million	15.1	20.1	29.0	31.0
	Cities of less than a 1 million	28.1	31.1	53.9	47.9
More developed regions	Total population	5.6	1.8	—	—
	Urban population	6.8	4.3	13.0	6.7
	Cities of 10 million or more	1.3	0.1	2.4	0.2
	Cities of 5 to 10 million	-0.7	0.4	-1.3	0.6
	Cities of 1 to 5 million	3.0	2.0	5.7	3.1
	Cities of less than a 1 million	3.2	1.8	6.2	2.8
Less developed regions	Total population	73.6	71.5	—	—
	Urban population	45.3	60.5	87.0	93.3
	Cities of 10 million or more	6.5	7.4	12.5	11.4
	Cities of 5 to 10 million	1.8	5.8	3.5	8.9
	Cities of 1 to 5 million	12.1	18.1	23.3	27.9
	Cities of less than a 1 million	24.8	29.2	47.7	45.1

In less developed regions, where most of the population still lives in rural areas, the proportion of people living in cities with less than a million inhabitants is 24 per cent currently and will likely rise to 27 per cent by 2015 (table 3).

18. In both the more and the less developed regions, the proportion of people living in large urban agglomerations is low, amounting to 6.3 per cent in the less developed regions and to 9.5 per cent in the more developed regions today. By 2015, the relative increase in that proportion will be greater for less developed regions, where it will rise to 8.5 per cent, a level that is closer to the 9.9 per cent that more developed regions will have at that time.

19. Not only do the largest cities account for relatively low proportions of the world population but in addition their share of the annual growth of the urban population is expected to be moderate. During 2000-2015 cities of 5 million inhabitants or more are expected to absorb 21 per cent of the annual increment in the urban population, whereas cities with less than a million inhabitants will absorb 48 per cent (table 4). In both cases, cities in the less developed regions will absorb most of that increase. Thus the large cities of developing countries are projected to account for 20 per cent of the increase in the world's urban population and cities with less than a million inhabitants in less developed countries will account for 45 per cent of that increase.

20. The increase in the proportion of the population living in large urban agglomerations is mostly the result of a rise in the number of such agglomerations rather than of the rapid growth of the population of most of them.

Table 5. Population and growth rate of the urban agglomerations with more than 10 million inhabitants, 1975-2015

Urban agglomeration	Population (in millions)				Growth rate (percentage)	
	1975	1999	2000	2015	1975-2000	2000-2015
1 Tokyo	19.8	26.4	26.4	26.4	1.2	0.0
2 Mexico City	11.2	17.9	18.1	19.2	1.9	0.4
3 Bombay	6.9	17.5	18.1	26.1	3.9	2.4
4 São Paulo	10.0	17.5	17.8	20.4	2.3	0.9
5 New York	15.9	16.6	16.6	17.4	0.2	0.3
6 Los Angeles	8.9	13.0	13.1	14.1	1.5	0.5
7 Shanghai	11.4	12.9	12.9	14.6	0.5	0.8
8 Lagos	3.3	12.8	13.4	23.2	5.6	3.7
9 Calcutta	7.9	12.7	12.9	17.3	2.0	1.9
10 Buenos Aires	9.1	12.4	12.6	14.1	1.3	0.7
11 Dhaka	2.2	11.7	12.3	21.1	6.9	3.6
12 Karachi	4.0	11.4	11.8	19.2	4.3	3.2
13 Delhi	4.4	11.3	11.7	16.8	3.9	2.4
14 Osaka	9.8	11.0	11.0	11.0	0.4	0.0
15 Beijing	8.5	10.8	10.8	12.3	0.9	0.9
16 Jakarta	4.8	10.6	11.0	17.3	3.3	3.0
17 Metro Manila.	5.0	10.5	10.9	14.8	3.1	2.1
18 Rio de Janeiro	7.9	10.5	10.6	11.9	1.2	0.8
19 Cairo	6.1	10.3	10.6	13.8	2.2	1.7

Thus, the number of cities with 5 million inhabitants or more will likely pass from 41 in 2000 to 59 in 2015. Among those cities, the number of "megacities" (those with 10 million inhabitants or more) is expected to increase from 19 in 2000 to 23 in 2015 (table 1). As is well known, most of the large cities are located in developing countries. In 2000, just 10 of the 41 cities with 5 million inhabitants or more belonged to developed countries and only one more, for a total of 11, will be located in developed countries by 2015.

21. Large urban agglomerations do not necessarily experience fast population growth. In fact, some of the fastest growing cities have small populations and, as population size increases, the growth rate of a city's population tends to decline. However, some of today's megacities have experienced rather high rates of population growth over the past 25 years. Thus, Dhaka in Bangladesh grew at an average annual rate of 6.9 per cent during 1975-2000 and Lagos, Nigeria, increased at a rate of 5.6 per cent annually over the same period. But they are exceptional cases. Among the 19 megacities of 2000, just 7 grew at rates above 3 per cent per year during 1975-2000 and 9 experienced moderate or low growth (below 2 per cent per year). In the future, just 4 of today's megacities are expected to experience growth rates above 3 per cent and 10 will be experiencing very low growth, at below 1 per cent per year (table 5).

Urban Hierarchy

Undoubtedly one of the major changes taking place in the distribution of the world population over the past two centuries is the concentration of large numbers of people in relatively small, highly urbanized areas known as urban agglomerations. Over the course of the twentieth century, the population of certain urban agglomerations grew to levels unprecedented in human history. Thus, it is estimated that by 2000 a total of 19 urban agglomerations had at least 10 million inhabitants each, so that the population of a single one of them surpassed the total population of countries such as Hungary, Portugal or Sweden. For that reason, such populous urban agglomerations have become known as mega-cities.

Yet, despite their size and importance, mega-cities still account for a relatively small share of both the world population and the world urban population. In 2000 the total population in the 19 mega-cities constituted 4.3 per cent of the world population and 9.2 per cent of the urban population (table 6) and, although the number of mega-cities is expected to rise to 23 by 2015, they will jointly account for 5.2 per cent of the world total population and 9.8 per cent of the urban population at that time.

Table 6. Distribution of the Urban Population of the World, the more developed regions and the less developed regions by size of urban settlement, 1975, 2000 and 2015

Development group	*Size class of urban settlement (number of inhabitants)*	*1975*	*2000*	*2015*
World	10 million or more	4.4	9.2	9.8
	5 million to 10 million	8.2	5.4	6.5
	1 million to 5 million	21.2	24.7	26.3
	500,000 to 1 million	11.4	10.5	9.8
	Fewer than 500,000	54.8	50.0	47.6

More developed regions			
10 million or more	4.9	7.4	7.1
5 million to 10 million	8.5	5.0	5.3
1 million to 5 million	19.8	24.3	25.8
500,000 to 1 million	9.4	10.0	9.9
Fewer than 500,000	57.4	53.2	51.9
Less developed regions 10 million or more	4.0	10.1	10.7
5 million to 10 million	7.9	5.7	6.9
1 million to 5 million	22.4	25.0	26.5
500,000 to 1 million	13.1	10.8	9.7
Fewer than 500,000	52.5	48.6	46.1
Least developed countries			
10 million or more	0.0	7.4	6.7
5 million to 10 million	0.0	3.0	10.0
1 million to 5 million	11.3	26.2	26.5
500,000 to 1 million	11.7	9.0	5.5
Fewer than 500,000	77.0	54.3	51.3

Between 1975 and 2000, the number of people living in mega-cities rose at an annual rate of 5.4 per cent, passing from 68 million to 263 million. Most of that increase resulted from the addition of urban agglomerations that had less than 10 million inhabitants in 1975 but crossed that threshold during the subsequent 25 years.

Thus, the number of mega-cities increased from 5 to 19 between 1975 and 2000. The most rapid growth occurred in less developed regions where the number of mega-cities increased from 3 to 15, and the population living in mega-cities rose from 33 million to 195 million. In the more developed regions, the number of mega-cities doubled from 2 to 4, and the population living in them rose from 36 million to 67 million. It is noteworthy that until 1995 there were no mega-cities in the least developed countries and that by 2000 only one urban agglomeration in those countries 'Dhaka in Bangladesh' had passed the 10 million mark.

Over the next 15 years, the number of megacities in the more developed regions will remain unchanged and so will that in the least developed countries, but four additional mega-cities are expected to emerge in the less developed regions.

As a result, the population living in the mega-cities of less developed regions is expected to increase at an average annual rate of 3 per cent per year during 2000-2015, reaching 306 million persons by the end of the period. In contrast, the number of persons living in the four mega-cities of the more developed regions will hardly change, passing from 67 million in 2000 to 69 million in 2015.

In addition, at the world level, cities with fewer than 500,000 inhabitants are the place of residence of the largest share of the urban population and are expected to account for a rising share of the world population. In both the more developed and the less developed regions, the proportion of persons living in cities with fewer than 500,000 inhabitants has been rising, reaching 40.5 per cent in the more developed regions and 19.4 per cent in the less developed regions by 2000. Because that trend is expected to continue, by 2015 a quarter of the world population is expected to live in small cities with populations that do not surpass 500,000 inhabitants.

In the highly urbanized more developed regions, such small cities have accounted for the largest proportion of the population since 1975 and by 2015 nearly twice as many people are expected to live in the small cities of the more developed regions than in their rural areas (503 million versus 246 million).

In contrast, rural areas will likely remain the main areas of residence of the inhabitants of the less developed regions, accounting for 52 per cent of the total population in developing countries in 2015 and having more than double the population of the small cities in the less developed regions (3,091 million versus 1,314 million). Because of the higher level of urbanization characterizing more developed regions, the proportion of their population living in urban settlements of any size class is larger than the equivalent proportion in less developed regions (table 6).

Consequently, to compare the population distribution of the two development group across the urban hierarchy it is better to consider only the urban population. The distribution of the urban population by size class of urban settlement shows that an important change occurred between 1975 and 2000 in the less developed regions. Thus, whereas in 1975 the urban population of less developed regions was somewhat less concentrated in urban agglomerations with at least 5 million inhabitants than that of more developed regions, by 2000 the urban dwellers of the less developed regions were more likely to live in large urban agglomerations than their counterparts in the more developed regions.

Specifically, in 1975, 13.4 per cent of the urban population of the more developed regions lived in urban agglomerations of 5 million inhabitants or more, compared to 11.9 per cent in the less developed regions. By 2000, the equivalent proportions were 12.4 per cent in the more developed regions and 15.8 per cent in the less developed regions; and the difference is likely to be accentuated further by 2015 when an expected 12.4 per cent of the urban population of the more developed regions will live in urban agglomerations with five million inhabitants or more and

17.6 per cent of that in the less developed regions will do so.

At the other end of the distribution, the urban population of the more developed regions has generally been more concentrated in small cities (with fewer than 500,000 inhabitants) than that of the less developed regions. In 2000, for instance, 53.2 per cent of the urban population of the more developed regions lived in small cities, compared with 48.6 per cent in the less developed regions. Furthermore, the more developed regions tended to have a lower proportion of the urban population living in cities with populations ranging from 500,000 to 5 million inhabitants than the less developed regions.

That is, in comparison to 1975, when the urban population of the less developed regions tended to be somewhat more concentrated in urban settlements of smaller size than that of the more developed regions, by 2000 the distribution the urban population of the less developed regions had shifted in the direction of urban settlements of higher population size, a tendency that is likely to continue until 2015 when 44.1 per cent of the urban population of the less developed regions is projected to live in urban agglomerations of at least a million inhabitants and just 38.2 per cent of that of the more developed regions will do so.

The case of the least developed countries, which are part of the less developed regions, illustrates in a more striking way the shift of distribution of the urban population across the urban hierarchy that the process of urbanization entails. In 1975, all the urban population of the least developed countries lived in cities with less than 5 million inhabitants. In fact, 77 per cent of the urban population lived in cities of fewer than 500,000 inhabitants. By 2000 the shift to higher size classes was clear: 10.4 per cent of the urban population of the least developed countries lived in urban agglomerations of 5 million inhabitants or more, and the proportion living in small cities of fewer than 500,000 inhabitants had dropped to 54.3 per cent.

The trend towards a higher concentration of the population in larger cities is expected to continue, though by 2015 still more than half of the urban population of the least developed countries is expected to live in small cities with fewer than half a million inhabitants.

In considering the redistribution of the population across the urban hierarchy it is important to bear in mind that urban agglomerations with large populations are relatively few and their passage from one size class to another causes important discontinuities in the total population allocated to each size class.

Such discontinuities are partic ularly relevant in the case of the less developed regions since, both the number of mega-cities and that of urban agglomerations with populations ranging from 5 million to 10 million inhabitants have changed and are expected to change substantially between 1975 and 2015.

The number of urban agglomerations with 5 million to 10 million inhabitants in the less developed regions, for instance, is not expected to rise steadily although, overall, their number will increase from 16 in 2000 to 29 in 2015. It is also worth noting that the number of cities with populations below 5 million grows rapidly and sharp discontinuities in population size in a given city-size class because of transfers of cities from one size class to the next are less likely.

Urban Hierarchy by Major Area

The differences existing between the distribution of the population across the urban hierarchy in the more developed and the less developed regions are accentuated when major areas are considered. In addition, the situation in Africa or Asia, major areas where the rural population still accounts for a large proportion of the total population, contrasts markedly with that of Europe or Northern America where the rural population constitutes at most one fourth of the total population and the overall level of urbanization is high. Mega-cities, for instance, are not equally distributed among all major areas, nor are they more likely to exist in the most highly urbanized ones.

Thus, only one of the five mega-cities that existed in 1975 was located in Northern America and there were none in Europe. At that time Asia and Latin America had two mega-cities each and among all major areas Asia had the largest number of inhabitants living in mega-cities (31 millionin 2 mega-cities). In 2000, Asia has more megacities than any other major area and the largest population living in mega-cities (150 million in 11 mega-cities). In addition, Latin America has 4 mega-cities, Northern America 2 and Africa, with 2 mega-cities, has become the fourth major area having such populous cities.

During 2000-2015 Asia is expected to continue having more megacities than any other major area and to have the largest population living in mega-cities. Yet the relative concentration of the population in megacities is and will continue to be considerably lower in Asia than in other major areas. Thus, just 4.1per cent of the population of Asia is estimated to live in mega-cities in 2000, whereas 11.4 per cent of that in Latin America and the Caribbean, and 9.6 per cent of the population of Northern America does so. In all major areas small cities with fewer than 500,000 inhabitants have been the residence of the highest proportion of urban dwellers and for Europe, Northern America, Oceania and Latin America and the Caribbean after 1975, the proportion of the total population living in small cities has been higher than that of persons living in rural areas.

In 2000, 47.1 per cent of the population of Europe is estimated to live in small cities, 35.9 per cent of that of Latin America and the Caribbean, 31 per cent of that of Oceania and 29.9 per cent of that of Northern America. In Asia and Africa the proportion of the total population living in small cities has been considerably lower, amounting to 16.9 per cent and 21.5 per cent respectively in 2000. By 2015 the proportion of the total population living in small cities with fewer than 500,000 inhabitants is expected to increase in all major areas except Oceania and the order of magnitude of that proportion for all major areas will be similar to that estimated for 2000. That is, the highest concentration of the total population in small cities will be found in Europe and Latin America and the Caribbean, while the lowest is expected in Asia.

Nevertheless, Asia is expected to experience one of the fastest rates of population growth in the cities with fewer than 500,000 inhabitants (2 per cent per year during 2000-2015), second only to that expected for small cities in Africa (3 per cent per year). Despite such rapid growth in the population of small cities, in both Africa and Asia the proportion of the population living in rural areas and the number of inhabitants of rural areas will be more than double those of persons living in small cities by 2015. Such a situation will contrast markedly with that of other major areas where the population of sma ll cities will generally surpass by wide margins the number of persons living in rural areas.

The distribution of the urban population by size class of urban settlement shows the varied profiles and trends experienced by the different major areas. Among the most urbanized major areas, Europe is characterized by an urban structure where the majority of the urban population (at least 63 per cent) lives in small cities with fewer than 500,000 inhabitants and where there has been a tendency for cities with populations ranging from 1 million to 5 million inhabitants to attract a growing share of the urban population to the detriment of larger cities. Furthermore, the number of large urban agglomerations (with more than 5 million inhabitants) in Europe has been small and constant since 1975 (there are only 5 in the continent).

In comparison with Europe, both Northern America and Latin America and the Caribbean have experienced a reduction of the proportion of the urban population living in small cities that has been accompanied by a higher concentration of the population in medium-sized cities, particularly those with populations ranging from 1 million to 5 million inhabitants, and in mega-cities. Furthermore, between 1975 and 2000 the proportion of the urban population in urban agglomerations with populations ranging from 5 million to 10 million inhabitants declined markedly in both major areas, partly as a result of the transfer of one or two agglomerations in this category to that of mega-cities (i.e. urban agglomerations with 10 million inhabitants or more).

During 2000-2015, Northern America is expected to experience a slight increase in the proportion of the urban population living in small cities with fewer than 500,000 inhabitants and declines in the proportions living in cities with 500,000 to 5 million inhabitants and in mega-cities. There will also be a rise in the proportion living in cities with populations of 5 million to 10 million inhabitants. In

Latin America and the Caribbean the distribution of the urban population will continue to shift towards a somewhat greater concentration in agglomerations with populations ranging from 1 million to 10 million inhabitants. Such increases will be counterbalanced by a reduction of the proportions of people living in cities with fewer than 1 million inhabitants and in mega-cities.

Asia has been experiencing a redistribution of the urban population towards greater concentration in larger urban agglomerations and partic ularly in mega-cities. Thus, the proportion of the urban population living in cities with fewer than one million inhabitants has been declining, while there has been a steady increase in the proportion living in urban agglomerations with populations ranging from 1 million to 5 million inhabitants and in those with more than 10 million inhabitants.

The reduction in the proportion living in urban agglomerations with 5 million to 10 million inhabitants is likely to be reversed in the future as the shift towards a greater concentration of the urban population in large agglomerations continues.

In Africa a similar trend is noticeable, particularly if one considers jointly the proportions of the urban population living in urban agglomerations with 5 million to 10 million inhabitants and that living in mega-cities. The overall proportion of the urban population in those agglomerations has increased from 5 per cent in 1975 to 9.8 per cent in 2000 and is projected to reach 12.4 per cent in 2015. There will also be a significant increase in the proportion of persons living in urban agglomerations with 1 million to 5 million inhabitants, whereas the proportion of people living in cities with less than 1 million inhabitants has been declining and is expected to experience further reductions by 2015.

For Oceania, the changes observed in the distribution of the urban population by size class are difficult to interpret because they are affected by the small number of cities in that major area and the discontinuities associated with the transfer of cities from one category to the next.

Those six cities account today for 55.9 per cent of the urban population of Oceania and are expected to have 51.5 per cent of the corresponding population in 2015. By 2015, Asia is expected to have 267 cities of that size, followed by Europe, Africa and Latin America and the Caribbean, each with slightly more than 60 cities in that category, and then by Northern America with 44. These numbers contrast markedly with the number of urban agglomerations with 5 million inhabitants or more that either exist today or are expected in the near future. Asia, with the highest number of such large cities, has today 23 urban agglomerations with more than 5 million inhabitants, 11 of which are mega-cities. By 2015, it is expected to have 35 agglomerations of that size, 15 of which will be mega-cities.

All other major areas have today and are expected to have in 2015 less than 10 large urban agglomerations each. Latin America and the Caribbean has 7 agglomerations with more than 5 million inhabitants today and is expected to have 9 by 2015; Northern America has 3 and is expected to have 4 in fifteen years;

distribution of the Urban Increment by City Size

Further proof of the importance of those two groups of urban settlements, namely, cities with fewer than 500,000 inhabitants and those with populations ranging from 1 million to 5 million inhabitants, can be obta ined by considering the distribution of the average annual increment of the urban population among cities or urban agglomerations grouped by size class. Also displayed is the distribution of the annual increment of the urban population by size of urban settlement.

Two types of distributions are presented. The first is the distribution of the urban increment for each development group (i.e. the percentages add to 100 for each development group, namely, the world, the more developed regions and the less developed regions). The second is the distribution of the world's urban increment among the urban agglomerations of the more developed regions and those of the less developed regions by size of urban settlement.

Both distributions show the same overall traits: at the world level, small cities with fewer than 500,000 inhabitants have absorbed and are expected to absorb the largest share of the annual increment of the world urban population: 44.3 per cent during 1975-2000 and 40.3 per cent during 2000-2015. They are followed by cities with populations ranging between 1 million and 5 million inhabitants that accounted for 29 per cent of the annual urban increment during 1975-2000 and are ex-pected to account for 31 per cent during 2000-2015. Mega-cities had the third largest share, absorbing 14.9 per cent of the annual urban increment during 1975-2000 and 11.5 per cent during 2000-2015.

The same pattern in the distribution of the average annual urban increment is found in the less developed regions, where small cities with fewer than 500,000 inhabitants have absorbed a considerably larger share of the urban increment than cities with populations ranging from 1 million to 5 million inhabitants and the latter have had a larger share than mega-cities. In the more developed regions, in contrast, cities with populations ranging from 1 million to 5 million inhabitants have absorbed and are expected to absorb a higher share of the average annual urban increment than small cities with fewer than 500,000 inhabitants (43.7 per cent versus 34.9 per cent during 1975-2000 and 46.8 per cent versus 33.7 per cent during 2000-2015). Furthermore, whereas the mega-cities of the more developed regions had the third largest share of the annual urban increment during 1975-2000 (18.7 per cent), over the next fifteen years their share of the annual urban increment is expected to decline markedly so that the third largest share will go to cities with populations ranging from 5 million to 10 million inhabitants.

The distribution of the overall urban increment among more developed and less developed regions shows that the latter have absorbed and are expected to absorb the major share of the urban increment of the world population, amounting to 87 per cent during 1975-2000 and 93.3 per cent during 2000-2015. Consequently, small cities in the less developed regions have recorded the greatest gains in population among all groups of urban settlements, having absorbed 39.8 per cent of the world urban increment during 1975-2000 and being expected to absorb 38.2 per cent during the next fifteen years (figure 1).

They are followed by cities with populations ranging from 1 million to 5 million inhabitants in the less developed regions whose share of the overall annual urban increment was 23.3 per cent in 1975-2000 and is expected to rise to 27.9 per cent in 2000-2015. Lastly, the mega-cities of the less developed regions account for the third largest share of the overall urban increment, absorbing 12.5 per cent of it in 1975-2000 and an expected 11.4 per cent during 2000-2015. In fact, in the less developed regions the next fifteen years are expected to witness a greater concentration of urban growth in cities with populations ranging from 1 million to 10 million inhabitants than in cities with more than 10 million inhabitants.

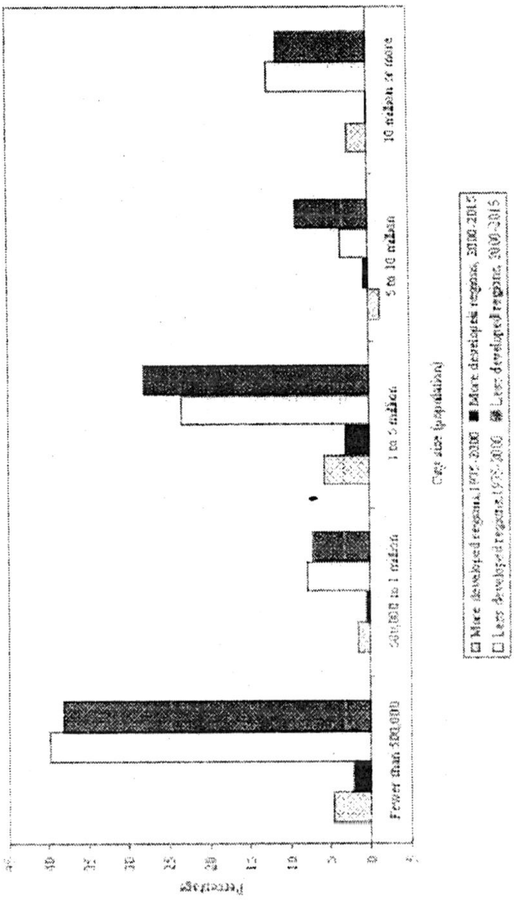

Figure 1. Percentage distribution of the overall annual urban increment among categories of urban settlements by size and development group, 1975-2000 and 2000-2015

In comparison with the cities of the less developed regions, those of the more developed regions will record very low population increases, especially because their overall share of the annual urban increment is expected to decline from 13 per cent during 1975-2000 to 6.7 per cent during 2000-2015. As already noted, the largest relative increases will be absorbed by cities with populations ranging from 1 million to 5 million inhabitants, but the magnitude of those gains will be small since they amount to 5.7 per cent of the overall urban increment during 1975-2000 and to just 3.1 per cent of that increment during 2000-2015. Small cities with fewer than 500,000 inhabitants, which have absorbed and are expected to absorb the second largest share of the overall urban increment among cities in the more developed regions, have recorded increases equivalent of 4.5 per cent of the global urban increment during 1975-2000 and will likely absorb just 2.3 per cent of the urban increment expected during 2000-2015.

These projections indicate that among all cities in the world, the small cities of developing countries (with fewer than 500,000 inhabitants) and the cities with populations ranging between 1 million and 5 million inhabitants in the less developed regions are the most likely to absorb the highest share of the annual increment of the world urban population (figure 1), amounting to nearly twothirds of total urban growth during 2000-2015. This outcome underscores the importance of fostering the development of sustainable economic activity and improving the services available in small and medium-sized urban settlements in the less developed regions of the world.

4

Urbanisation and Rural Population Growth

The world urban population is estimated to have reached 2.9 billion in 2000, a figure nearly four times as large as that estimated for 1950 (0.8 billion). Indeed, over the second half of the twentieth century, the world urban population increased at an average annual rate of 2.67 per cent, implying that it doubled, on average, every 26 years. In comparison, the total population of the world increased at an average annual rate of 1.75 per cent, doubling every 40 years.

The difference between those two rates of growth, that is, between the speed of growth of the urban and that of the total population, determines the speed of growth of the proportion urban. Thus, between 1950 and 2000, the world population urbanized rapidly, with the proportion urban rising at a rate of 0.91 per cent per year and passing from 29.7 per cent in 1950 to 47 per cent in 2000.

As a result of these unprecedented trends the population of the world, which during most of human history had lived mainly in rural settlements, is on the verge of crossing the threshold that will make it urban in its majority. According to the current projections, half of the world population will be urban in 2007. Although the urbanization of the world population is expected to continue, neither the urban population nor the proportion urban is expected to grow as rapidly in the future as it did in the recent past.

During 2000-2030, the world urban population is projected to increase at a rate of 1.8 per cent per year, nearly a full percentage point lower than the urban growth rate estimated for 1950-2000. The decline in the speed of growth will be smaller for the proportion urban, which is expected to rise at a robust 0.83 per cent per year during 2000-2030, with the result that by 2030 the population of the world will likely be 60.3 per cent urban and urban dwellers will number 4.9 billion.

In contrast with the rapid rise of the urban population, the growth of the world rural population has been slowing markedly. In 1950, 7 of every 10 persons on earth lived in rural areas, and they numbered 1.8 billion. Over the course of the next fifty years, rural population growth averaged 1.19 per cent per year and the rural population nearly doubled, reaching an estimated 3.2 billion by 2000. However, over the coming thirty years (2000-2030), rural population growth is expected to be minimal so that by 2030 the number of rural inhabitants will be hardly changed, remaining at 3.2 billion.

These trends imply that virtually all the population growth expected at the world level during 2000-2030 will be concentrated in urban areas. During that period the urban population will likely increase by 2 billion persons, passing from 2.9 billion to 4.9 billion, the same number that will in all probability be added to the whole population of the world, which is projected to rise from 6.1 billion in 2000 to 8.1 billion in 2030. Since natural increase is generally lower in urban than in rural areas and is expected to decline in both, the substantial growth still expected in the urban population is most likely to be fueled by both rural-urban migration and the geographical expansion of urban settlements, particularly through the transformation of rural villages into cities.

That process has been and will continue to be especially important for the developing world where the potential for the emergence of new urban settlements is still high. Indeed, one of the crucial factors in assessing the future of urbanization is to consider the contrasting experiences of the more and the less developed regions of the world. The following section discusses in some detail the past and future patterns of urban and rural growth in those regions.

Striking differences are apparent between the more developed and the less developed regions with respect to their patterns of urbanization. While most of the population of the less developed regions currently lives in rural areas, the large majority of the population of the more developed regions resides in urban areas. Moreover, the urban population of the less developed regions has been growing considerably faster than that of the more developed regions and, as a result, its share of the world urban population has been rising (figure 1).

In 1950 the urban population of more developed regions was considerably higher than that of the less developed regions (446 million versus 304 million), so that the more developed regions accounted for 60 per cent of the world urban population at a time when they had just 32 per cent of the world's inhabitants. But already in the 1950s the patterns of growth of the urban populations of the more developed and the less developed regions were showing signs of divergence, with the former growing rather slowly compared to the latter. As a consequence, by 1975 the urban population of the less developed regions had surpassed that of the more developed regions (810 million versus 734 million) and the difference between them increased rapidly thereafter. In 2000, 1.94 billion urban dwellers are estimated to live in the less developed regions and just 0.9 billion in the more developed regions.

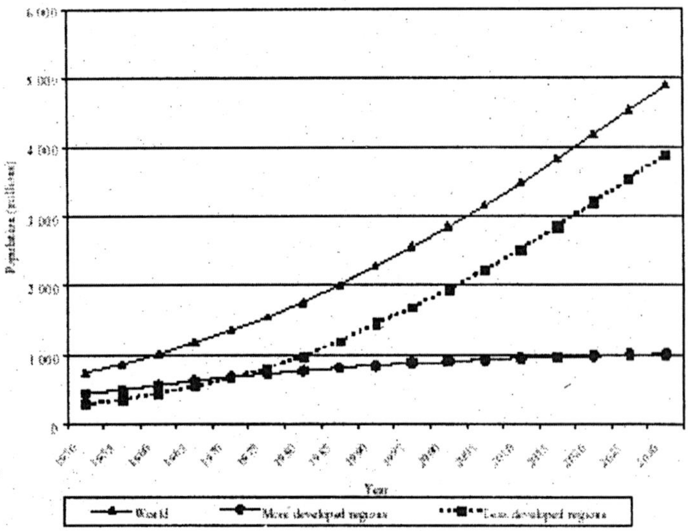

Figure 1. Estimated and projected urban population in the world, the more developed and the less developed regions, 1950-2030

Today, the less developed regions account for 68 per cent of the world urban population and 80 per cent of the total population. As the world becomes increasingly urbanized, the difference between these two figures will decline further. By 2030, with 3.9 billion urban dwellers, the less developed regions will have 79 per cent of the world urban population and 85 per cent of the total. Correspondingly, with 1 billion urban dwellers, the more developed regions will account for 21 per cent of the world urban population and 15 per cent of the total. Sustained high fertility and declining mortality were at the root of the fast population growth experienced by the less developed regions until 1970 and, still today, despite substantial reductions of fertility, the population growth of less developed regions remains high.

Table 1. Distribution of the total, urban and rural population of the world between the more developedand the less developed regions, 1950-2030

	Percentage of the world population			
Development groupings	*1950*	*1975*	*2000*	*2030*
Total population				
More developed regions	32.2	25.7	19.6	14.9
Less developed r`egions	67.8	74.3	80.4	85.1
Urban population				
More developed regions	59.5	47.5	31.7	20.7
Less developed regions	40.5	52.5	68.3	79.3
Rural population				
More developed regions	20.7	12.4	8.9	6.2
Less developed regions	79.3	87.6	91.1	93.8

The urban populations of developing countries, in spite of being generally characterized by lower fertility than the overall population, have experienced particularly high growth because of high rural-urban migration and the expansion of urban localities through the transformation of rural settlements into cities. As a result, the urban areas of the less developed regions have been absorbing a rising share of the annual increment to the world urban population. The ne xt 25 years are expected to see a steady rise of the annual increment of the urban population until it reaches 72 million in 2020-2025 and then drops slightly to 71 million in 2025-2030.

The overall increase of the annual increment of the urban population has been accompanied by a dramatic change in its distribution between the more and the less developed regions. Whereas in 1950-1955 the urban areas of the less developed regions absorbed 55 per cent of the annual increment of the world urban population, by 1995-2000 they were absorbing 91 per cent and by 2025-2030 they are expected to absorb 97 per cent (figure 2). For, just as the absolute increase of the urban population of less developed regions has been rising, that of the population in the cities of the more developed regions has been slowing down. In 1995-2000, the urban areas of more developed regions grew by 5 million persons annually whereas 52 million were added every year to the urban areas of less deve loped regions. By 2025-2030 it is expected that 69 million persons will be added annually to the urban population of the less developed regions whereas the urban areas of more developed regions will gain just 2 million new residents every year.

Not only are the urban areas of less developed regions absorbing most of the population growth occurring in urban areas worldwide, they are also increasingly absorbing most of the growth of the total world population. Thus, whereas in 1950-1955 the increase in the population of the urban areas of the less developed regions accounted for 28 per cent of the total increment to the world population, by 1995-2000 that increase accounted for 67 per cent of the annual increment to the world population and by 2020-2025 it will surpass the latter. Indeed, as figure 3 shows, in contrast with

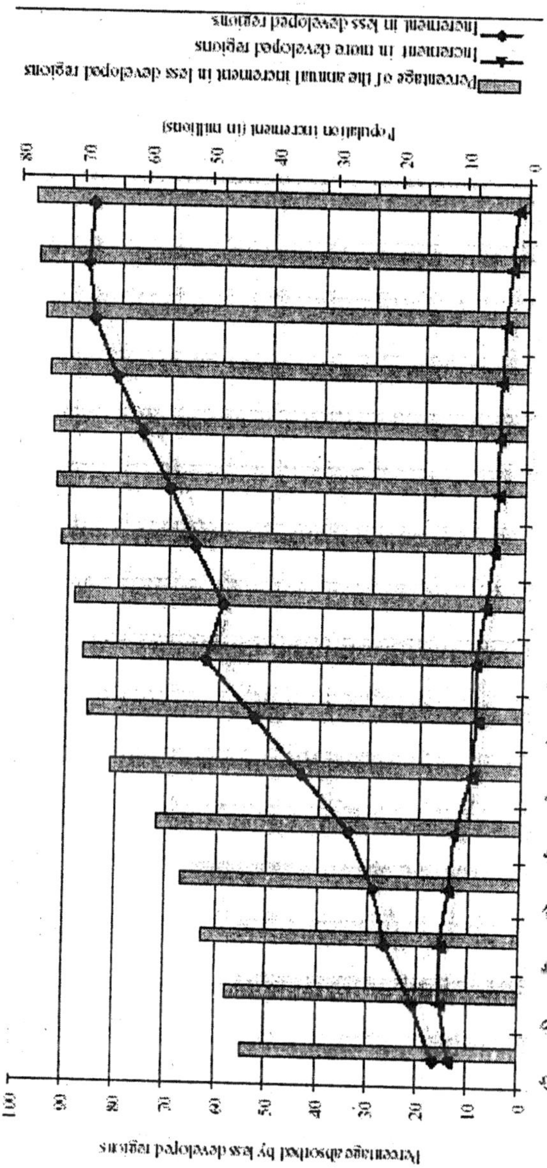

Figure 2. Annual urban increment in the more developed and the less developed regions and percentage of total urban increment represented by the urban increment of the less developed regions

the annual increment to the world population, which began a steady decline after 1985-1990 when it reached a peak of 86 million, the annual increment to the urban population of the less developed regions is expected to increase steadily after 1995 so that by 2025-2030 it will have surpassed the annual increment of the world population by 19 per cent. Such an outcome is consistent with a net transfer of population from rural to urban areas in the less developed regions, either through migration or as a result of the territorial expansion of urban settlements and the transformation of rural villages into cities.

Urban areas are also absorbing most of the growth occurring within regions. In the more deve loped regions, only the urban areas gained population during 1950-1995, while the rural areas lost population. In contrast, both the urban and the rural populations of less developed regions have been growing steadily, though urban areas are absorbing a rising share of the annual population increment. In 1950-1955 their annual population gain amounted to 36 per cent of the total, a figure that rose to 70 per cent in 1995-2000. By 2025-2030 the annual increase in the urban population of less developed regions is expected to surpass that of the total population of those regions by 17 per cent. At that time, the urban areas of more developed regions will barely be growing, but their growth, even if slight, will contrast sharply with the overall de-cline of their total population and the persistent decrease of their rural population.

The contrasting trends in urban growth between the more and the less developed regions are also apparent when population growth rates are considered. Furthermore, whereas the urban growth rate of the more developed regions has been declining fairly steadily since 1950, that of the less developed regions fluctuated during 1950-1995 showing no marked tendency to decrease before 1990.

The first major drop of the urban growth rate in the less developed regions occurred between 1985-1990 and 1990-1995 when it declined by nearly 0.8 percentage points, from 3.8 per cent per year to 3 per cent per year. For 1995-2000, the urban growth rate in the less developed regions is estimated at 2.9 per cent per year, equivalent to five times that estimated for the more deve loped regions (0.56 per cent per year) and the divergence between the two is expected to be accentuated in the future, so that by 2025-2030, the growth rate of the urban population of the less developed regions is projected to be 1.85 per cent per year, nearly ten times the one projected for the urban population of more developed regions (0.19 per cent per year).

One way of assessing the implic ations of the differences in urban growth rates between the more developed and the less developed regions is to note that, if the urban population of the less developed regions were to continue growing at the average annual rate expected during 2000-2030, it would double in 60 years. In contrast, given the low rate of growth expected for the urban population of the more developed regions after 2000, it would take more than a thousand years for it to double.

An intriguing feature of past trends in the urban growth rate of less developed regions is its fluctuating pattern before 1995. Thus, the urban growth rate of the less developed regions excluding China shows no fluctuations: it rises initially from 3.9 per cent per year in 1950-1955 to 4.2 per cent per year in 1960 1965 and then declines steadily to reach 3 per cent in 1995-2000. In contrast, the urban growth rate for China has fluctuated markedly, passing from 4.3 per cent per year in 1950-1955 to 2.2 per cent per year in 1970-1975, rising again to reach 5 per cent in 1985-1990 and then dropping abruptly to 2.7 per cent in 1990-1995. As figure 3 shows, the trends in urban population growth in China do not reflect similar changes in overall population growth.

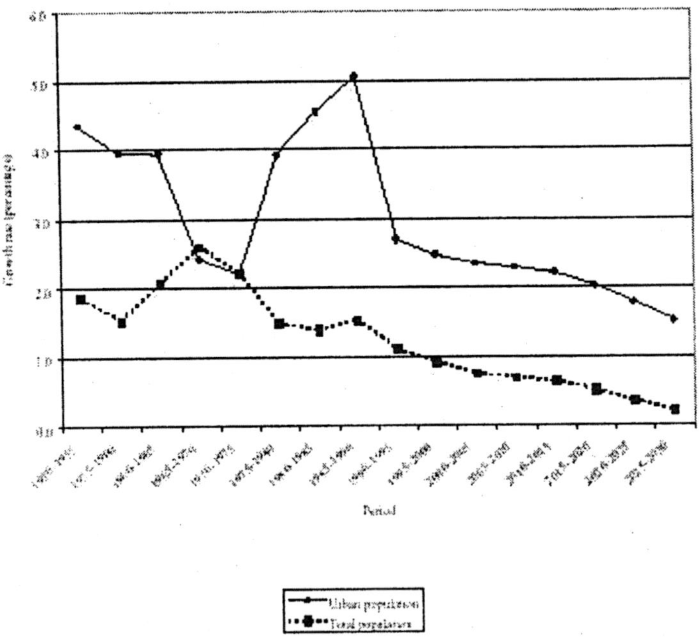

Figure 3. Growth rates of the urban and total population of China compared, 1950-2030

Instead, the decline in urban population growth stems largely from the virtual stagnation of the proportion urban during 1960-1970 and its subsequent rise is associated with the increases in the proportion urban recorded in 1980-1990. The period of sharp decline in urban growth (1965-1970), when even the proportion urban declined slightly, coincides with the initial phase of the Cultural Revolution, a programme of radical political and socio-economic reform that resulted in considerable instability and civil strife in the cities of China and was accompanied by the forceful relocation of large numbers of urban dwellers to rural areas. The reduction of the proportion urban reflects both the effects of this programme and the use of an official definition of urban localities and urban population that might not have provided an adequate measure of the actual changes taking place in the urban system. Lack of census information for the period 1960-1980 limits the possibility of assessing the accuracy of the official estimates available.

The census conducted in 1982 provides the first comprehensive source of data on the urban population of China, its cities and towns since the 1950s. However, starting in 1983, the official criteria to determine the geographical demarcation of cities and towns have changed several times, leading to an increase in the number of localities considered as urban and producing sharp rises in the urban population. Reclassification has therefore played an important role in determining urbanization trends in China since 1980. Such considerations should be borne in mind in interpreting the trends in urban growth experienced by that country as well as their effect on the overall growth of the urban population of the less deve loped regions.

The more and less developed regions also differ markedly in the trends experienced by their rural populations. Thus, whereas the rural population of more developed regions has been declining steadily during most of the twentieth century, that of less developed regions has been growing. In fact, the growth rate of the rural population of less developed regions peaked at 2.13 per cent per year in 1965-1970 and has been declining ever since. By

1995-2000, the rural growth rate of less developed regions stood at just 0.78 per cent per year and is expected to drop to 0.02 per cent by 2015-2020 before becoming negative.

Table 2. Percentage urban and growth rate of the Urban and total population, China, 1950-2030

Period	*Percentage urban at the beginning of the period*	*Growth rate (percentage)*	
		Urban population	*Total population*
1950-1955	13.4	4.34	1.87
1955-1960	15.1	3.95	1.53
1960-1965	16.8	3.93	2.07
1965-1970	17.5	2.42	2.61
1970-1975	17.4	2.21	2.21
1975-1980	18.5	3.90	1.48
1980-1985	21.3	4.53	1.38
1985-1990	25.2	5.04	1.53
1990-1995	28.5	2.70	1.10
1995-2000	30.9	2.47	0.91
2000-2005	33.4	2.34	0.75
2005-2010	36.2	2.28	0.69
2010-2015	39.1	2.21	0.64
2015-2020	42.3	2.02	0.51
2020-2025	45.5	1.78	0.35
2025-2030	48.7	1.51	0.21

As a consequence, the rural population of less developed regions will be declining in 2025-2030 at a pace similar to that experienced by the rural areas of more developed regions during 1950-1960. The diverging patterns of growth of the rural populations of the more and the less developed regions have resulted in a significant redistribution of the rural population among the two development groups. In 1950, the 367 million rural dwellers in the more developed regions constituted 21 per cent of the rural population of the world, whereas by 2000, the projected number of rural dwellers in the more developed regions (285 million) barely accounted for 9 per cent of the world rural population. By 2030, the share of the rural population of more developed regions is expected to drop further (to 6 per cent) and the rural population is projected to be 200 million persons. That is, between 1950 and 2030, the rural population of the more developed regions is expected to decline by nearly 45 per cent.

Table 3. The Distribution of Countires or areas in more developed and less developed regions by the proportion of the Population living in Urban areas compared, 1950, 1975, 2000 and 2030

	1950	*1975*	*2000*	*2030*
Less developed regions				
Lower extreme	0.0	0.0	0.0	0.0
Lower quartile	9.7	19.3	32.4	49.4
Median	22.8	35.3	48.6	64.3
Upper quartile	37.5	53.5	71.2	81.5
Upper extreme	100.0	100.0	100.0	100.0
More developed regions				
Lower extreme	13.7	20.0	22.6	40.9
Lower quartile.	27.8	51.5	63.0	74.3
Median	50.1	65.6	74.7	81.6
Upper quartile	70.0	81.5	86.7	90.7
Upper extreme	100.0	100.0	100.0	100.0

In comparison, the growth of the rural population of less developed regions has been impressive. The number of rural dwellers in less developed regions rose from 1.4 billion in 1950 to 2.9 billion in 2000, more than doubling over those 50 years. But the next 30 years are expected to witness a major reduction in rural population growth. As a result, between 2000 and 2020, the rural population of less deve loped regions will increase by just 170 million persons to reach 3.1 billion and it is expected to start declining thereafter so that by 2030 it will stand at 3 billion, just 98 million higher than in 2000. As a consequence of the contrasting patterns of growth of the urban and rural populations of the more and the less developed regions, the two groups of regions have experienced and are expected to experience different trends in the growth of the proportion urban.

As already noted, the more deve loped regions were already highly urbanized by 1950, when 55 per cent of their population lived in urban areas. At that time, the less developed regions were barely urbanized, having just 18 per cent of their inhabitants living in cities. However, because the growth of the urban population of less developed regions was rapid in relation to that of the total population, between 1950 and 2000 the proportion urban had more than doubled, reaching 40 per cent. In the more developed regions, the proportion urban rose by a more modest amount, passing from 55 to 76 per cent between 1950 and 2000.

Consequently, the difference between the proportion urban of the more developed regions and that of the less developed regions became smaller. The future is expected to see a further reduction of that difference, since the proportion urban in less deve loped regions is expected to rise to 56 per cent by 2030 and that of the more developed regions is projected to reach 84 per cent. These results imply that by 2030 there will still be ample room for the expansion of the proportion urban in the less deve loped regions whereas that of the more developed regions will be nearing an upper limit. Such a contrast is made clearer by considering the rate of urbanization (i.e. the growth rate of the proportion urban). In contrast, the rate of urbanization of the less developed regions, which was mostly of the order of 1.8 per cent to 1.9 per cent per year before 1990, is expected to remain above 1 per cent per year until 2025 and will still be 0.98 per cent in 2025-2030. At that rate, the proportion urban in the less developed regions would reach 70 per cent by 2050. The differences in the levels of urbanization between the more developed and the less developed regions are also apparent when one considers the distribution of countries and areas in each group according to the proportion urban.

In 1950, three-quarters of the 173 countries or areas in the less developed regions had at most 37.5 per cent of their population living in urban areas whereas half of the 55 countries or areas in the more deve loped regions had already more than 50 per cent of their population living in urban areas. By 2000, in half of the countries or areas of the less developed regions at least 48.6 per cent of the population is estimated to live in urban areas and in three-quarters more than 32.4 per cent do so. That is, the bulk of the distribution of less developed countries by level of urbanization has shifted upward. And there has also been a significant upward shift of the distribution of countries in the more developed regions, with three-quarters of them exhibiting a proportion urban at or above 63 per cent. By 2030, even the least urbanized country in the more developed regions will have attained a level of urbanization higher than 40 per cent and in three-quarters of the developed countries, over 74 per cent of the population is expected to live in urban areas. In the less developed regions, a few small island countries are expected to remain mostly rural even by 2030, but three-quarters of all countries or areas in those regions will likely exhibit levels of urbanization above 49 per cent.

The marked upward shift of the distributions of countries by level of urbanization make plain the momentous change that has taken place over the course of the twentieth century and that is expected to lead to a highly urbanized world during the twenty-first century. Nevertheless, there is and will continue to be considerable variation among countries and among major areas and regions in terms of the level of urbanization attained. The next section explores those differences in terms of major areas.

Patterns of Urban and Rural growth

The different patterns of urbanization observed at the level of more developed and less developed regions are the result of the varying experiences of the major areas that constitute them. Europe and Northern America, being part of the developed world, exhibit high levels of urbanization (i.e. high proportions of the population living in urban areas) and slowing rates of urban population growth. In the developing world, Africa and Asia remain largely rural, whereas Latin America and the Caribbean considered jointly have a high proportion of their population living in cities. Oceania, which straddles the developed and the developing world, is also highly urbanized. Yet high levels of urbanization do not correlate well with the number of urban dwellers in each major area. Asia, albeit characterized by having the lowest proportion urban (36.7 per cent in 2000), has the largest number of persons living in urban areas (1.4 billion). It is followed by Europe, with 545 million urban dwellers; Latin America and the Caribbean with 391 million; and Africa with 297 million. Because of the high growth rates of the urban population expected in Africa and Asia, by 2030 those two major areas will have the largest numbers of urban dwellers in the world: 2.6 billion in Asia and 766 million in Africa, although they will still be the least urbanized major areas of the world.

In 1950 Asia was the second least urbanized major area, with 17.4 per cent of its population living in cities. By 2000 that proportion is expected to have risen to 36.7 per cent but is still one of the lowest of the world and, despite the robust rate of urbanization that Asia is expected to experience during 2000-2030 (1.25 per cent per year, the highest of any major area), the proportion urban in Asia will be the lowest among major areas by 2030, standing at 53.4 per cent.

Africa, which in 1950 was the major area with the lowest proportion of its population living in cities, experienced the fastest rate of urbanization of any major area during 1950-2000 and saw that proportion rise from 14.7 per cent in 1950 to 37.9 per cent in 2000. Although Africa's average rate of urbanization over the next 30 years is expected to be lower than during the second half of the twentieth century (1.21 per cent per year instead of 1.89 per cent per year), it will still be among the highest experienced by all major areas and will result in a level of urbanization of 54.5 per cent by 2030. That is, if the projected trends hold, by 2030 the level of urbanization in both Africa and Asia will have passed the 50 per cent mark and their populations will have become more urban than rural.

Compared to Africa and Asia, the urbanization of Latin America and the Caribbean was already fairly advanced by 1950 when the region had 41.4 per cent of its population living in urban areas. Although this level of urbanization was lower than that characterizing Europe or Northern America in 1950, over the next 50 years Latin America and the Caribbean experienced a rapid increase of the proportion urban, averaging 1.2 per cent per year. Consequently, by 2000, the proportion urban in Latin America and the Caribbean had reached levels similar to those characterizing Europe and Northern America. With nearly three-quarters of their populations already living in cities, those three major areas are expected to experience a marked decline of the rate of urbanization, and the proportion urban is expected to rise moderately to reach values in the range of 82.6 to 84.4 per cent by 2030. It is noteworthy that by that date, the second most urbanized major area of the world is expected to be Latin America and the Caribbean.

Oceania, the major area with the smallest population, was the second most urbanized area in 1950, when already 61.6 per cent of its population lived in cities. Since then it has experienced the lowest rate of urbanization in the world, amounting to 0.26 per cent per year. Such a low rate of growth of the proportion urban resulted in a level of urbanization of 70.2 per cent in 2000 and, because the rate of urbanization is expected to decline further during 2000-2030, by 2030 the proportion urban will not be as high as that expected for Europe or Northern America. Thus, instead of reaching a level of urbanization of 80 per cent or more, the proportion of Oceania's population living in urban areas is expected to be 74.4 per cent in 2030.

A more detailed picture of the trends in urbanization experienced by the major areas can be obtained by considering changes in the rate of urbanization over time. The rate of urbanization, being the growth rate of the proportion urban, is equivalent to the difference between the growth rate of the urban population and that of the total population. Consequently, its trajectory over time is very likely to reflect the changes taking place in the urban growth rate. Only Latin America and the Caribbean displays a smoothly declining trend in the rate of urbanization: it drops steadily from 1.8 per cent per year in 1950-1955 to 0.26 per cent per year in 2025-2030.

In Africa, whose rates of urbanization have generally been the highest in the world, the rate of urbanization declines markedly from 1960 to 1980, passing from 2.35 per cent per year in 1960-1965 to 1.6 per cent per year in 1975-1980. After 1985 it experiences a slight recuperation, rising to 1.73 per cent per year by 1990-1995. From there on the rate of urbanization in Africa is projected to follow a smooth downward trend that reaches 0.99 per cent per year by 2025-2030. In contrast with Africa or Latin America and the Caribbean, the rate of urbanization in Asia shows no clear trend before 1995, having fluctuated sharply over the period.

The urbanization trends in China, which is the home of 30 per cent of the urban population in Asia, are the cause of such fluctuations. As discussed earlier in relation to the urban growth rate of the less developed regions, such fluctuations stem both from histor ical events that retarded or even reversed urbanization in China during the late 1960s and early 1970s, and from the official definition of urban used in China until the 1980s which in all likelihood did not reflect adequately the expansion of existing cities and the emergence of new cities in that country. In general the urbanization rates experienced by Europe, Northern America and Oceania have been considerably lower than those exhibited by the major areas of the developing world. Furthermore, the respective rates of urbanization of those three major areas declined markedly between 1960 and 1975 or 1980. In Oceania, that decline led to negative rates of urbanization as of 1975-1980, and even by 1990-1995, after a slight recuperation of the urbanization rate, the proportion urban in Oceania was still declining.

In Northern America the urbanization rate dropped to nearly zero in the 1970s and by 1990-1995 had risen to a low 0.22 per cent per year. Europe maintained higher urbanization rates than the other two major areas over the whole 1950-1995 period but, even so, by 1990-1995 it had a rate of urbanization of just 0.35 per cent per year. Over the projection period all three major areas are expected to see their urbanization rate converge to values ranging from 0.26 to 0.31 per cent per year. Such projected values imply a fairly important rise in the rate of urbanization for Oceania, a slight recuperation for Northern America and a modest decline for Europe.

The reduction of the urbanization rates experienced by Europe, Northern America and Oceania between 1960 and 1980 can be related to the phenomenon known as "counter-urbanization" which entailed a shift in population distribution down the urban hierarchy. Although, strictly speaking, counter-urbanization involves a redistribution of the population within the urban system and not a return of urban dwellers to rural areas, in highly urbanized countries counter-urbanization was associated with a faster aggregate growth of nonmetropolitan populations in relation to the growth of the population in metropolitan areas, and in some countries an increase of the rate of growth of the rural population was also noticeable.

A more significant increase occurred in both Northern America and Oceania where the rural growth rate increased markedly between 1965-1970 and 1970-1975. Furthermore, in Oceania the rural growth rate continued to increase for another decade and was still 1.72 per cent per year in 1990-1995, higher than the 1.43 per cent per year at which the urban population was growing at the time. In Northern America the growth spurt of the rural population recorded in the early 1970s lasted for just a decade before a decline set in, so that by 1990-1995 the rate of rural population growth stood at 0.33 per cent per year.

In the major areas of the less developed world, two types of trends are discernible in terms of the rural growth rate. The major area constituted by Latin America and the Caribbean has seen its rural growth rate decline steadily so that by 1990-1995 it was just 0.05 per cent per year. Africa and Asia, in contrast, both experienced an increase of the rate of growth of the rural population during the 1950s and 1960s. In the case of Africa, declining mortality combined with sustained high fertility produced the increase in the rural population growth rate, which reached a peak of 2.22 per cent per year in 1975-1980 and is estimated to have declined to 1.64 per cent per year in 1990-1995.

In Asia, the highest growth rate of the rural population occurred in 1965-1970, when rural growth reached 2.18 per cent per year, largely as a result of events in China and the high rural growth rate experienced by that country. Since then, the growth rate of the rural population of Asia has been declining steadily so that by 1990-1995 it had reached 0.93 per cent per year. For all major areas, the projections of rural population growth entail a steady reduction of the rural growth rate, but it is noteworthy that by the end of the projection period the major areas will vary considerably in terms of the rate of growth of their rural populations. Thus, by 2025-2030, Europe's rural population is expected to be declining at a rate of -1.69 per cent per year; that of Northern America will be decreasing at a rate of -0.89 per cent per year; those of Asia, Latin America and the Caribbean, and Oceania will be experiencing a reduction in size at rates ranging from -0.55 to -0.11 per cent per year; and only the rural population of Africa will still be experiencing positive growth, increasing at a rate of 0.47 per cent per year.

As a result of such trends, the number of rural inhabitants in Africa is expected to more than triple between 1950 and 2030, rising from 188 million in 1950 to 487 million in 2000 and reaching 640 million by the end of the projection period. In Asia, the major area with the largest number of rural inhabitants, the rural population is estimated to have grown from 1.2 billion in 1950 to 2.3 billion in 2000, and although it is expected to reach 2.4 billion by 2010, it will likely decline to slightly less than 2.3 billion by 2030. Latin America and the Caribbean are expected to see their rural population drop from 128 million in 2000 to 122 million in 2030, and the relative reductions of the rural population will be more marked in Northern America and Europe.

Thus, the number of rural dwellers in Northern America will likely be cut by 18 per cent during 2000-2030, dropping from 71 million to 58 million; and Europe will experience a 35 per cent reduction of the rural population (from 184 million to 120 million). Only in Oceania will the reductions be minimal, so that the rural population is still expected to increase from 9 million in 2000 to 11 million by 2030. Changes in the size of the rural population of the major areas will result in a significant redistribution of the rural population of the world by major area.

The share of Northern America will also be cut significantly, from 3.5 per cent in 1950 to 2.2 per cent in 2000 and to an expected 1.8 per cent in 2030. Latin America and the Caribbean will also see its share drop by nearly two percentage points, from 5.5 in 1950 to 3.8 in 2030. In contrast, the shares of Africa and Asia will increase markedly. By 2030, Africa is expected to be the home of nearly 20 per cent of the world rural population, almost double the figure that the continent accounted for in 1950 (10.6 per cent); and Asia will remain as the home for the vast majority of the world's rural dwellers. By 2030, 70.5 per cent of the world rural population will live in Asia, a somewhat lower proportion than the one the continent houses today (72.6 per cent) but still considerably higher than the share Asia had in 1950 (65.4 per cent).

The redistribution of the world urban population over time in many ways parallels that of the rural population. Africa, for instance, has experienced and is expected to experience the highest urban and rural growth rates in the world. Asia has experienced the second highest rate of rural growth and the third highest in terms of urban growth. It is followed by Latin America and the Caribbean in terms of rural growth and preceded by it in terms of urban growth. At the other extreme, Europe has been characterized by the lowest rates of both urban and rural population growth. Africa's urban growth rate has been very high, averaging 4.4 per cent per year over 1950-2000 and is expected to remain above 3 per cent per year over most of the projection period. The urban growth rate of Latin America and the Caribbean started at a level close to that of Africa in 1950-1955, but has declined rapidly, reaching 2.36 per cent in 1990-1995 and being expected to drop to 1.07 per cent by 2025-2030.

In Asia, the urban growth rate shows the fluctuations associated with the urbanization trends experienced by China and remains relatively high until 1990, averaging 3.4 per cent per year during 1950-2000. By 1990-1995, the urban growth rate in Asia stood at 2.78 per cent per year and it is expected to decline to 1.74 per cent per year by 2025-2030. In Europe, Northern America and Oceania, the urban growth rate declined markedly between approximately 1960 and 1980, dur ing the period of counter-urbanization but, whereas it showed signs of recuperation or stabilization in Northern America and Oceania after 1980, in Europe it kept on declining. As a result, by 1990-1995, the urban population of Europe was growing at just 0.51 per cent per year, whereas that of Northern America was increasing at 1.24 per cent per year and that of Oceania at 1.43 per cent per year.

Further reductions of the urban growth rate are projected for these three major areas so that by 2025-2030 the urban population of Europe will be declining slowly, and those of Northern America and Oceania will be growing at rates of 0.7 and 1.07 per cent per year, respectively. The rapid urban growth experienced by the major areas of the developing world has resulted in large numbers of urban dwellers. Africa's urban population increased nine-fold between 1950 and 2000, rising from 32 million to 297 million in the course of half a century. The urban populations of Asia and Latin America and the Caribbean increased by more than five-fold each, from 244 million to 1.4 billion in Asia, and from 69 million to 391 million in Latin America and the Caribbean.

The number of urban dwellers in Northern America more than doubled (from 110 million to 239 million) and so did the number of those in Oceania (rising from 8 million to 21 million). Even the urban population of Europe, whose growth rates were fairly low, increased by 90 per cent, passing from 287 million to 545 million during 1950-2000. Yet, owing to the large differences in urban growth rates among major areas, a significant redistribution of the world urban population resulted. Africa's share of the urban population more than doubled, rising from 4.3 per cent in 1950 to 10.4 per cent in 2000.

Asia gained 15 percentage points, seeing its share increase from 32.5 per cent to 47.5 per cent. Latin America and the Caribbean also recorded an increase, so that by 2000 their urban population accounted for 13.7 per cent of the world urban population, up from the 9.2 per cent in 1950. But those rising shares were counterbalanced by sharp declines in the shares of Europe and Northern America. The former saw its share of the world urban population drop from 38.3 per cent to 19.2 per cent, and Northern America's share declined from 14.6 per cent to 8.4 per cent.

Over the next thirty years, the differentials in urban population growth will further accentuate the redistribution of the urban population that took place from 1950 to 2000. Africa's urban population will increase by 2.6 times between 2000 and 2030, and Asia's will nearly double. With 766 million urban dwellers in 2030, Africa will have 15.7 per cent of the urban population, and Asia will have 53.3 per cent amounting to 2.6 billion persons. Between the two, they will account for 69 per cent of the world urban population. All other major areas are expected to see their share of the world urban population decline, even though their urban populations are projected to increase substantially.

The urban population of Latin America and the Caribbean, for instance, will increase by 50 per cent, rising from 391 million in 2000 to 604 million in 2030, but its share of the world urban population will decline from 13.7 per cent to 12.4 per cent. Similarly, the share of Northern America is expected to decline from 8.4 per cent to 6.4 per cent although its urban population will likely increase by 30 per cent. But the major reduction expected is in Europe's share, which will decrease from 19.2 per cent to 11.7 per cent between 2000 and 2030 as a result of the very low increase of Europe's urban population over the period.

Given their high urban growth rates and their growing shares of the world urban population, Africa and Asia account for a large proportion of the increment of the urban population. During 1950-2000, 65.5 per cent of the 41.9

million persons that, on average, were added annually to the urban population of the world was absorbed by the urban areas of Africa and Asia. And the shares of both major areas are expected to increase over the next thirty years.

Thus, during 2000-2030, Asia alone will account for 61.3 per cent of the annual increment to the world urban population while Africa will account for 22.9 per cent. That is, Africa and Asia will together absorb 84.2 per cent of the average annual increase of the urban population over the next thirty years (amounting to 57.4 million persons annually). All the other major areas are expected to see their share of the average annual increment to the urban population decline.

In Latin America and the Caribbean the reduction expected will be of 32 per cent, meaning that its share will drop from 15.4 per cent in 1950-2000 to 10.4 per cent in 2000-2030. For Oceania and Northern America the reductions in share will be of the order of 17 and 42 per cent respectively, but for Europe, they will amount to 90 per cent. That is, Europe is expected to see its share of the average annual increment of the urban population in 2000-2030 reduced to one tenth of the value it had in 1950-2000: from 12.3 per cent to 1.3 per cent. Indeed, Europe is the only major area expected to experience a reduction of its urban population by 2030, amounting to a loss of 150,000 persons between 2025 and 2030.

The rapid growth of the urban population of Africa, Asia and Latin America and the Caribbean combined with the expected reduction of population growth in rural areas has important implic ations for the geographical distribution of overall population growth. Between 1950 and 2000, the average annual increment of the urban population of Asia accounted for 31 per cent of the average annual increment of the total population of the world, which is estimated at 71 million. During 2000-2030, when the world population is expected to increase annually by 69 million, the urban areas of Asia will absorb 61 per cent of that increment, Similarly, the share of the urban areas of Africa will increase markedly, passing from 7.5 per cent of the average annual population increment in 1950-2000 to 22.6 per cent of that expected during 2000-2030. Consequently, between 2000 and 2030, the urban areas of Asia and Africa will jointly absorb 83 per cent of the increment in the world population.

Urban and Rural Population Growth at Regional Level

In Oceania, for instance, Australia/New Zealand, the most urbanized region of the world (85 per cent urban in 2000), coexists with Melanesia, the least urbanized (24 per cent urban). Micronesia and Polynesia have intermediate but still low levels of urbanization (ranging from 40 to 45 per cent). In Europe, Northern Europe and Western Europe are among the most highly urbanized regions of the world (more than 82 per cent urban) but Eastern Europe and Southern Europe have significantly lower levels of urbanization.

In the Americas, South America has a slightly higher level of urbanization than Northern America (over 77 per cent each) but Central America and the Caribbean are considerably less urbanized. Nevertheless, in all the regions of Europe and the Americas, urbanization is far advanced and the proportion urban in each is at or above 63 per cent. In Africa and Asia, only Western Asia, with 70 per cent of its population urban, has reached a level of urbanization similar to those in Europe or the Americas. Among the other regions, urbanization levels are moderately high in Northern Africa and Southern Africa (at about 50 per cent) but they are considerably lower in the rest of Africa and Asia. Aside from Melanesia, Eastern Africa and South-central Asia are the least urbanized regions of the world, and urbanization levels are just slightly higher in Middle Africa, South-eastern Asia and Eastern Asia.

With low levels of urbanization and large populations, most of the regions of Asia account for high proportions of the rural population of the world. About a third of all rural inhabitants of the world live in South-central Asia, whereas Eastern Asia accounts for a further 29 per cent and Southeastern Asia for 10 per cent. Eastern Africa and Western Africa follow, each accounting for about 5 per cent. That is, in 2000, 4 out of every 5 rural dwellers live in these five regions and that proportion is unlikely to change significantly during 2000-2030, despite the fact that the rural populations of most of the regions of Africa and of South-Central Asia will increase and those of Eastern Asia and South-eastern Asia will decline. Although rural population growth is expected to decline in all regions, it will still be sizeable in Eastern Africa, Middle Africa and Western Africa, as well as in Melanesia, Micronesia, Polynesia and Western Asia. Slow rural growth is likely to characterize South-central Asia, Central America and Northern Africa, but in all other regions, the rural population is expected to decline by 2030.

Particularly rapid reductions of the rural population are likely in all the regions of Europe. The urban population is also concentrated in a few regions, but it is not as highly concentrated as the rural population. Despite their low levels of urbanization, Eastern Asia and South-central Asia have the largest urban populations of the world and they jointly account for 36 per cent of all urban dwellers. South America, Northern America, Eastern Europe, South-eastern

Asia and Western Europe, in decreasing order, follow as the regions housing the largest urban populations of the world but together with Eastern Asia and South-central Asia, they account for just 74 per cent of all urban dwellers. By 2030, seven regions will also account for approximately 73 per cent of the urban population, but they will include Western Asia and Western Africa instead of Eastern Europe and Western Europe.

Indeed, during 2000-2030, the urban population of all regions of Europe is expected to increase very slowly, at rates lower than 0.21 per cent per year. No other region will exhibit such low rates of urban population growth. The urban populations of Australia/New Zealand and Northern America, whose growth rates are also expected to be on the low side, will grow at 0.9 per cent per year. All other regions are expected to have urban growth rates above 1.3 per cent per year. Particularly high urban growth rates, above 3 per cent per year, are likely in Eastern Africa, Middle Africa and Western Africa, as well as in Melanesia and Micronesia. The urban populations of South-central Asia, South-eastern Asia, Western Asia, Northern Africa and Polynesia are also expected to growth moderately fast. The different patterns of urban and rural population growth at the regional level will result in a redistribution of the urban and rural population at the world level and will lead to different patterns of urbanization

Urban Population Growth

In 1950, the most urbanized regions of the world were those of Europe, Australia/New Ze aland and Northern America and they generally had large numbers of urban dwellers. However, because of their large populations, certain regions of the developing world also had large numbers of urban dwellers even if their levels of urbanization were low. Thus, in 1950 Eastern Asia had the largest urban population in the world although its level of urbanization was a modest 18 per cent.

Similarly, South-central Asia, with 16.6 per cent of its population living in urban areas, ranked fifth among all regions when ordered by urban population size. In addition, South America, with an urbanization level of 42.8 per cent in 1950, higher than that of Eastern Europe, ranked seventh. But despite those exceptions, most of the regions with large numbers of urban dwellers in 1950 were in the developed world:

Northern America and the four regions of Europe, in particular, were among the eight regions with the highest number of urban inhabitants in 1950 when their levels of urbanization varied between 39.3 per cent in Eastern Europe and 72.7 per cent in Northern Europe. In 2000, only three of the more developed regions remain among the eight with the largest urban populations (Northern America, Eastern Europe and Western Europe) and they all have seen their ranks drop as the growth of their urban populations has failed to keep pace with that of the number of urban dwellers in certain developing regions.

Thus, South-central Asia has moved to second place, South America has moved to third place, South-eastern Asia to sixth, and Western Asia to eighth. In addition, Eastern Asia remains as the region with the largest number of urban dwellers in the world. Consequently, all the regions of Asia are among those having the largest numbers of urban inhabitants, particularly among those in the developing world. At the other end of the spectrum, Melanesia, Micronesia and Polynesia remain as the regions with the smallest urban populations, largely because their overall populations are also small (table 4). Among regions with medium-sized urban populations, Central America with 91 million urban dwellers has maintained its rank at number 10, and the Caribbean with 24 million urban dwellers has passed from fifteenth to sixteenth place between 1950 and 2000. More important changes in rank have occurred among the regions of Africa, particularly Eastern Africa and Middle Africa, which moved to fourteenth and fifteenth place in 2000 after having ranked seventeenth or higher in 1950.

Over the projection period the urban population of South-central Asia is expected to grow more rapidly than that of Eastern Asia so that by 2030 the former will have the largest urban population of the world (table 1). South America will keep its third rank, but South-eastern Asia and Western Asia will move up the ranks to fourth and sixth place, respectively. Furthermore, Western Africa will rise to seventh place and Eastern Africa to ninth. As a consequence, the more developed regions will see their ranks drop further. Only Northern America and Eastern Europe will remain among the eight regions with the largest urban populations, and Western Europe will drop to eleventh place, following Northern Africa. Southern Europe will drop from ninth place in 2000 to fourteenth place in 2030, and Northern Europe will move from thirteenth place to fifteenth.

Only Australia/New Zealand will not experience a change of rank, largely because of the large drop it experienced between 1950 and 2000 when it passed from thirteenth to eighteenth place. Changes in the ranks of regions according to urban population size are produced by the differential growth rates that those populations have experienced in the past and are expected to experience over the projection period.

Table 4. The regions of the world according to the size of their urban populationsin 1950, 2000 and 2030

Rank	Region	Urban population (millions) 1950	Rank	Region	Urban population (millions) 2000	Rank	Region	Urban population (millions) 2030
1	Eastern Asia	120.8	1	Eastern Asia	571.7	1	South-central Asia	1 026.6
2	Northern America	109.7	2	South-central Asia	455.5	2	Eastern Asia	932.9
3	Western Europe	95.6	3	South America	275.9	3	South America	418.6
4	Eastern Europe	86.3	4	Northern America	239.0	4	South-eastern Asia	397.4
5	South-central Asia	82.9	5	Eastern Europe	218.6	5	Northern America	313.7
6	Northern Europe	56.8	6	South-eastern Asia	192.7	6	Western Asia	247.9
7	South America	48.4	7	Western Europe	151.4	7	Western Africa	241.7
8	Southern Europe	48.2	8	Western Asia	132.0	8	Eastern Europe	225.6
9	South-eastern Asia	26.9	9	Southern Europe	95.8	9	Eastern Africa	205.3
10	Central America	14.7	10	Central America	90.9	10	Northern Africa	173.7
11	Western Asia	13.4	11	Western Africa	88.2	11	Western Europe	160.2
12	Northern Africa	13.1	12	Northern Africa	87.9	12	Central America	149.7
13	Australia/New Zealand	7.6	13	Northern Europe	79.1	13	Middle Africa	109.0
14	Western Africa	6.2	14	Eastern Africa	64.6	14	Southern Europe	100.5
15	Caribbean	6.0	15	Middle Africa	33.9	15	Northern Europe	84.3
16	Southern Africa	6.0	16	Caribbean	24.0	16	Southern Africa	36.1
17	Middle Africa	3.7	17	Southern Africa	22.5	17	Caribbean	35.7
18	Eastern Africa	3.4	18	Australia/New Zealand	19.3	18	Australia/New Zealand	25.4
19	Melanesia	0.1	19	Melanesia	1.5	19	Melanesia	4.1
20	Polynesia	0.1	20	Polynes ia	0.3	20	Micronesia	0.6
21	Micronesia	0.0	21	Micronesia	0.2	21	Polynesia	0.5

Clearly, between 1950 and 2000, the urban populations of less developed regions have grown faster than those of more developed regions. Particularly high rates of urban population growth have been recorded in the regions of Africa (with the exception of Southern Africa) and in Western Asia, South-eastern Asia and Melanesia.

Urban growth rates in these seven regions during 1950-2000 ranged from 3.8 per cent per year in Northern Africa to 5.9 per cent per year in Eastern Africa. In fact, Eastern Africa, Western Africa and Melanesia have all experienced sustained annual rates of urban growth above 5 per cent.

As a result, the urban population of Eastern Africa increased from just 3 million persons in 1950 to 65 million in 2000, and that of Western Africa increased nearly fifteen-fold, rising from 6 million in 1950 to 88 million in 2000. But, despite such rapid growth in the urban population, Eastern Africa remains among the least urbanized regions of the world, with just 26 per cent of its population living in urban areas today, and Western Africa has reached only a moderate level of urbanization (40 per cent).

Consequently, there is still considerable room for the continued increase of their urban populations and, both regions are expected to experience some of the highest rates of urban population growth projected after 2000. Indeed, by 2030, both regions are projected to have jointly an urban population of 447 million, larger than the urban population expected for Eastern and Western Europe combined.

Middle Africa has also experienced fast urban population growth during 1950-2000. Increasing at an annual average rate of 4.4 per cent, its urban population rose from 4 million in 1950 to 34 million in 2000 and is expected to experience the most rapid increase of any region during

2000-2030, growing at a rate of 3.9 per cent per year. At that speed, the urban population will reach 109 million in 2030, a number just slightly higher than that expected for the urban population of Southern Europe.

Fast urban growth has also characterized and is expected to remain characteristic of Melanesia and Micronesia but, given their small urban populations, the numbers involved are not as striking as those relative to Africa. Nevertheless, since many of the countries or areas in these two regions are small isla nds, the rapid urban growth expected may strain available resources.

In 2000, Melanesia is estimated to have 1.5 million urban dwellers and Micronesia 200,000. During 2000-2030, the urban population of each region is expected to increase at more than 3 per cent per year, rising to 4.1 million by 2030 in the case of Melanesia and to 600,000 in Micronesia.

In Western Asia, the urban population increased tenfold, from 13 million to 132 million. Even though the rate of urban population growth is expected to decline substantially in both regions, the size of the urban population already attained by 2000 ensures that even modest rates of growth will produce substantial increases in absolute terms.

Thus, South-eastern Asia, with an expected urban growth rate of 2.4 per cent per year, is projected to have 397 million urban dwellers in 2030, while Western Asia, whose rate of urban population growth is expected to drop by more than half (to 2.1 per cent per year), will attain an urban population of 248 million persons. These changes imply that by 2030 these two regions combined will have more urban dwellers than the whole of Europe.

Rapid urban growth has also occurred in Northern Africa, the most urbanized region of the African continent today. Growing at 3.8 per cent per year, the urban population of the region increased from 13 million to 88 million between 1950 and 2000 and, although its growth rate is expected to fall by 40 per cent between 1950-2000 and 2000-2030, to an average of 2.3 per cent per year, its urban population is projected to rise to 174 million in 2030. Just as in the case of Northern Africa, Central America and South America have also experienced urban growth rates above 3 per cent per year during 1950-2000.

As a result, their urban populations that, especially in the case of South America, were already moderate in size in 1950, increased considerably, to reach 91 million in Central America and 276 million in South America by 2000. Although the urban growth rates expected for both regions during 2000-2030 will be markedly lower than those of all regions that have preceded in this discussion (of the order of 1.4 to 1.7 per cent), the large population base already attained means that the absolute increases expected will be sizable. Thus, Central America is expected to attain 150 million urban dwellers by 2030 and South America 419 million.

Eastern Asia, Polynesia and South-central Asia are the other three regions exhibiting moderately high urban growth rates during 1950-2000. Polynesia, just as the other developing regions of Oceania, has a very small urban population that is estimated today at 300,000 and will likely rise to half a million by 2030. In contrast, Eastern Asia and South-central Asia have the two largest urban populations in the world, at 572 million and 455 million respectively. Given the large total population of these two regions and their considerable potential for urban growth because of their still low to moderate levels of urbanization, it is not surprising that they will both maintain ascendancy over other regions in terms of urban population size. However, they will differ considerably with regard to their expected future rates of urban growth.

South-central Asia, whose urban population is estimated to have grown at 3.4 per cent per year during 1950-2000, is expected to experience a rate of urban growth of 2.7 per cent per year during 2000-2030, whereas Eastern Asia, whose 1950-2000 annual rate of urban growth was 3.1 per cent, is expected to see it decline to 1.6 per cent per year. The difference in expected urban growth rates produces the reversal already noted in the ranks of the two regions with respect to population size: by 2030 South-central Asia, with 1,027 million urban dwellers, will have surpassed Eastern Asia's urban population of 933 million by almost 100 million.

Only two less developed regions, the Caribbean and Southern Africa, experienced moderately low rates of urban population growth during 1950-2000, of the order of 2.7-2.8 per cent per year. The low overall rate of population growth of the Caribbean coupled with its moderate level of urbanization even as early as 1950 (35 per cent) explains the relatively low growth of the urban population. Nevertheless, the urban population of the Caribbean increased four-fold from 1950 to 2000 and is expected to rise by 50 per cent over the next thirty years when the average annual rate of urban growth in the region is projected to be 1.3 per cent.

In Southern Africa, the most urbanized region of the continent in 1950, the low rate of urban growth stems from a very low rate of urbanization coupled with the lowest rate of overall population growth recorded in Africa. Both figures are likely to reflect mostly the situation in the

Republic of South Africa, which accounts for 86 per cent of the population in the region. Population growth has been lower in Southern Africa because its fertility has tended to be lower than in rest of Africa and, more recently, because of increasing mortality due to the high prevalence of HIV/AIDS. Furthermore, the increase in the level of urbanization has been slower than previously expected. Nevertheless, Southern Africa is and is expected to remain the second most urbanized region of Africa and its urban population, which stands today at an estimated 23 million persons is expected to increase at an annual rate of 1.6 per cent during 2000-2030 to reach 36 million in 2030.

The regions having the lowest rates of urban population growth during 1950-2000 are those belonging to the more developed world. Among them, Australia/New Zealand and Eastern Europe exhibited the highest urban growth rates, at nearly 1.9 per cent per year. In contrast, the urban populations of Western Europe and Northern Europe grew at average rates lower than one per cent per year during 1950-2000. During 2000-2030, average growth rates in all the more developed regions will be below one per cent and those of all regions of Europe are expected to be lower than 0.25 per cent per year.

Only the urban populations of Australia/New Zealand and Northern America are expected to grow at an average of 0.9 per cent per year. As a result, whereas the urban populations of these two regions are expected to increase by about a third in each case (from 19 million to 25 million in the case of Australia/New Zealand and from 239 million to 314 million in the case of Northern America), those of the regions of Europe will barely change, increasing by 5 to 6 per cent in most cases. The lowest rate of growth is expected in Eastern Europe where the urban population is projected to increase by just 3 per cent over the next thirty years. The slow growth of the urban population in the regions of Europe is the result of both low rates of urbanization and the expected decline of the total population, which implies that, even if the proportion urban is increasing moderately, it is being applied to a declining overall number of inhabitants.

The different patterns of urban growth at the regional level lead to changes in the distribution of the world urban population among the regions.

As a result, whereas in 1950 those three less developed regions accounted for 34 per cent of the world urban population, by 2000 they accounted for 46 per cent. The next thirty years are expected to see only a small change in this share, which will rise to nearly 49 per cent. Concomitantly, the joint shares of Northern America, Western Europe, Eastern Europe, Northern Europe and Southern Europe, which in 1950 accounted for 53 per cent of the world urban population, declined to 28 per cent in 2000 and will likely drop to 18 per cent by 2030. In addition, nearly all the other less developed regions, except those in Oceania, saw their shares of the world urban population increase between 1950 and 2000 but during 2000-2030 only the shares of the regions of Asia and those of Africa (with the exception of Southern Africa) will increase.

Rural Population Growth

Echoing the differences among regions in terms of urban population growth, the differences in the growth rates of their rural populations are also sharp. In general, the regions of Africa and the less developed regions of Oceania have tended to experience the highest rural growth rates whereas the lowest are observed in the regions of Europe (table 5).

Table 5. Rural Population and Rural Growth rate by region, 1950-2030

	Rural population (in millions)			*Rural rate of growth (%)*	
Region	*1950*	*2000*	*2030*	*1950-2000*	*2000-2030*
Eastern Africa	61.4	182.4	259.9	2.18	1.18
Middle Africa	22.6	61.8	96.1	2.01	1.47
Northern Africa	40.2	85.3	88.6	1.51	0.13
Southern Africa	9.6	24.3	22.1	1.86	-0.31
Western Africa	54.7	133.5	173.6	1.78	0.88
Eastern Asia	550.3	913.5	776.3	1.01	-0.54
South-central Asia	415.7	1035.3	1 116.7	1.83	0.25
South-eastern Asia	155.1	325.9	313.4	1.48	-0.13
Western Asia	36.8	56.1	65.5	0.84	0.52
Eastern Europe	133.0	88.4	55.9	-0.82	-1.52
Northern Europe	21.3	15.3	11.1	-0.66	-1.08
Southern Europe	60.8	48.4	31.2	-0.46	-1.47
Western Europe	45.3	32.0	22.2	-0.70	-1.22
Caribbean	11.0	14.1	13.0	0.50	-0.28
Central America	22.3	44.3	47.5	1.38	0.23
South America	64.6	69.9	61.0	0.16	-0.45
Northern America	62.0	70.6	58.1	0.26	-0.65
Australia/New Zealand	2.6	3.4	3.2	0.58	-0.20
Melanesia	2.0	4.9	6.4	1.83	0.89
Micronesia	0.1	0.3	0.4	1.94	1.06
Polynesia	0.2	0.4	0.4	1.39	0.57

But there is considerable diversity within major areas. Furthermore, as in the case of the urban population, the size of the rural population does not display a high correlation with its rate of growth. The rapid rural population growth experienced by South-central Asia, at 1.8 per cent per year, led to such an outcome and because the rural population of South-central Asia is expected to continue growing during 2000-2030, it will remain larger than the rural population of Eastern Asia, which is expected to decline.

The most interesting development within the group is that, whereas the rural population of Australia/ New Zealand was the largest in the group in 1950, by 2000 it had been surpassed by that of Melanesia and will remain in second place until 2030 despite the negative growth rate it is expected to experience during 2000-2030. Indeed, the low rural growth rates that have characterized Australia/New Zealand contrast markedly with those of the less developed regions of Oceania, all of which have experienced and are expected to experience rural growth rates that are among the highest in the world.

Nevertheless, the small population base of these regions implies that their share of the world rural population is and will remain very low (of the order of 0.2 per cent). In contrast with the three largest regions of Asia and those of Oceania, the position of all other regions in terms of the size of their rural populations has changed considerably.

In 1950, the rural populations of Eastern Europe, South America and Northern America ranked fourth, fifth and sixth, but by 2000 they all had seen their ranks increase because of the slow growth or even the negative growth that their rural populations experienced. In Eastern Europe, the rural population declined by a third, passing from 133 million in 1950 to 88 million in 2000, a reduction that produced the lowest rate of rural population growth in the world during 1950-2000, at -0.8 per cent per year.

In comparison, the rural populations of Northern America and South America grew at moderate rates, though both rates were close to zero (0.2 and 0.3 per cent per year, respectively). During 2000-2030 all three regions are expected to experience a reduction of the rural population, with Eastern Europe evincing again the lowest rate of rural population growth in the world at -1.5 per cent per year. As a consequence, the rural population of Eastern Europe, which ranked fourth in the world in 1950 and sixth in 2000 is expected to rank eleventh by 2030, with both the rural populations of South America and Northern America having surpassed it by then. In 1950, the rural populations of the regions of Africa alternated with those of the regions of Europe in terms of the ranks they occupied above the sixth place. Eastern Africa had the largest rural population in the continent, followed by Western Africa and Northern Africa.

Southern Europe and Western Europe had rural populations similar in size to those of these regions of Africa. But over the next fifty years, the rural populations of the regions of Africa would experience some of the highest rural growth rates in the world whereas the rural growth rates of the European regions would be negative and among the lowest in the world.

Consequently, by 2000 the African regions ranked higher than those of Europe. By 2000, the rural populations of Eastern Africa and Western Africa had become the fourth and fifth largest in the world, with 182 million and 134 million persons respectively. Furthermore, because both regions are projected to experience relatively high rates of rural growth during 2000-2030, they are expected to maintain their present ranks until 2030. Northern Africa and especially Middle Africa have also moved up the ranks as their rural populations have increased at a rapid pace.

The growth rates experienced by the rural popula tion of Middle Africa have been and are expected to be particularly high (slightly above 2 per cent per year in 1950-2000 and 1.5 per cent per year in 2000-2030), leading to a four-fold increase of the rural population from 1950 to 2030 and making of Middle Africa the region with the sixth largest rural population in 2030, one rung above Northern Africa.

As a result, by 2030, these four regions of Africa will follow the three largest regions of Asia as the regions of residence of the highest number of rural dwellers. By that time, Eastern Africa, Western Africa, Middle Africa and Northern Africa will account for 19 per cent of the world rural population, nearly double the share they had in 1950 (10 per cent). In contrast with the regions of Africa, the regions of Europe, with their declining rural populations, will account for a decreasing proportion of the world rural population. Eastern Europe and Southern Europe, which in 1950 accounted for 11 per cent of the world rural population are expected to see their share decline to less than 3 per cent by 2030.

The equivalent figures for Western Europe and Northern Europe considered jointly are 4 per cent and 1 per cent. In terms of the rate of decrease of the rural population, Eastern Europe has had the highest and Southern Europe the lowest during 1950-2000, but during 2000-2030 both regions will have high and fairly similar rates of decrease, leading to very marked reductions of the rural population. Although both regions will continue to have the largest rural populations in Europe, their rapid decrease will be fueled as much by the continued rise of the proportion urban as by the expected reductions of the total population of each region.

Although a declining total population is also expected in the case of Western Europe, the rate of decline projected for the total population of that region is lower than in the case of Eastern Europe and Southern Europe, so that its effects on rural population decline are less marked. It is important to underscore that whereas during 1950-2000 only the regions of Europe experienced a reduction of the rural population, during 2000-2030 nearly half of all regions of the world are expected to experience such reductions.

Among the less developed regions, Eastern Asia and South-eastern Asia, the Caribbean and South America, as well as Southern Africa are expected to have negative rates of rural population growth. The cases of the regions of Asia and of South America have already been discussed above. In the Caribbean and Southern Africa, negative rural growth is related to the relatively low rate of increase expected for the total population of those regions and to the still sizable increase projected for the proportion urban.

As mentioned in discussing urban growth in Southern Africa, the reduction of overall population growth in the region is partly the result of the growing HIV/AIDS epidemic. In sum, with the rising urbanization of the world, the growth of the rural population has been dampened in every region and, especially in the most highly urbanized regions, rural population growth has been low or negative over the past fifty years. The future is expected to witness an accentuation of those trends with the proviso that certain regions with low to moderate levels of urbanization and whose overall population growth remains robust (mainly Eastern Africa, Middle Africa and Western Africa) will still experience a moderate to high rate of rural population growth.

In 14 of the 21 regions of the world, the rate of growth of the rural population is projected to be 0.25 per cent per year or lower during 2000-2030 and in 10 of them the rate will be negative. A decreasing rural population will characterize all the regions of Europe, two of the regions of Asia (Eastern Asia and South-eastern Asia), Northern America, the Caribbean, South America and Southern Africa. In 2030, nearly 7 out of every 10 rural dwellers will live in the three largest regions of Asia and another 2 will live in the four largest regions of Africa.

Proportion Urban Population

Changes in the proportion of the population living in urban areas are the result of differential rates of growth between the urban and the rural populations of a region. In fact, the rate of increase of the proportion urban (also known as the urbanization rate) is equivalent to the difference between the rate of growth of the urban population and that of the total population. The latter, by encompassing the growth of both the urban and the rural components of the population, reflects the effects of the differential between the two.

In 1950 there were already considerable differences among the regions with respect to the level of urbanization attained. Western Europe with 68 per cent urban and Northern America with 64 per cent were also highly urban at the time. In comparison, the other regions of Europe (Southern Europe with 44 per cent urban or Eastern Europe with 39 per cent urban) or the regions of Latin America (Central America with 40 per cent urban and South America with 43 per cent urban) were considerably less urbanized, not to mention most of the regions of Africa, Asia or developing Oceania, whole levels of urbanization were generally well below 25 per cent.

Between 1950 and 2000, all regions experienced an increase in the proportion urban, but its rate of growth varied considerably among regions. Generally, the rate of urbanization declines as the level of urbanization rises. The relation between the two is illustrated in figure 4 where the proportion urban in 1950 is plotted against the average annual rate of urbanization estimated for the period 1950-2000.

The curve superimposed on the observed points represents a logarithmic function fitted to the data. As the value of R2 presented on the graph indicates, the fitted curve explains 88 per cent of the variance in the observed values, implying that the fit is good. However, the experience of several regions deviates noticeably from the fitted curve.

The best fit is obtained at high levels of urbanization, where regions with more than 60 per cent of the population living in urban areas experience very low rates of urbanization (below 0.4 per cent per year). In the next group of regions, where the proportion urban varies from 35 per cent to 45 per cent, Southern Africa, with a proportion urban of 38 per cent in 1950 experienced a very low rate of urbanization in relation to the fitted values.

Constraints on the free movement of people that prevailed in the Republic of South Africa during the period of apartheid are likely to be at the root of this diverging experience. Most of the other regions in the group, namely, the Caribbean, Central America, South America and Eastern Europe, experienced urbanization rates averaging more than 1 per cent per year which, according to the fitted curve, are slightly above what would be expected given their level of urbanization. Only Southern Europe, with a rate of urbanization of 0.8 per cent per year matched the fitted values.

In the next group, distinguished by a proportion urban varying between 14 per cent and 27 per cent, two regions deviate markedly from the fitted values: South-central Asia whose rate of urbanization at 1.2 per cent per year seems too low in relation to the low percentage of the population that lived in urban areas in 1950 (16.6 per cent), and Western Asia whose rate of urbanization of 1.9 per cent per year appears as too high in relation to the moderate proportion urban already attained by 1950 (27 per cent).

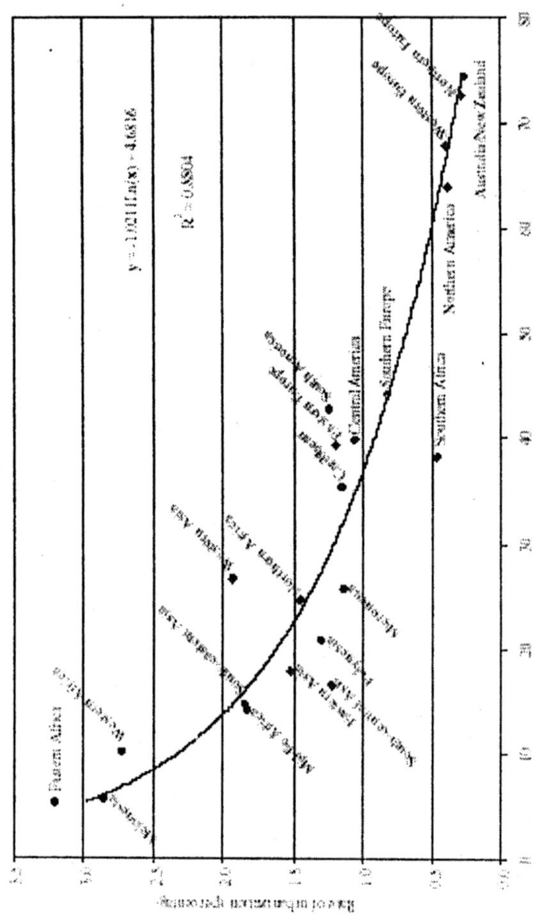

Figure 4. Relation between the percentage urban in 1950 and the rate of urbanization during 1950-2000

Among the other regions in the group, Eastern Asia, Micronesia and Polynesia, all experienced rates of urbanization that are on the low side in relation to the proportions urban that they had initially, whereas in Middle Africa, Northern Africa and South-eastern Asia the urbanization rates observed are closer to those expected on the basis of the proportions urban that those regions had in 1950. All regions in this group experienced urbanization rates varying between 1.1 per cent and 2 per cent per year.

Lastly, the three regions with the lowest percentage urban in 1950 experienced the highest rates of urbanization during 1950-2000. Except for the case of Melanesia, the fitted curve does not approximate well the observations at this end of the range. In particular, the high urbanization rate experienced by Eastern Africa (3.2 per cent per year) is not reached by the fitted curve (the fitted value is less than 3 per cent). There is also the suggestion that Western Africa, where 10 per cent of the population lived in urban areas by 1950, experienced a relatively high urbanization rate during 1950-2000 in relation to that initial level.

Only Melanesia, with a starting proportion urban of 6 per cent and a rate of urbanization of 2.9 per cent per year was close to the fitted values. The same analysis can be carried out for the period 2000-2030 using as initial proportion urban that estimated for 2000.

For regions with proportions urban above 75 per cent, the urbanization rate is projected to be very low (at or below 0.3 per cent per year). This group is headed by Australia/ New Zealand, which remains the most highly urbanized region of the world, followed by Northern Europe, Western Europe, South America and Northern America. The more developed regions in this group were already highly urbanized by 1950 (with proportions urban above 63 per cent) but that was not the case for South America whose proportion urban was a low 42.8 per cent. It is noteworthy therefore that, according to present estimates, by 2000 the proportion urban for South America has surpassed that for Northern America. Furthermore, projected values show that Northern America will remain as the least urbanized area in the group, with 84.4 per cent urban in 2030. South America is projected to have 87.3 per cent of its population living in urban areas by that time and Western Europe and Northern Europe will have higher values still, with Australia/New Zealand heading the group with a level of urbanization nearing 89 per cent.

Among the five regions that in 2000 are estimated to have proportions urban ranging from 63 to 72 per cent, the rate of urbanization is projected to vary between 0.39 and 0.51 per cent per year leading to projected values ranging from 73.3 per cent urban in the Caribbean to 80.1 per cent urban in Eastern Europe by 2030. Western Asia with 79.1 per cent urban in 2030, Southern Europe with 76.3 per cent and Central America with 75.9 per cent are the other regions in the group. Clearly, just as South America, Western Asia, the Caribbean and Central America have also achieved and are expected to maintain levels of urbanization comparable to those characterizing the more developed regions.

The remaining less developed regions display a wide range of levels of urbanization in 2000, going from 23.7 per cent in Melanesia to 50.8 per cent in Northern Africa. The group includes all the regions of Africa, all those of Asia except Western Asia, and all the developing regions of Oceania. Their levels of urbanization are expected to increase at a moderately rapid pace since most of these regions are projected to have urbanization rates above 1 per cent per year. As a consequence, by 2030 only three regions will still have less than half of their population living in urban areas, namely, Melanesia, Eastern Africa and Southcentral Asia. The most urbanized regions in this group will be in Africa and in Oceania, each of which will have between 58 and 67 per cent of its population in urban areas. Two of the regions with large rural populations, Eastern Asia and South-eastern Asia, are expected to attain levels of urbanization of the order of 54 to 56 per cent. Consequently, by 2030, the most populous regions of the developing world will have barely gone past the midway point toward a highly urbanized society, implying that the potential for further urban growth will remain high.

Rural Population Growth at the Country Level

Urbanization patterns at the country level are even more varied than at the regional level. Furthermore, for the majority of countries, the changes experienced over the second half of the twentieth have been remarkable. Thus, whereas in 1950 only a quarter of the 228 countries or areas in the world had more than 46 per cent of their population living in urban areas, by 2000 more than half of them had 56 per cent or more of their population liv ing in urban areas, and if the country-level projections presented in this volume hold, by 2030 three-quarters of all countries or areas will have more than 55 per cent of their population in urban areas.

In most countries the urban population has grown in parallel to the proportion urban. However, because the large majority of countries have small or medium-sized populations, their urban population remains small. Thus, in 2000 threequarters of all countries and areas had urban populations of less than 7.4 million persons.

There are relatively few countries with large urban populations. In 2000, 25 countries accounted for 75 per cent of the urban population in the world. China and India had the largest urban populations in the world, at 410 million and 288 million urban inhabitants respectively. The other countries with large urban populations included mostly populous developing countries with low to moderate levels of urbanization and medium-sized developed countries with high levels of urbanization.

Most of the developed countries with large urban population in 2000 have exhibited low to moderate rates of urban population growth during 1950-2000 (below 2 per cent per year), whereas most developing countries in the group have experienced rates of urban growth ranging from 2 per cent to 5 per cent per year. Particularly high rates of urban growth were estimated for Bangladesh (5.8 per cent per year) and Nigeria (5.5 per cent per year). In 2030, 28 countries are expected to account for 75 per cent of the world's urban population.

China and India will again head the list with projected urban populations of 752 million and 633 million respectively. Only 7 of the 28 countries with large urban populations in 2030 are located in the more developed regions, down from 9 in 2000. That is, the majority of countries with large urban populations in 2030 will be in the developing world and most of them will have, as today's highly urbanized countries, complex urban systems where single cities can have populations of several million persons.

The rural population of the world is also largely concentrated in developing countries. Although three-quarters of all countries or areas of the world had rural populations of less than 7.3 million persons in 2000, the largest rural populations were considerably higher than the largest urban populations: 868 million in China and 725 million in India. Just 16 countries accounted for 75 per cent of the rural population in the world, only two of which were developed countries.

In comparison to the urban growth rates of the 25 countries that comprised 75 per cent of the urban population in 2000, the growth rates of the rural population among those 16 countries during 1950-2000 were considerably lower. Thus, only three countries experienced rural growth rates above 2 per cent per year (the Democratic Republic of the Congo, Ethiopia and Pakistan) and for two countries the average annual rural growth rates over the 50-year period were negative (Brazil and the Russian Federation).

During 2000-2030, more than half of the countries or areas of the world are expected to experience negative growth rates of the rural population, implying that their rural population will decrease. Among the 17 countries that are expected to account for 75 per cent of the world's rural population in 2030 only five-Afghanistan, the Democratic Republic of the Congo, Ethiopia, Nepal and Uganda-are likely to experience rural growth rates above 1 per cent per year.

Although the rural populations of some populous countries, such as Bangladesh, India and Pakistan, are still expected to increase, that of China is projected to decline significantly, so that by 2030 it will have been surpassed by that of India (744 million vs. 749 million respectively). Most countries that are projected to see their rural population rise by 2030 are located in Africa, South-central Asia or developing Oceania. For the rest of the world, the rapid rise of urbanization coupled with a reduction of overall population growth will result in reductions of the rural population.

Level of Urbanisation

Not only are the world's regions at very different stages of the transition to a largely urban population but the differences among them are amplified when one considers conditions at the country level. To analyse major trends in urbanization among the 228 countries or areas of the world, their distribution according to the level of urbanization is considered (table 6). Figure 5 displays schematically the changing distribution over time, showing for each time point the interquartile range of the distribution as a central box and the lengths of the upper and lower quarters of the distribution as the lines that extend beyond the upper and lower boundaries of the central box. The position of the median is indicated within the box by a symbol. The distributions presented are for the level of urbanization of countries and areas in 1950, 1975, 2000 and 2030. In all cases, the extremes of the distribution are 0 and 100, since there have always been and there are expected to remain a few countries or areas that are totally rural (i.e., where the level of urbanization of zero) and some that are totally urban and have therefore a level of urbanization of 100 per cent.

The interquartile range holds the central half of the distribution, that is, 50 per cent of the countries or areas have urbanization levels falling within the range of values delimited by the upper and lower boundaries of the box. A further 25 per cent of the countries or areas have levels of urbanization whose values range from zero to the lower boundary of the box (the range indicated by the line that "tie s" the box to the lower axis) and another 25 per cent have levels of urbanization whose values range from the upper boundary of the box to 100 per cent. The median is the central value of the distribution, meaning that half the countries or areas have levels of urbanization above and half below the median.

Table 6. Indicators of the distribution of countires and areas according to the proportion urban in 1950,1975, 2000 and 2030

	Percentage urban			
Indicator	*1950*	*1975*	*2000*	*2030*
All countries or areas				
Lower extreme	0.0	0.0	0.0	0.0
Lower quartile	12.5	21.6	35.9	54.7
Median	28.0	43.0	56.4	70.9
Upper quartile	46.1	62.8	75.6	84.1
Upper extreme	100.0	100.0	100.0	100.0
Interquartile range	33.6	41.3	39.7	29.4
Countries with more than 150,000 inhabitants in 1995				
Lower extreme	0.3	3.2	6.2	14.2
Lower quartile	10.6	21.3	35.6	54.9
Median	26.9	43.4	57.1	71.0
Upper quartile	43.0	62.8	75.3	83.6
Upper extreme	100.0	100.0	100.0	100.0
Interquartile range	32.4	41.5	39.7	28.7
Countries with less than 150,000 inhabitants in 1995				
Lower extreme	0.0	0.0	0.0	0.0
Lower quartile	17.9	24.9	37.3	53.0
Median	37.9	38.6	52.7	69.8
Upper quartile	54.0	65.5	80.1	86.7
Upper extreme	100.0	100.0	100.0	100.0
Interquartile range	36.2	40.6	42.8	33.8

As table 6 and figure 5 show, the median of the level of urbanization has been rising steadily from 1950 to 2000, passing from 28 to 56 per cent, and is projected to reach 71 per cent in 2030. Concomitantly, the position of the central part of the distribution has been moving upward as the level

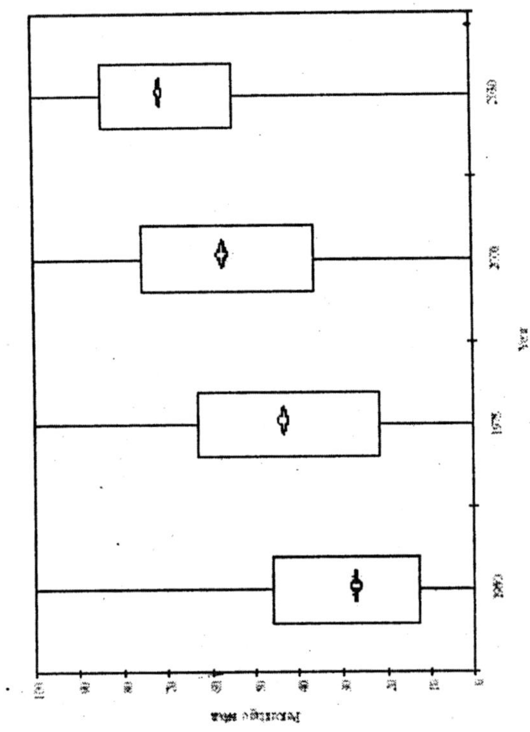

Figure 5. Distribution of countries by level of urbanization, 1950, 1975, 2000 and 2030

of urbanization of most countries has risen. Furthermore, the length of the box (the interquartile range), which indicates the amount of variation around the median, has been changing.

In 1950, most countries had low urbanization levels (in 3 out of every 4 countries the proportion urban was below 46 per cent) and there was relatively small variation around the median because the process of differentiation in terms of level of urbanization was still at its initial stages. By 1975, not only had the median increased markedly (from 28 per cent to 43 per cent) but, in addition, the interquartile range had risen from 33.6 percentage points to 41.3, indicating that the variation around the median had increased as some countries experienced faster urbanization rates than others. But as more and more countries caught up with the rapidly urbanizing ones, the degree of variation around the median began to decline.

By 2000 the interquartile range stood at 39.7 percentage points, still higher than the value it had in 1950 but lower than in 1975 (table 6). If the projected paths toward increased urbanization hold, by 2030 the median level of urbanization will be 71 per cent and the proportion urban for half of the countries or areas in the world will be within a range of 55 per cent to 84 per cent, implying that the interquartile range will have declined to 29 percentage points, lower than the value it had in 1950 and indicative of an increasing homogeneity among countries in terms of the levels of urbanization attained.

Furthermore, by 2030 the upper quarter of the distribution will be more concentrated than ever before, ranging from 84 per cent to 100 per cent. However, the lower quarter of the distribution will be considerably more extended than in the past, varying between a proportion urban of 0 and one of 54.7 per cent and implying that the least urbanized countries will be more diverse than ever before. One of the possible reasons for the growing diversity in the level of urbanization at the lower end of the distribution is that countries or areas with small territories and small populations may be more likely to maintain a rural character for longer than countries or areas with larger populations, probably because small rural societies with limited natural resources face more constraints than better endowed countries to engage in a rapid process of urbanization.

A comparison of the two sets of indicators shows that in 1950 the small countries or areas tended to have higher levels of urbanization than the large countries. Thus, the median level of urbanization for the small countries was 37.9 per cent whereas that of the larger countries was 26.9 per cent. In addition, both the lower and the upper quartiles of the distribution of the small countries were higher than those of the large countries.

Over time, the median of the distribution of small countries has fallen below that of large countries, but the upper quartile has been and is expected to remain above that of large countries, implying that at the upper end of the distribution small countries tend to display higher levels of urbanization than large ones. However, at the lower end of the distribution, small countries show consistently greater dispersion than large countries. Thus, the difference between the lower quartile and the lower extreme of the distribution of small countries has been and is expected to continue being considerably larger than the corresponding value for the distribution of large countries.

In 1950, for instance, the lower quarter of the distribution of small countries ranged from 0 to 17.9 per cent whereas that of large countries had a range of 0.3 per cent to 10.6 per cent, considerably narrower. By 2000, large countries in the lower quarter of the distribution had levels of urbanization ranging between 6.2 per cent and 35.6 per cent, a narrower range than the 0 to 37.3 per cent corresponding to small countries, and in 2030, the respective ranges are expected to be 14.2 per cent to 54.9 per cent for large countries and 0 to 53 per cent for small ones. That is, small countries are responsible for extending the lower part of the distribution of all countries to zero and thus increasing its dispersion. This finding indicates that at least some small countries are indeed slow at embarking on the urbanization process.

Thus, they are the countries with levels of urbanization within the range determined by 0 and half the distance between the lower extreme and the lower quartile of the distribution of large countries (table 6). Consequently, the reduction in the length of the list over time is indicative of the increasing levels of urbanization that characterize large countries as time elapses. Furthermore, whereas in 1950 a low level of urbanization was of the order of a few percentage points, because of the general tendency for the level of urbanization to rise, by 2000 a "low" level has become anything below 20 or 21 per cent, and by 2030 "low" will be anything below 36 per cent. That is, in the world of 2030, where most countries are expected to have a level of urbanization of at least 55 per cent, having a proportion urban below 36 per cent means having a low level of urbanization in relation to the position of the majority of countries.

Consequently, among the five small countries listed as least urbanized in 2000, four experienced either no change in the level urbanization or a reduction of that level between

1950 and 2000. Although their experience suggests that some small populations face constraints in pursu-ing urbanization, the number of deviant cases is too small to conclude that a small population, per se, represents a drawback to urbanization. In fact, small populations are fairly likely to live in places that are highly urbanized.

Thus, among the most highly urbanized countries in the world, the proportion of countries or areas with small populations (less than 150,000 in 1995) or with populations ranging from 150,000 to one million inhabitants is large. The cut-off point for each list is given by the mid-point of the interval between the upper quartile and the upper extreme of the corresponding distribution for all countries (table 6). As in the case of the least urbanized countries, this approach produces lists of different lengths for different periods, lengths than in themselves indicate changes over time in the distribution of countries by level of urbanization. The rising values of the cut-off points clearly reflect the overall increase in urbanization levels among most countries.

As expected, 12 out of the 19 most urbanized countries in 1950 were either small countries or countries with less than a million inhabitants, and among the remaining countries or areas, Hong Kong Special Administrative Region of China, Singapore and Uruguay each had between 1 million and 3 million inhabitants in 1950; Australia, Belgium and the Netherlands each had a population ranging from 8 million to 11 million; and only the United Kingdom had more than 50 million inhabitants.

By 2000, 31 countries or areas were identified as most urbanized, having at least 88.5 per cent of their respective populations living in urban areas, and 21 of them had a population of less than one million inhabitants. Among the others, the United Kingdom and Argentina had the largest populations, with 58 million and 37 million respectively. They were followed by the Netherlands (16 million) and Belgium (10 million). The rest were small countries or areas with populations ranging from 2 million in Kuwait to 7 million in Hong Kong Special Administrative Region of China. That is, very high urbanization remains associated with fairly small populations and that pattern is not expected to change markedly in the future.

Accordingly, the countries or areas projected to be the most urbanized by 2030 are the same as those for 2000, except that Oman is expected to replace San Marino. Therefore, 20 of the 31 most urbanized countries or areas in 2030 will have a population of less than a million and among the 11 others, Argentina with 49 million and the United Kingdom with 60 million inhabitants will be the largest. Most of the rest will have populations ranging from 2 million to 10 million inhabitants. It also bears noting that six small countries or areas plus Singapore have been totally urban since 1950 and that by 2000 they were joined by the Hong Kong Special Administrative Region of China, the most populous area with 100 per cent of its population living entirely in an urban environment.

The rest are located in Oceania, South-central Asia and South-eastern Asia. Table 7 permits an assessment of the differences among major areas by comparing the distributions of the countries located in them by level of urbanization. Perhaps the most interesting feature revealed by those distributions is not the relative level of urbanization in each major area, but the degree of homogeneity that exists within major areas or, in other words, the amount of variation among the countries or areas that constitute each major area. Africa, for instance, displays the lowest amount of variability around the median, although the interquartile range has been increasing.

Table 7. Indicatorsof the distribution of countries and areas by major area, according tothe proportion urban in 1950, 1975, 2000 and 2030

	Percentage urban			
Indicator	*1950*	*1975*	*2000*	*2030*
Africa				
Lower extreme	0.3	3.2	6.2	14.2
Lower quartile	4.8	15.2	29.9	49.4
Median	9.6	21.3	39.0	57.3
Upper quartile	18.7	33.8	50.3	67.0
Upper extreme	67.8	68.5	95.4	98.2
Interquartile range	13.9	18.6	20.4	17.5
Asia				
Lower extreme	2.1	3.5	7.1	15.0
Lower quartile	12.4	19.5	27.6	43.9
Median	25.9	44.3	57.4	71.6
Upper quartile	38.9	61.9	81.1	89.7
Upper extreme	100.0	100.0	100.0	100.0
Interquartile range	26.5	42.4	53.6	45.9
Europe				
Lower extreme	13.7	20.0	22.6	40.9
Lower quartile	24.5	48.3	59.6	71.3
Median	42.6	58.3	68.6	79.0
Upper quartile	62.5	77.1	86.4	90.4
Upper extreme	100.0	100.0	100.0	100.0
Interquartile range	38.1	28.8	26.9	19.1
Americas				
Lower extreme	10.0	10.0	12.0	26.3
Lower quartile	28.8	38.7	48.4	63.2
Median	37.9	49.9	67.9	80.3
Upper quartile	56.3	70.7	80.5	87.3
Upper extreme	100.0	100.0	100.0	100.0
Interquartile range	27.5	32.0	32.2	24.1
Oceania				
Lower extreme	0.0	0.0	0.0	0.0
Lower quartile	9.0	19.7	21.1	37.9
Median	23.2	31.3	44.3	59.0
Upper quartile	46.8	54.5	62.5	73.4
Upper extreme	100.0	100.0	100.0	100.0
Interquartile range	37.8	34.8	41.4	35.5

That is, in 1950 most countries of Africa had very low levels of urbanization and displayed a large degree of homogeneity in that respect. By 2000, although they had grown somewhat more heterogeneous, the levels of urbanization of the countries of Africa were still highly concentrated around the median. The range of the distribution, however, had become very wide, spanning the interval between 6.2 per cent and 95.4 per cent. In the future a reduction of the variation around the median is expected but the overall range of variation will remain large, going from 14.2 per cent to 98.2 per cent.

Asia and the Americas, which includes Latin America, the Caribbean and Northern America, displayed a medium level of variation around the median in 1950 when urbanization levels in Asia were still on the low side and those in the Americas were already moderately high. But whereas the variation around the median has been rising markedly in Asia, to reach 53.5 percentage points in 2000, that for the Americas has shown a very small increase (from 27.5 percentage points in 1950 to 32.2 in 2000).

These results reflect the growing heterogeneity among the urbanization levels of the countries or areas of Asia, a continent that comprises at the same time small countries or areas that are very highly urbanized and many of the most populous countries in the world whose levels of urbanization remain low.

In the Americas, in contrast, there has been a rapid increase of urbanization levels in almost every country and the result is a convergence to the high levels of urbanization typical of the developed world, as the distribution for 2030 reveals. Europe, as the only major area comprising only more developed regions, is also the only one displaying a declining variation around the median as time elapses. That reduction is a reflection of the high degree of homogeneity among European countries regarding patterns of urbanization and of the advanced stages that they have reached in the transition to a nearly universal urban way of life.

Thus, by 2030, more than three quarters of the countries in Europe will have at least 70 per cent of their populations living in urban areas and the least urbanized country in the continent will be 40.9 per cent urban. Lastly, in Oceania, where small countries predominate, the distribution is affected by the bimodal nature of the distribution of those countries.

Consequently, Oceania is the only major area where the lower extreme remains at 0 and forces the lower part of the distribution to become more and more elongated over time. Furthermore, although some small areas are highly urbanized and so are Australia and New Zealand, the larger part of the countries or areas in Oceania remain less urbanized than their counterparts in the Americas or even in Asia. Because of the co-existence of such different groups, by 2000 Oceania displays the second highest degree of varia tion around the median and is still expected to evince a high degree of heterogeneity in 2030.

Size and Growth of the Urban Population

Countries differ not only in the level of urbanization that they have attained, but also with respect to the size of their urban populations. As the distribution of countries and areas according to urban population size shows, the range of variation of the urban population has been increasing steadily. Both the unprecedented population growth that many countries have experienced during the second half of the twentieth century and their rising levels of urbanization have resulted in increasing numbers of people living in urban areas. Yet, in the majority of countries or areas the number of urban dwellers remains modest.

Thus, the median urban population size stands at 2.1 million persons in 2000, up from 288,000 in 1950, and three-quarters of all countries or areas have at most 7.4 million urban dwellers today. Although both the median and the upper quartile of the distribution of countries by urban population size are expected nearly to double by 2030, most countries will have fairly small urban populations: in half of them the number of urban dwellers is not expected to exceed 3.9 million and in three-quarters it will likely be below 14.5 million.

In addition, in a quarter of all countries or areas of the world the urban population is expected to have at most 403,000 persons. However, although the urban populations of most countries are small and are expected to remain small, countries at the upper end of the distribution have large numbers of urban dwellers living in complex urban systems where single cities can have populations of several millions.

Most of the world's most populous countries belong to this group and some countries with intermediate population sizes and high levels of urbanization have also been part of it. In 1950, when most countries were still at the early stages of the urbanization process, 17 countries accounted for three-quarters of the world urban population.

The United States headed the list with 101 million urban dwellers. It was followed by China and India, both of which had very low levels of urbanization at the time (12.5 per cent and 17.3 per cent, respectively), though their large total populations produced large numbers of urban dwellers. The next six slots corresponded to developed countries (Germany, the Russian Federation, the United Kingdom, Japan, Italy and France).

In total, 11 of the 17 countries in the list were developed countries, most of them located in Europe. The list for 1950 included also three countries in Latin America (Brazil, Mexic o and Argentina in order of population size) and three developing countries in Asia (China, India and Indonesia, ordered according to population size). By 2000, along with the overall increase in the urban population of the world, the number of countries accounting for three-quarters of it had increased to 25, 10 of which were located in the developed world.

China and India headed the list, having seen their urban populations increase nearly six-fold and five-fold respectively. Indonesia had risen from fifteenth to seventh place, and Pakistan, Turkey, the Philippines, Iran, the Republic of Korea and Bangladesh, in order of urban population size, had joined the group. There had also been additions from Africa (Nigeria and Egypt) and from Latin America (Colombia). Furthermore, several of the developed countries with large urban populations in both 1950 and 2000 had experienced a change in rank between the two dates. The urban population of the Russian Federation had surpassed that of Germany and that of the Ukraine had become larger than that of Spain. The faster urbanization rates experienced by the Russian Federation and the Ukraine produced such changes.

In 2030, 28 countries are expected to account for 75 per cent of the world urban population and most of them are located in the developing world. Indeed, only 7 of the 11 developed countries appearing in the lists for 1950 and 2000 are expected to remain in the list of 2030 and all of them, except the United States, are expected to see their ranks drop as they are displaced by the larger urban populations of developing countries. Among the latter, China and India will continue to head the list, but Brazil, Indonesia, Pakistan and Nigeria are also expected to rank high, occupying places fourth to seventh. Furthermore, all the developing countries included in the list for 2000 remain in that for 2030 with the addition of three African countries, namely, the Democratic Republic of the Congo, Ethiopia and Algeria, and three Asian countries?Saudi Arabia, Viet Nam and Iraq. That is, in 2030, there will be 12 devel-oping countries from Asia in the list of the countries with the largest urban populations in the world.

A comparison of the countries accounting for three-quarters of the urban population with those accounting for the same proportion of the total population of the world reveals some interesting differences. In 1950, 6 of the 21 countries that accounted for 75 per cent of the world population were not among the 17 countries accounting for three-quarters of the urban population mainly because, despite their large populations, their levels of urbanization were too low. They were, in order of population size, Bangladesh, Pakistan, Nigeria, Viet Nam, Egypt and the Philippines. Conversely, Argentina and the Netherlands were in the list of countries accounting for most of the urban popula tion but not in that of the most populous countries in the world.

In 2000 only four of the most populous countries were not in the list of those with the highest numbers of urban dwellers, namely, the Democratic Republic of Congo, Ethiopia, Thailand and Viet Nam. However, five highly urbanized countries appeared in the list of countries with large numbers of urban dwellers although their overall population did not qualify them for the list of most populous countries, namely, Argentina, Colombia, Poland, the Republic of Korea and Spain. By 2030, three of the most populous countries (Myanmar, Thailand and the United Republic of Tanzania) are not expected to be among those with the largest numbers of urban dwellers and four of the latter (Algeria, Argentina, Iraq and Saudi Arabia) are not expected to be among the most populous countries.

However, despite the differences between the two sets of countries, the large degree of overlap between the two indicates that the urban population tends to be concentrated in the same geographical areas as the overall population of the world. That is, the concentration of most of the world's urban population in a few countries largely parallels that of the total population.

Today the most urbanized countries with large urban populations include several in the less developed regions. Indeed, in 2000 Argentina is estimated to have the highest level of urbanization in the group of countries with large urban populations, at nearly 90 per cent, and Brazil, Colombia, Mexico, the Republic of Korea and Turkey all have more than 70 per cent of their populations living in urban areas.

However, most of the highly urbanized countries with large urban populations in 2000 still belong to the more developed regions. Among the 16 countries with large urban populations and a level of urbanization of 65 per cent or more, 10 are located in Europe or Northern America. The rest of the 25 countries with large urban populations in 2000 have considerably lower levels of urbanization. Only Iran and the Philippines are more than 50 per cent urban. The other seven countries, located in Africa and Asia, have levels of urbanization ranging from 24.5 per cent (Bangladesh) to 45.2 per cent (Egypt). But the urbanization levels of most of the countries with large urban populations are like ly to rise considerably in the future. By 2030, 18 of the 28 countries with large urban populations are expected to have over 73 per cent of their populations living in urban areas and only 7 of them will be countries in the more developed regions.

High levels of urbanization will be common among a number of large developing countries although the most populous will still have relatively low proportions of the population living in urban areas. In Bangladesh and India, for instance, the urban population will constitute 43.8 per cent and 45.8 per cent of the total, respectively. In general, countries that have already reached high levels of urbanization tend to experience low rates of urbanization because a high proportion urban cannot keep on rising at a fast pace for long.

Size and Growth of the Rural Population

Countries vary considerably according to the size of their rural populations. Furthermore, although over the past fifty years the rural population of every country has grown at lower rates than the urban population, rural growth has nevertheless been robust in many developing countries with the result that the range of variation of the rural population has increased steadily since 1950.

As a result, the largest rural population in the world (that of China) has risen from 485 million in 1950 to 867 million in 2000. Similarly, in the course of the past fifty years there has been a consistent increase of the median and the quartiles of the distribution of countries or areas according to size of the rural population. Yet, in 2000 half of the countries or areas in the world had less than 1.72 million rural inhabitants each and in three-quarters of them the rural population did not surpass 7.3 million. Over the next thirty years, the median and the upper extreme of the distribution of countries or areas by size of the rural population are expected to decline as a result of reductions in the rural population of a growing number of countries.

Consequently, by 2030 half of the countries or areas in the world are each expected to have less than 1.4 million inhabitants in rural areas and the largest rural population in the world, which will then correspond to India, will likely be lower than 750 million. Highly urbanized countries in the developed world have been experiencing reductions of the rural population for a long time.

In Europe, such reductions have meant that the distribution of countries by rural population size has become more compressed as the range of variation has diminished. Europe is the only major area where all the location parameters of the distribution of countries by rural population size have been declining steadily since 1950.

By 2030 the largest rural population in Europe will stand at barely 20 million, down from 33 million in 2000. No other major area has as yet experienced reductions of the rural population such as those characterizing the countries of Europe, but between 2000 and 2030 the majority of countries in the Americas are expected to follow similar trends.

Consequently, the largest rural population in the Americas is projected to pass from 63 million in 2000 to 52 million in 2030 and the other location parameters of the distribution for the Americas will also decline. In Asia a reduction of the largest rural population in the continent (i.e., the upper extreme) is expected but other location indicators are not expected to decrease, implying that most Asian countries are unlikely to experience reductions of the rural population during 2000-2030.

Furthermore, the interquartile range for Asia is expected to increase between 2000 and 2030, indicating that the variability in the rural population size of Asian countries will grow. The main indicators of the shapes of the distributions of countries or areas in Africa and Oceania by rural population size have generally shown a steady increase between 1950 and 2000, consistent with the continued rise of the rural population in most of the countries in those two continents. Furthermore, those trends are expected to continue into the future so that, overall, most countries in Africa and Oceania are expected to experience the sustained growth of their rural populations until 2030.

The different patterns of rural population growth experienced by countries or areas result in considerable variability with respect to their rates of rural population growth. Between 1975 and 2000, the rural growth rates of countries or areas varied between -13.4 per cent and 6.7 per cent, and during 2000-2030 they are projected to range between -2.5 per cent and 3.5 per cent, implying that the wide range of variation of rural growth rates among countries or areas over the past fifty years is unlikely to be emulated in the future. Furthermore, for three-quarters of all countries or areas, the rural growth rates are expected to vary between -0.8 per cent and 3.5 per cent in 2000-2030, about half the range over which the equivalent set of rural growth rates varied in 1975-2000 (-0.5 per cent to 6.7 per cent).

A key feature of the distribution of countries by the rate of rural population growth is the increase in the number of countries exhibiting negative rates and therefore experiencing net reductions of the rural population. During 1950-1975 there were 49 such countries, less than a quarter of the 228 countries or areas in the world. By 1975-2000, the number of countries with declining rural populations had increased to 74 and it is expected that during 2000-2030, 116 countries or areas will experience negative rural growth rates, that is, more than half of all countries or areas are expected to see their rural populations decrease over the course of the next thirty years.

During 1950-2000, 11 of the 25 countries in that group were small countries or areas with overall populations of less than one million in 1995. A further 10 were countries of Europe whose low rates of overall population growth coupled with the continued increase of the urban population through rural-urban migration and reclassification resulted in a declining rural population. Another two, the Republic of Korea and Uruguay, also fit that description, and in the two other cases, Gabon and Lebanon, the reduction of the rural population was brought about by very rapid urbanization.

Those types of transitions happen in countries with small populations, specifically China, Hong Kong SAR; Falkland Islands (Malvinas); Guadeloupe; Niue; St. Pierre and Miquelon. decline include 11 countries or areas with small populations and 13 European countries experiencing very low or even negative overall population growth. Once more, a number of small countries or areas with populations below one million in 1995 are prominent in both periods. Some of them tend to experience the highest sustained rates of growth of the rural population, mainly because they start with very small numbers of rural inhabitants.

Of greater importance are the high rural growth rates experienced by countries with at least a million inhabitants in 1950. There are 11 such countries, six of them located in Africa, four in Asia and one, Guatemala, in Latin America. During 2000-2030, the 16 countries with more than a million rural dwellers among the 25 expected to experience high rates of rural population growth included 13 in Africa and three in Asia (Afghanistan, Bhutan and Yemen).

As in the case of the urban population, the countries experiencing the highest rates of rural population growth are usually not those with the largest rural populations. Because many of the countries with large rural populations experienced low rates of rural population growth during 1950-2000, the degree of concentration of the rural population in a few countries increased between 1950 and 2000.

Thus, whereas 20 countries were needed to account for 3 out of every 4 rural dwellers in 1950, by 2000 the same fraction could be accounted for by just 16 countries. Furthermore, most of the developed countries that in 1950 had had sizable numbers of rural inhabitants were no longer in the list in 2000. France, Germany, Italy, Japan and the Ukraine were among that group. In addition, developing countries that experienced rapid urbanization during 1950-2000 also dropped from the list (e.g., Mexico, the Republic of Korea and Turkey).

As a result by 2000, 14 out of the 16 countries accounting for threequarters of the rural population belonged to the less developed regions (the exceptions being the Russian Federation and the United States), and among them only one, Brazil, was in Latin America and three were in Africa (the Democratic Republic of the Congo, Egypt and Nigeria). That is, the largest rural populations in the world are mostly concentrated in Asian countries, with China, India, Indonesia, Pakistan, Bangladesh and Viet Nam heading the list.

As of 2000, China and India account jointly for about half of the total rural population of the world and the six Asian countries with the largest rural populations account for nearly 62 per cent of the world's rural population. By 2030, 17 countries are expected to account for three-quarters of the rural population of the world. Among them, only the United States belongs to the more developed regions and among the other 16, five are located in Africa (the Democratic Republic of the Congo, Egypt, Ethiopia, Nigeria and Uganda) and the rest in Asia. The rural population of China, which is expected to reach 744 million by 2030, will have been surpassed by that of India (749 million) and Pakistan, Bangladesh and Indonesia will occupy third, fourth and fifth places, respectively. Those five countries will account jointly for 56.7 per cent of the world's rural population, with the share of China and India having declined to 46.3 per cent.

In general, the countries having large rural populations have been and are expected to remain highly rural. By 2030, that number had risen to seven out of 17 and included China, Egypt and Pakistan with proportions rural in the range of 40 per cent to 50 per cent; Indonesia and Nigeria, each with 36.5 per cent rural; the Philippines with 26.2 per cent rural, and the United States with 15.5 per cent rural. In addition, during 1950-2000 most of the countries that in 2000 accounted for three-quarters of the world's rural population exhibited rates of rural population growth ranging from 1.4 per cent to 2.6 per cent. China and Indonesia had somewhat lower rural growth rates (of the order of 1.16 to 1.17 per cent), and the United States, Brazil and the Russian Federation had very low or negative rates of rural population growth.

5

International Migration

According recent estimates of international migration, an estimated 150 million persons reside outside of their country of birth or nationality. This number does not include the additional millions of people who make short visits as tourists or business travellers to other countries. Longer-term international migrants belong to two broad groups: voluntary migrants and forced migrants. Fuelled by a combination of push factors in source countries and pull factors in receiving countries, voluntary migration is sustained by well-developed networks that link the supply of labour with the demand of businesses for both highly skilled and unskilled workers. Forced migration is fuelled by conflicts, human rights abuses and political repression that displace people from their home communities.

Scale of International Migration

The number of long-term international migrants (that is, those residing in foreign countries for more than one year) has grown steadily in the past four decades. According to the UN Population Division, in 1965, only 75 million persons fit the definition, rising to 84 million by 1975 and 105 million by 1985. There were an estimated 120 million international migrants in 1990, the last year for which detailed international statistics are available.

An examination of data from selected countries of in-migration indicates that international migration continued with about the same rate of growth in the 1990s. As of the year 2000, according to estimates prepared by this author for the International Organisation for Migration, there are 150 million international migrants.

Between 1965 and 1975, the growth in international migration (1.16% per year) did not keep pace with the growth in global population (2.04% per year). However, overall population growth began to decline in the 1980s while international migration continued to increase significantly. During the period from 1985 to 1990, global population growth increased by about 1.7 percent per year, whereas the total population of international migrants increased by 2.59 percent per year.Even with the numbers of international migrants large and growing, it is important to keep in mind that fewer than three percent of the world's population have been living outside of their home countries for a year or longer. The propensity to move internationally, particularly in the absence of compelling reasons such as wars, is limited to a small proportion of humans.

International migrants come from all parts of the world and they go to all parts of the world. In fact, few countries are unaffected by international migration. Many countries are sources of international flows, while others are net receivers and still others are transit countries through which migrants reach receiving countries. Such countries as Mexico experience migration in all three capacities, as source, receiving and transit countries. Migration tends to be within regions, with migrants often remaining within the same continent. More than half of international migrants traditionally have moved from one developing country to another. In recent years, however, migration from poorer to richer countries has increased significantly. While the traditional immigration countries – the United States, Canada and Australia – continue to see large-scale movements, as a result of labour recruitment that began in the 1960s and 1970s, Europe, the oil rich Persian Gulf states and the "economic tigers" of east and Southeast Asia are now also major destinations for international migrants.

The industrialised countries belonging to the Organisation for Economic Cooperation and Development (OECD) experienced significant growth in their immigrant population during the 1990s. In 1986/87, about 36 million international migrants (some of whom subsequently naturalised) lived in the US, France, Germany, Canada, Australia and the United Kingdom. A decade later, more than 46 million international migrants were reported to be living in these same countries, more than a 25 percent increase.

The most rapid growth in the number of international migrants tends to occur as a result of refugee crises. Massive numbers of refugees may cross a border within a very short time, often into areas with little prior immigration. The more than 800,000 refugees who fled from Kosovo to Albania and the former Yugoslav Republic of Macedonia in 1999 represents one of the most recent manifestations of this phenomenon.

One of the most significant trends has been the feminisation of migration streams that had heretofore been primarily male. Significantly, many of the new female migrants relocate as principal wage earners, rather than as accompanying family members. Whereas Orlando Patterson could write in 1978 that "the greater propensity of women to move is a pattern peculiar to the New World," by the 1990s, Stephen Castles and Mark Miller's observation about Asian migration could be applied more generally: "A key development in recent years has been the increasing feminisation of migration: about 1.5 million Asian women were working abroad by the mid-1990s, and in many migratory movements they outnumber men." For example, more than 60 percent of migrants from Sri Lanka are women, employed primarily in domestic service. Women heads of household are also disproportionately represented in many refugee contexts.

Categories of Migrants

Migrants generally fall into two, though sometimes overlapping, categories: voluntary and forced migrants.

Voluntary Migrants

There are two major groupings of voluntary migrants:

a) labour migrants and

b) family members of prior migrants.

Labour Migrants

Many of today's international migration streams began with the recruitment and employment of foreign workers. During the 1940s to 1960s, the United States operated a guest worker program with Mexico, called the Bracero Program. In the 1960s and 1970s, many European countries instituted their own guest worker programs, bringing in labour from Turkey, northern Africa, and southern Europe. During the same period, oil-rich Libya and Persian Gulf states recruited workers from other Muslim countries, as well as south, east and Southeast Asia. South Africa recruited migrants from Mozambique and Lesotho to work in the mining industry. Some migrants were recruited for seasonal work, often in agriculture. Others filled short-term labour shortages in a wider range of industries produced by burgeoning economies. Often, the international migrants were hired to perform jobs that natives would not do, particularly for the low wages or poor working conditions offered. In some situations – the oil producing regions, for example – they provided technical skills not readily available within the native population.

Even after active labour recruitment ended, labour migration often continued. European countries withdrew their labour contracts after the 1973 oil crisis and resulting recession, but many of their guest workers remained. Employers who were pleased with the performance of their existing staff did not want to train new workers to fill posts held by guest workers; many employees who had established roots did not want to return to their home countries.

When the Bracero Program ended in 1965, migration patterns shifted towards unauthorised routes. During the more recent financial crisis in Southeast Asia, governments found it difficult to terminate temporary work programs that had been in operation for years.

Today, labour migration is highly complex. Several distinct categories of workers migrate, differentiated by their skills, the permanence of their residence in the host country and their legal status. At the lower end of the skills spectrum, international migrants pick fruits and vegetables, manufacture garments and other items, process meat and poultry, work as nursing home and hospital aides, clean restaurants and hotels, do gardening and construction, take care of children and the elderly, and provide myriad other services. They provide these types of services in a wide range of receiving countries in almost all parts of the globe. At the higher end of the skill spectrum, international migrants engage in equally diverse activities. They fill jobs requiring specialised skills, run multinational corporations, teach in universities, provide research and development expertise to industry and academia, practice medicine, and design, build and program computers, to name only a few activities. Again, they can be found undertaking such assignments throughout the world.

In most countries, migrants are admitted as temporary workers and they are granted work authorisation for specified periods. They have no right to remain in the destination country beyond the period of authorised employment. This is particularly true in the Persian gulf states and East and Southeast Asia.

In some cases, particularly in Europe, if a permit is renewed several times, the international migrant is allowed to remain indefinitely. The traditional immigration countries, the U.S., Canada and Australia, also have mechanisms for direct admission of foreign workers for permanent settlement.

In addition to legal avenues of entry for labour migrants is unauthorised migration. Statistics on unauthorised migration are hard to find in most countries since these movements are generally clandestine, but it appears that the numbers are substantial.

Unauthorised workers can be found in almost as diverse a range of jobs and industries as authorised workers, with agricultural and food processing jobs, light manufacturing, construction and service jobs being the most common types of employment. In many cases, unauthorised migrants are smuggled into countries by professional rings that specialise in human trafficking.

Migration for Family Reunification

The second major type of voluntary migration is for family reunification. Governments often permit close family members of those already in the country to enter through legal channels although this policy is found more frequently in the traditional immigration countries than in those authorising contract labourers only. The anchor relative in the host country may have been married and had children at the time of arrival but left his or her family members behind. Having determined to remain in the host country, he or she petitions for family reunification. Alternately, a citizen or international migrant already living in the host country marries a foreign national and seeks his or her admission.

The willingness of states to authorise family reunification is supported by international human rights law. Article 16(3) of the Universal Declaration of Human Rights states clearly that "the family is the natural and fundamental group unit of society and is entitled to protection by the society and the state."

Splitting families apart deprives each member of the fundamental right to respect of his or her family life. Since the family unit is often the principal support to its members, separating families also undermines other rights. Children and women, in particular, become vulnerable to exploitation when they are separated from their relatives.

Family reunion is often seen to be a consequence of labour migration. For example, in the years after guest worker programs ended in Europe, most officially sanctioned international migration consisted of family reunion as former guest workers brought their relatives to join them. Similarly, a substantial share of the migration into the United States in the past decade has been the family members of unauthorised migrants who gained legal status through the Immigration Reform and Control Act of 1986.

Family reunion is also a cause of still further migration. Many would-be labour migrants learn of employment prospects through their family members in other countries and then seek authorised or, in some cases, unauthorised entry to take the jobs. Moreover, once family members obtain residence status in a new country, they are often able to bring in additional relatives through family reunification programs. This process is called chain migration.

Although few countries permit legal immigration of extended family members, some migration systems do authorise admission of parents and adult siblings of already resident immigrants. To take one scenario, an international migrant with long-term residence sponsors his new spouse for admission; they then sponsor each of their parents, who in turn, sponsor their other children who enter with their spouses, who in turn sponsor their parents, and the chain continues.

Aside from its strong humanitarian basis and despite the potential for chain migration, host countries value family reunification because it is generally an effective mechanism for helping immigrants adapt to their new society. Already resident family members help new arrivals find jobs, housing, and other needed assistance.

New immigrants may add their earnings to augment household income. Parents of immigrants often take care of young grandchildren, thereby allowing both spouses to be gainfully employed. Families pool their savings to open businesses. At the same time, however, family migration may result in fiscal costs for the host society. Aged parents may require health services or income support that immigrant families cannot afford. Immigrants often have more children than natives and the children may have special need for language or other instruction, increasing costs for public education. These costs may be an investment in the future but they are also a current expenditure.

Eligibility for family reunification is not universal, however. Many contract labour arrangements preclude admission of family members. Admission rules often restrict family reunification for asylum seekers and those granted temporary protection, even in traditional immigration countries.

Forced Migrants

A large number of international migrants have been forced to leave their home countries and seek refuge in other nations. Many leave because of persecution, human rights violations, repression or conflict. They depart on their own initiative to escape these life-threatening situations although in a growing number of cases, they are driven from their homes by governments and insurgent groups intent on depopulating or shifting the ethnic, religious or other composition of an area. In other cases, migrants are forced to move by environmental degradation and natural and human-made disasters that make their homes inhabitable for at least some period. Because the legal frameworks for responding to these forms of forced migration differ, the two groups will be discussed separately.

Refugees have a special status in international law. A refugee is defined by the 1951 UN Convention Relating to the Status of Refugees as "a person who, owing to well-founded fear of being persecuted for reasons of race, religion, nationality, membership of a particular social group or political opinion, is outside the country of his nationality and is unable or, owing to such fear, is unwilling to avail himself of the protection of that country." Refugee status has been applied more broadly, however, to include others persons who are outside their country of origin because of armed conflict, generalised violence, foreign aggression or other circumstances which have seriously disturbed public order, and who, therefore, require international protection.

Environmental degradation and natural disasters uproot another type of forced migrant. Unlike the refugees described above, environmental migrants do not need protection from persecution or violence, but like refugees, they are unable to return to now uninhabitable communities. Most environmental migrants move internally, some relocating temporarily until they are able to rebuild their homes and others seeking permanent new homes. Some environmental migrants, however, cross national boundaries. The specific environmental factors that precipitate movements vary.

Mass migration may result from such natural phenomena as earthquakes, volcanic eruptions, flooding, hurricanes and other events that destroy housing, disrupt agriculture, and otherwise make it difficult for inhabitants to stay within their communities, particularly until reconstruction is completed. For example, periodic floods in Bangladesh have uprooted hundreds of thousands of persons. Hurricanes Georg and Mitch provoked massive displacement in the Caribbean and Central America, respectively. While most of these flood victims are internally displaced, the recurrent environmental problems provide an impetus for external movements as well.

Man-made disasters also precipitate mass movements. Large-scale industrial and nuclear accidents, such as those that occurred in Bophal and Chernobyl, can displace thousands of people within a very short period. Other manmade environmental problems lead to more gradual movements.

Global warming, acid rain, pollution of rivers, depletion of resources, soil erosion and desertification all hold the potential to uproot millions of people who can no longer reside or earn a living in their home communities. While some of this environmental degradation may be reversible, the most severe problems will require sustained attention and significant resources for reclamation. In the meantime, both internal and international migration can be expected.

Trends in International Migration

Seven principal trends now affect international migration and global responses, including asylum policies and practices:

— growing economic integration and globalisation;

— changing geo-political interests in the post-Cold War era;

— changing demographic trends and gender roles;

increasing transnationalism as migrants are able to live effectively in two or more countries at the same time;

— increasing technological innovation;

— growing reliance on smugglers, traffickers and other intermediaries; and

— harmonisation of migration policies through regional and international mechanisms.

Economic Globalisation

Economic globalisation is not new. Nor is the role of international migration in stimulating and being affected by global markets. More than 500 years ago, European exploration, conquest and colonisation of continents with rich natural resources were connected integrally with the growth of a new mercantile, capitalist economy. Supported by new technologies that made circumnavigation of the earth possible, migration played a critical role in the expansion of global trade. Europeans settled new territories where, too often, they used migrants as well as indigenous populations as slave labour to mine minerals, grow agricultural products, cut down trees or engage in other activities that would fuel growing manufacturing sectors.

Today's economic globalisation, however, gives new meaning to this old phenomenon. The growth in communications and transportation technologies, combined with the willingness of states to enter into binding trade commitments and businesses to establish multinational entities, has permitted an integration of economies that had heretofore operated in separate, differentiated spaces.

The ramifications of economic globalisation and integration for international migration are considerable as is the role that migration plays in furthering globalisation. As Saskia Sassen has written, "Immigration is, in my reading, one of the constitutive processes of globalisation today, even though not recognised or represented as such in mainstream accounts of the global economy."

Movement of labour within the global economy, by definition, requires new thinking about the role of states in regulating migration as well as the rules and regulations that govern entry and exit. Russell and Teitelbaum make the point that "international migration is not only a factor in the competitive production of manufactures for trade, international migration is central to international trade in services."

Economic trends influence migration patterns in a number of ways. The growth in multinational corporations, for example, has put pressure on governments to facilitate the inter-country movements of executives, managers and other personnel. Similarly, corporations use contingent labour and contract out assignments at an unprecedented rate. In manufacturing, it is not unusual for components of a single product to be made in several different countries. The corporate interest in moving its labour force to meet the demands of this type of scheduling often runs into conflict with immigration policies.

Bilateral, regional and international trade regimes are beginning to have a profound effect on migration. The European Union's evolution of a harmonised migration regime to serve as a counterpart to its customs union is but one example. The Asia-Pacific Economic Cooperation (APEC) Committee on Trade and Investment, spurred by the Business Advisory Council, has overseen exchange of information on business visa requirements and is identifying mechanisms for regional co-operation to facilitate mobility.

The North American Free Trade Agreement (NAFTA) includes potentially important migration-related provisions permitting freer movement of professionals, executives, and others providing international services from signatory countries. Although movements of lesser-skilled workers are not regulated by NAFTA, the issue is likely to be revisited as economic integration grows. The General Agreement on Trade in Services (GATS) is another example of trade negotiations affecting migration policy. To give one example, in GATS, the US guaranteed a minimum of 65,000 visas per year for admission of foreign professionals who are authorised to remain in the US for up to three-year stays.

The growth in global trade and investment has import for major source countries of migration as well as the receiving countries. The issues raised in this connection are far more difficult because they relate to the often-unauthorised movements of unskilled workers. It has long been held that economic development, spurred by access to global markets and capital, is the best long-term solution to emigration pressures in poor countries.

While negotiating NAFTA, former President Salinas of Mexico described his hope that "more jobs will mean higher wages in Mexico, and this in turn will mean fewer migrants to the United States and Canada. We want to export goods, not people." In more colourful language, Salinas cited his preference for Mexico to export tomatoes instead of tomato pickers.

Academicians exploring the relationship between economic development and emigration tend to agree that improving the economic opportunities for people in source countries is the best long-term solution to illegal migration. Almost uniformly, however, they caution that emigration pressures are likely to remain and, possibly, increase before the long-term benefits accrue: "The transformations intrinsic to the development process are at first destabilising. They initially promote rather than impede migration. Better communications and transportation and other improvements in the quality of life of people working hard to make a living raise expectations and enhance their ability to migrate."

Several researchers posit what economist Philip Martin refers to as an "immigration hump." As levels of income rise, emigration would at first increase, then peak and decline. The experience of such countries as Italy and Korea in transitioning from emigration to immigration countries gives credence to this theory.

Changing Geo-political Interests

The post Cold War era presents new opportunities as well as new challenges for migration regimes. The effects are most profound with regard to treatment of forced migration. Most current refugee and asylum policy was formulated following World War II with the lessons of the Nazi era in mind and tensions between East and West growing.

To a large degree, refugee policy was seen as an instrument of foreign policy at both international and domestic levels. Admission of refugees for permanent resettlement, asylum for victims of persecution and repression, and international aid to victims of surrogate Cold War fights (Central America, Ethiopia, Vietnam, etc.) were all part of the fight against communism.

The Cold War also made all but impossible some of the solutions to refugee crises, whether defined as attacking root causes or promoting return of refugees. With the end of the Cold War, new opportunities emerged. Many decades-old civil wars came to an end. Democratisation and increased respect for human rights took hold in numerous countries throughout the globe. As a result, repatriation became a possibility for millions of refugees who had been displaced for years.

One of the most significant changes in recent years has been in the willingness of countries to intervene on behalf of internally displaced persons and others in need of assistance and protection within their home countries. Classic notions of sovereignty, which formerly precluded such intervention, are under considerable pressure. International human rights and humanitarian law have growing salience in defining sovereignty to include responsibility for the welfare of the residents of one territory.

Intervention may be expected when the actions of a sovereign state threaten the security of another state. What is new is the recognition that actions that prompt mass exodus into a neighbouring territory threaten international security. In a number of cases, beginning with Resolution 688 that authorised intervention in northern Iraq, the Security Council has determined that the way to reduce the threat to a neighbouring state is to provide assistance and protection within the territory of the offending state.

The changing geo-political scene is a two-edged sword, however. The need for humanitarian intervention also is linked to the end of the Cold War. Rabid nationalism has replaced communism in some countries, while others have so destabilised that no government exists to protect the civilian population.

Addressing these new situations is made all the more challenging now that the ideological supports for generous refugee responses have unravelled. That the principles of asylum and non-refoulement (non-return to places of persecution) appear to be under growing attack in Europe and North America is one manifestation of this issue. Further, as the failure of the international community to protect the so-called safe havens in Bosnia showed, humanitarian interests alone are often an insufficient substitute for political will.

Demographic and Gender Trends

Additional global trends affecting future migration pertain to demography and gender roles. World-wide, fertility rates are falling although many countries in the developing world continue to see rapid population growth. In most developed countries, fertility levels are well below replacement rates – that is, couples are having fewer than two children. These countries can foresee a time in which total population will decrease, leading some demographers to refer to a looming population implosion.

They can also expect an ageing population. The United Nations Population Division projects that the number of persons aged 60 or older will increase from 600 million in the late 1990s to 2 billion in 2050. The population of older persons will exceed that of children for the first time in history. At the same time, the number of working age persons per each older person will decline.

Along with these changes in population growth and age distribution are changes in the role of women within society. Women are increasingly pursuing educational opportunities, working outside of the home and participating in civil society. The 1994 Cairo Conference on Population and Development recognised that women's education and ability to generate income are essential elements of any strategy to restrain rapid population growth. Not surprisingly, as women gain greater autonomy through education and work, they are also migrating not just as reunifying spouses but also as principal applicants for work visas.

Demographic trends affect international migration in two respects. First, they are an important factor in explaining emigration pressures in many countries. Societies with rapid population growth often are unable to generate sufficient employment to keep pace with new entries into the labour force. Environmental degradation may also result, particularly when land use policies do not protect fragile eco-systems. Such natural phenomena as hurricanes and earthquakes often have disproportionately negative effects on densely populated areas, particularly in poor countries, with large numbers displaced from homes destroyed by these events.

Second, demographic trends influence the receptivity towards and impact of migration on countries of destination. The direction of these effects is not necessarily straightforward, however. For example, a country with low fertility rates and an ageing population may benefit from the admission of working-age international migrants, but as the migrant population becomes a larger share of total population, there may be a backlash against the newcomers. This pattern is seen particularly where the migrants are of a different race, ethnicity or religion than the native population.

Trans-nationalism

A fourth trend affecting migration is trans-nationalism. Partly because of the technological revolution of the second half of the 19th century, migrants can far more easily today live in two societies at the same time. While circular migration has been a notable aspect of migration for much of the past century, when travel was more difficult, migrants tended to live sequentially in one country or the other. Now they can maintain two homes, shuttling easily between them.

This phenomenon can be seen in migration from north Africa and Turkey into Europe; Mexico, Central America and the Caribbean into the United States; China into Canada, Australia and the United States; and Mozambique and Lesotho into South Africa.

Money flows between immigrants and those who remain at home is another important aspect of trans-nationalism. Remittances often exceed any other form of trade, investment or foreign aid available to the source countries of migrants.

According to the International Monetary Fund, an estimated $77 billion was remitted in 1997. The decision to remit and the amount remitted varies depending on the location of family members, earnings abroad, costs of migration and destination country living expenses, duration of stay, and other similar factors. Maintaining the flow of these resources is often an important consideration in immigration policy-making.

Perhaps the most visible aspect of trans-nationalism is the growing acceptance of dual nationality. Several major emigration countries, including Mexico and the Dominican Republic, have shifted from opposition to dual nationality to active support for it. A change in Mexican law permits nationals who naturalise in another country to retain their Mexican nationality.

Making a distinction between nationality and citizenship, Mexico does not, however, intend to permit naturalised citizens to vote in Mexican elections. By contrast, the Dominican Republic, which also recognises dual nationality, permits absentee voting by Dominicans who naturalise elsewhere.

Technological Innovations

The communications, information and transportation revolutions transforming society are likely to have mixed effects on migration trends. On the one hand, travel is cheaper and easier than ever before, increasing the likelihood that migrants can move far distances. Similarly, global communications systems enable would-be migrants to monitor the economic, social and political situations in distant countries and determine whether and where they wish to relocate.

Inexpensive transport and telephone systems also permit migrants to remain in touch with their families at home, making migration a less radical step than it was in earlier periods. These factors contribute not only to increased migration but also to the trans-nationalism discussed above.

On the other hand, such innovations as the Internet will permit people to obtain good paying jobs without moving long distances. Although a certain portion of even high-tech information technology jobs require physical proximity to other workers, other positions can be filled at long distances. Moving such jobs to companies in developing countries is far less expensive, in financial and social terms, than moving workers to the jobs. At the same time, as the economies of developing countries improve with investment of this type, the economic incentives for migration should diminish. The process will take time, however, to be measured in generations in some cases.

Technological innovations may reduce the demand for inexpensive unskilled labour in some industries. In the United States, for example, the growers of sugar cane had been highly dependent on temporary foreign workers admitted from Caribbean states. Mechanisation of the sugar cane harvest, though, sharply reduced the need for this labour. At present, the availability of foreign workers often acts as a disincentive to make technological investments because it can take several years to amortise these costs. As the cost of technology reduces, however, the interest in a steady supply of foreign workers may well diminish.

Smuggling and Trafficking

It has long been recognised that three factors must be present for international migration to occur: demand/pull from receiving countries; supply/push from source countries; and networks to link the supply with the demand. The networks explain why certain migrants move to certain locations. They also explain why the same set of push or pull factors in different countries lead to very different migration experiences. If the networks are not functioning, the supply and demand never find each other.

Networks are often familial or community-based. Migrants tend to go to places in which their relatives, friends and community members are already located. Those already settled in the new country provide many needed services, not least of which is finding jobs or helping the newcomer obtain other sources of support. Sometimes, labour contractors serve this purpose. Working on behalf of companies in receiving countries, they seek out labourers and facilitate their migration. Certainly, the large-scale migration of Mexicans to the United States or migrants from North Africa to Europe began with such labour recruitment.

A particularly troubling trend in recent years has been the emergence of professional smuggling and trafficking operations as such facilitators of migration. Smuggling is, of course, one of the world's oldest professions. When nation states established borders and sought to regulate traffic across them, they created markets for the smuggling of humans as well as goods. What is new is the scale of smuggling, measured in both numbers and profits, as well as an emerging pattern of increasing professionalisation. This pattern may vary by the type and location of the smuggling.

At the most informal levels, aliens are helped by individuals whom they know to traverse the border. At a slightly more organised level, local agents may be used to link migrants to more formal smuggling operations. The local contacts, who are generally well known to the migrants, tell them who to contact at the border to help them gain entry into the receiving country.

Several types of services may be offered: assistance in crossing without inspection; houses in which they can hide from the authorities; transportation to interior locations; links to employers. Smugglers may sell or rent fraudulent documents to be used in obtaining entry and to verify eligibility for lawful employment or receipt of services. The use of the types of smuggling operations varies by gender and financial resources. Often, smugglers act like legitimate business people, guaranteeing their services and agreeing to receive final payment when the migrant reaches the final destination.

Other smuggling/trafficking operations are far less benign. Smugglers pack large numbers of migrants into small, unventilated spaces to cross borders or reach ports. Fearing apprehension by border authorities, smugglers have left migrants without water or protection from the hot sun.

The most troubling form of smuggling involves human trafficking, where the smugglers not only bring migrants across borders but exploit and abuse their labour in the process. As smuggling fees increase, and migrants find it difficult to pay all costs at once, smugglers "sell" migrants to businesses who cover the fees in exchange for indentured labour. This can amount to virtual slavery, particularly for women and children forced into sexually exploitive occupations.

Another new element is the cost of smuggling and the profits derived from it. Migrants smuggled from the Fujian province of China reportedly pay upwards of $50,000 per person, often finding that it takes several years to repay their debt. These operations may yield profits of as much as $5-7 billion per year. Smugglers have the advantage over governments at the moment because of the lack of an international migration regime in which governments co-operate to prohibit and prosecute smugglers of humans. Smugglers can easily exploit the gaps in the institutional structures of international co-operation as well as the fragmentation of domestic government law enforcement efforts. It is also to their advantage that except for the violence they may inflict their basic service of supplying cheap labour for receiving countries is widely tolerated even though illegal. Their advantage over migrants is the migrants' dependence, ignorance and lack of recourse when agreements are not fulfilled.

Harmonisation Trends

Historically, states have seen immigration policy as a matter of national interest, often adopting unilateral policies aimed at regulating entry and exit. Nations treat the admission of immigrants and control of unauthorised migration as quintessential matters of sovereignty. After all, immigration policy deals with fundamental issues of national identity as well as national security. The protection of one's borders is key to a state's definition of itself.

While few would question that states do, in fact, have both the authority and the responsibility for making decisions regarding immigration, there is increasing recognition that sovereignty limits the ability of states to address the realities of today's international migration. In 1995, the UN General Assembly asked the Secretary General to report on the feasibility and desirability of convening an international conference on international migration and development.

After consulting with member governments, the Secretary General concluded that there was insufficient consensus about what could be accomplished at such a conference: "The disparate experiences of countries or sub-regions with regard to international migration suggest that, if practical solutions are to be found, they are likely to arise from the consideration of the particular situation of groups of countries sharing similar positions or concerns with the global international migration system... In the light of this, it may be expedient to pursue regional or sub-regional approaches whenever possible."

During the past decade, regional mechanisms have been established in the Americas, Europe, East Asia, Africa, and elsewhere, in which receiving, source and transit countries address issues of mutual concern. The European Union has had the longest experience in this respect. Free movement of labour within the European Community first came into force in 1968. During recent years, however, discussions turned to broader themes raised by a common immigration policy. Debate about visa policy is a case in point.

The intergovernmental Schengen Agreement, originally signed among five EU members in 1985, called for the abolition of internal borders between member states, largely to facilitate trade by reducing long waits at border crossings.

The agreement contained the first provisions for the establishment of a single "Schengen visa" for travel throughout most of Western Europe.

The 1991 Maastricht Treaty on the European Union defined a common, European visa policy as essential for the realisation of the Union's long-term goal of establishing a single market in goods, capital, and labour. The later Amsterdam Treaty (1997) included the Schengen Agreement into the EU's formal political architecture. Five years after the treaty's entry into force, it is envisioned that decisions on visa issuance will be decided by majority vote.

Less developed multilateral approaches to migration are to be found in other regions, some arising from the migration ramifications of economic integration and others focusing on alien trafficking, illegal migration, mass migration emergencies, and other security concerns related to large-scale movements of people.

The Regional Migration Conference, referred to as the "Puebla Group", brings together all the countries of Central and North America for regular, constructive dialogue on migration issues, including an annual session at the vice-ministerial level. The Plan of Action calls for co-operation in exchanging information on migration policy, exploring the links between development and migration, combating migrant trafficking, returning extra-regional migrants, and ensuring full respect for the human rights of migrants, and reintegrating repatriated migrants within the region, equipping and modernising immigration control systems, and training officials in migration policy and procedures. An early and continuing issue on the agenda is averting movements of extra-regional migrants through Central America, Mexico and the Caribbean to the United States and Canada.

In East and Southeast Asia, two regional migration consultation processes, are ongoing. One, known as the "Manila Process", is co-ordinated by IOM and focuses on irregular migration and trafficking in East and Southeast Asia. Since 1996, it has brought together each year seventeen countries for regular exchange of information.

The second Asian regional process, known as the Asia-Pacific Consultations (APC), is co-sponsored by IOM and UNHCR. It provides for consultations amongst governments in Asia and Oceania on a broad range of population movements in the region. Both of these ongoing dialogues were strengthened by the ministerial-level International Symposium on Migration that the Royal Thai Government hosted in Bangkok. The search for solutions to the many migration-related problems affecting the region becomes of particular relevance in light of the economic crisis affecting parts of Asia.

Other such processes are in the making in the Southern Cone of South America, in southern Africa and in the Mediterranean. They intend to bring together the governments of all countries involved in the migration process, origin, transit and receiving.

To date, much of the harmonisation sought through these regional mechanisms pertains to management of unauthorised migration. Among the policies adopted through or supported by these mechanisms are: mandatory visa requirements, sanctions against carriers transporting improperly documented migrants, pre-inspection clearance programs, interdiction of vessels, diversion of arrivals to transit countries (e.g., safe third countries), exclusion from future admission, and detention. Although broadly applied to all unauthorised migrants, some of these mechanisms have been targeted at persons who would be likely to apply for asylum if granted admission. For example, States have invoked visa requirements on nationals of certain countries because of increases in asylum applications.

Refugee Protection

The global trends described above have particular importance for the refugee protection system. The trends are clearer regarding numbers and destinations than they are in predicting policy responses. All States can expect to see significant levels of international migration in the future. Some of this migration will be among the wealthier countries, as multinational corporations adopt global labour policies and countries follow the lead of the European Union in facilitating such practices.

Other migration will continue within the developing world and particularly within States, as the poorest migrants and refugees find themselves unwilling or unable to move long distances or even cross borders for either work or protection. However, as has been the case in the past few decades, an increasing proportion of migration will be from developing to developed countries.

Technological innovation, growing economic integration and increasingly more effective networks (including smugglers) will permit people with some capital, transnational contacts or willingness to indenture themselves the opportunity to move across vast distances as well as within economically-joined regions.

Most of the trends described above affect forced migrants as well as those moving voluntarily for economic reasons. Economic integration and development is occurring even among and within countries with vastly different political systems, protection of human rights, and demographic trends.

Persons able to find economic opportunities in wealthier partner countries because of economic integration and slowing population growth may be motivated to leave or remain outside of their countries because of repression and violations of rights. Certainly, many forced migrants will be as likely as economic migrants to take advantage of inexpensive transportation and communications, be members of transnational communities and have access to or even be recruited by smugglers and traffickers.

The global trend that will have the most impact on forced migration is the changing geo-political relations discussed above. At present, there appears to be little prospect of a slowing down in the type of nationalist and religious conflicts that generated millions of refugees and internally displaced in the 1990s.

Instability in the Balkans, Caucuses and Central Asian republics of the former Soviet Union continues. Religious fundamentalism continues to take hold in countries, in some cases precipitating the mass flight of religious minorities and secularists. Wars of liberation gave way to surrogate Cold War conflicts in parts of Africa, Latin America and Asia, which are now giving way to sometimes prolonged civil conflicts fuelled by illicit sales of diamonds, drugs and other commodities. All of these developments herald likely continued forced migration.

This is not to say that migration is inevitable nor that once begun, migration will not stop. The economic trends discussed above may well result in reduced movements from many countries. Formerly emigration countries such as Italy and Ireland, having significantly improved economies, have transformed themselves into immigration countries.

Demographic and economic projections for such current emigration countries as Mexico, Morocco and the Philippines demonstrate that a similar process is underway. However, it is likely to take at least a generation, if not longer, for economic development to progress to a point where migration patterns are reversed. In fact, if generally agreed upon theories are correct, one can expect increased migration to occur as the economies grow before the expected reduction takes place. Similarly, democratisation and greater respect for human rights may well lead to increased migration as previously repressive governments loosen restrictions on their citizens and permit greater contact with other societies.

Will increased migration of both forced and voluntary migrants necessarily lead to increased demands for asylum or other forms of protection? There the evidence is less clear and may be determined not by the interest of individual migrants but instead by the actions of States and such intermediaries as smugglers and traffickers. Let us take four scenarios that reflect the same broad trends. The first two reduce the number of asylum applications. However, the first scenario is beneficial to the bona fide refugee seeking protection while the second places the same refugee in some jeopardy. A third scenario shows relatively little change in asylum applications and leaves refugees in much the same situation as today. A fourth scenario shifts course and examines State responses to forced migration in the context of geo-political relations rather than economic and demographic trends.

Scenario 1: To take perhaps the more rosy scenario, some trends, such as economic integration and decreasing population growth in wealthier countries, may encourage States to provide alternative avenues of admission for migrants whose only option now is to apply for asylum.

Recognising that many now unauthorised migrants could fill jobs that may otherwise be unfilled because of labour shortages or the unwillingness of native workers to take the positions at prevailing wages or working conditions, the receiving States legalise at least part of the flow of migrants. Migrants whether voluntary or forced who also seek economic opportunities may avail themselves of these new options. States feeling less pressure on their asylum systems, particularly from those with weaker claims, may then be more willing to provide adequate protection to the presumably smaller number of applicants for asylum.

Scenario 2: A less promising scenario could also flow, however, from these same trends. Rather than increase legal avenues for admission, States tolerate unauthorised migration because of presumed labour shortages as long as the migrants are willing to work at lower wages or under less desirable working conditions. It would be fair to say that this response has occurred in the United States, which has taken steps in the context of very low unemployment to reduce the level of enforcement of sanctions against employers hiring unauthorised workers. Some smuggling operations that now encourage migrants to apply for asylum, as the only mechanism for admission, instead develop contacts with employers willing to pay the smuggling fees in exchange for inexpensive labour. Bona fide refugees who may have prevailed in asylum determinations are indentured to employers in order to pay off their smuggling fees. The State sees a reduction in asylum applications, but the number of unauthorised migrants does not change – or even increases to include new migrants drawn by the employment magnet and able to migrate because of the smuggling networks. Of course, there are costs to the State as well as the migrants in this scenario. The credibility of the State to manage migration is undermined; moreover, its ability to control unauthorised migration in the event of changing economic conditions is severely impaired.

Scenario 3: Under the third scenario, as in the first, States increase legal immigration opportunities in response to economic integration and declining population growth. However, the new admission categories give preference to migrants with certain specified skills and/or who come from countries that are trading partners. Even with broad admission criteria and generous quotas or ceilings, neither full employer demand nor full migrant supply is likely to be met. Would-be migrants from other countries or without specified skills do not qualify for admission, but they may well have the networks and capacity to migrate. In fact, the new admission categories may soon become oversubscribed; in the meantime, they may have raised expectations and created new networks that encourage qualified applicants to circumvent processing and attempt unauthorised entry. Some of those admitted, for example for seasonal work, may find that moving into unauthorised work in urban areas provides them more lucrative full-time, all-year opportunities. The lesson here is that legal immigration, which may offer many advantages for a receiving country, will not necessarily serve as a substitute for unauthorised migration and, under certain conditions, may even increase unauthorised movements. To the extent that asylum applicants in particular do not meet the criteria for legal admission, there is no reason to assume that increased legal immigration will divert them from the asylum system.

Scenario 4: The likelihood that forced migration pressures will increase or reduce asylum applications could be profoundly affected by future decisions to intervene or not intervene in source countries of conflict and repression.

Hints as to future trends can already be seen in decisions to intervene militarily in northern Iraq, Haiti, East Timor and the Balkans. Since Resolution 688 explicitly referenced that forced movements into Turkey and Iran presented a threat to international peace and security, countries have been debating the circumstances under which Chapter VII intervention is appropriate and politically and militarily feasible. To the extent that States opt to follow the northern Iraq precedent, requests for asylum and other forms of protection may decline significantly. States are also looking towards less intrusive ways to protect persons still inside home countries or neighbouring countries. Examples include safe havens (presumably with greater protection than has been the case in Bosnia and other places where they have been tried), regional protection centres, in-country processing for admission as refugees, and enhanced use of refugee resettlement, particularly for those with strong ties in more developed countries or no prospect for local integration or repatriation.

Policy Issues

One of the most surprising things about migration is how few people move, not how many people move. Push, pull and network factors affect far more people than those who actually migrate. State policy has much, though not all, to do with whether migration occurs and, even more so, in what manner it occurs. This is a point worth emphasising because too often governments choose draconian measures to control movements because they fear they are impotent to manage migration otherwise.

A second point is that refugee protection, far from being at odds with immigration control, is an essential element in managing migration flows.Whether and where migrants go is affected by complex factors: push, pull and networks. It is important to emphasise that being pulled or smuggled to Western Europe or other highly developed countries does not negate that the push factor may well be persecution, torture or conflict. While these causes do not necessarily obligate a State to admit someone for permanent settlement, they do generally prevent them from returning the individual to the country where they would be endangered. In some cases, the States have a legal obligation (i.e., under the Refugee Convention and Convention Against Torture); in other cases, the practical barriers to repatriation – particularly to conflict areas or to countries without stable governments –are formidable.

When States dismiss all migration as unauthorised movements, without giving recognition that there may be valid grounds to permit certain migrants to remain within their territory, the credibility of their immigration policies come under attack. At the same time, policies that make it harder for asylum seekers to exit their countries or to reach their destination merely shifts responsibility from one State to another, or to the broader international community, without solving the basic problem of refugee protection.

It is essential that governments have multiple tools to deal with complex flows of people. If the asylum system is the only avenue to provide protection, it will appear to be flawed since many, if not most, of those who cannot return home fall outside of the 1951 Refugee Convention definition of persecution. Even more so, if asylum is the only avenue of entry for those seeking economic opportunities, ensuring the credibility of the asylum system is made all the more difficult. Smugglers and others will take advantage of any weaknesses in the asylum system in order to ensure that their clients reach the intended destination. In the meantime, if States find it difficult to keep up with the asylum applications, those with bona fide claims to refugee status may find themselves waiting an inordinately long time to gain recognition.

Having said that States need multiple tools in their immigration and asylum systems, it is also important to emphasise that there are no easy or quick fixes in managing migration or protecting refugees. Those who argue that increasing access to legal immigration will solve unauthorised migration are bound to be disappointed. Only if borders were totally open, and governments placed no numerical or qualitative barriers (e.g., public health, welfare or criminal grounds) to entry, would legal immigration substitute perfectly for unauthorised movements. Since it is unlikely that States will take such action, there will continue to be would-be migrants who do not fit the criteria for entry and attempt to by-pass lawful immigration procedures.

Those who recommend ratcheting up control mechanisms should equally recognise that these policies and practices often have unintended consequences that make migration management all the more difficult. The U.S. experience in border control is a case in point. Since 1994, the United States has increased the presence of the Border Patrol and taken other steps to make it more difficult for migrants to cross without authorisation into urban areas along the border.

The new policies shifted crossings into more difficult terrain, resulted in multiple apprehensions before a successful crossing and inadvertently increased reliance on professional smuggling operations. All of these raised the costs but did not stop unauthorised migration. An unintended consequence has been that unauthorised migrants remain for longer periods in the United States.

Another unintended consequence has been an increase in deaths along the border as migrants continue to try to cross but face much more difficult terrain as well as smugglers willing to leave them behind if apprehension of the whole group is at risk.

Comprehensive Approach to Migration

What are the elements of a comprehensive approach to migration that will most effectively promote refugee protection? Four aspects must be considered: ameliorating the causes of unauthorised migration, with particular focus on forced movements; strengthening mechanisms that enhance protection while minimising abuses; managing all forms of migration flows and doing so in a manner that involves source, transit and receiving countries; and resolving the longer-term status of migrants.

Ameliorating the causes of unauthorised migration

Ultimately, reducing the push and pull factors is the most sensible way to address increasing migration pressures. Peace, respect for human rights, and reduction in income differentials between rich and poor countries are the best long-term solutions to uncontrolled migration. Given the large number of people fleeing internal conflict and insecurity, and as Sadako Ogata said before the Carnegie Commission on Preventing Deadly Conflict, UNHCR "has an obvious interest in the prevention or mitigation of deadly conflict. Not only are we in direct contact with the suffering of those who manage to escape persecution and mass violence, but we also witness the shrinking willingness to offer them sanctuary."

The role that UNHCR can play regarding prevention is a limited but important one. Clearly, UNHCR has not the resources nor the capacity to prevent conflict, ensure human rights or promote economic security. The agency can, however, 1) advocate alleviation of the causes of forced migration; 2) stimulate early warning of and response to refugee emergencies to prevent displacements and mitigate longer-term impacts; 3) utilise humanitarian assistance in a manner that reduces tensions, stabilises communities, limits the potential for its diversion to military purposes, and reaches those in need without unnecessarily requiring their movement towards the aid; and 4) encourage safe and orderly repatriation in a manner that supports peace and reconciliation. At the same time, UNHCR must continue to reiterate that prevention does not mean preventing people from seeking safety and protection abroad.

Strengthening mechanisms that promote protection

UNHCR generally defines its protection role in relationship to the 1951 UN Convention Relating to the Status of Refugees and its 1967 Protocol. The core, fundamental precepts of protection are: non-refoulement, including non-rejection of asylum seekers at the frontier; admission to safety; access to fair and efficient procedures for determination of refugee status; basic standards of treatment that accord with human dignity and integrity; and appropriate lasting solutions. Key to ensuring such protection is UNHCR's unhindered access to asylum-seekers and refugees to monitor their situation and treatment. Reinforcing these protection principles is one of UNHCR's principal responsibilities. Given that numerous countries have not yet signed the refugee Convention nor implemented policies and procedures to protect refugees, UNHCR should continue to encourage signatories. UNHCR should also continue to work with States to develop and implement policies and procedures that are consistent with the protection precepts described above. Further, UNHCR should continue to encourage the broadest application of the Convention , particularly to include persecution by non-State actors and in collapsed States with no functioning government and persecution based on gender – two areas where State practices vary greatly.

Even with full accordance to the 1951 Convention, however, gaps in international protection will be seen. The Convention definition is narrow in scope, referencing a well-founded fear of persecution on specific grounds. Persons who flee generalised conflict, violence and abuses do not necessarily fit the 1951 Convention definition. Although the OAU Convention and the Cartagena Declaration widen the scope to include those fleeing such situations, and UNHCR considers them to be of concern, States do not consistently apply the broader criteria.

Moreover, the Convention refers only to those who are already out of their countries of origin. It does not pertain to those who are still at home, even if they are subject to the type of conditions that would make them refugees if they left. In effect, the refugee system presents a fundamental dilemma for UNHCR and States concerned with protection: only those who manage to flee are covered by the refugee Convention, but flight often requires refugees to break immigration laws and to subject themselves to danger and sometimes exploitation at the hands of smugglers and traffickers.

A challenge for UNHCR is to broaden the scope of refugee protection to fill these gaps, and to do so in a manner that ensures the continued integrity of asylum while protecting the broadened system from potential abuse. A number of different approaches could be considered: Encourage adoption of forms of protection that complement asylum, with these complementary protection regimes focusing in particular on persons who flee generalised conflict and violence.

UNHCR should work with States to set out minimum standards of treatment for those granted the complementary status, encouraging States to afford similar protections to those spelled out in the Convention. The principal obligation of States should be non-return of migrants to conditions in which they would be endangered. If such conditions continue for some time, however, States should be encouraged to permit those granted the complementary status to remain permanently.

Complementary statuses serve not only to protect the large number of asylum seekers who flee conflict rather than persecution, they also facilitate both the appearance and reality of migration control. At present, it appears as if States have less control over their asylum systems than is the case. Although a sometimes small minority of applicants are accorded asylum, a much larger number are permitted to remain on other humanitarian grounds. Because the policies are framed solely as asylum policies, however, these other forms of relief tend to be disregarded. They do have value, apart from their humanitarian one, in allowing States to keep track of persons within their territory, determine what rights accrue to specific statuses, and require return if conditions permit.

Encourage development of mechanisms for in-country protection to minimise the negative effects of such migration controls as visa requirements and carrier sanctions. In particular, UNHCR should explore the feasibility of establishing procedures through which would-be asylum seekers can request protection prior to departure.

Several options should be considered: creating special "refugee" visas that embassies and consulates would grant to persons who do not qualify for regular visas but who can demonstrate that they are or will be endangered if they do not leave their home countries; establishing UNHCR offices in countries of origin where would-be asylum seekers could request protection, with the understanding that they would be evacuated to countries willing and able to receive them; and broadening the responsibilities of pre-inspection personnel and other immigration officials assigned to overseas locations so that they can assess the asylum claims of persons seeking to board aircraft and other carriers without proper documentation.

These various mechanisms are largely untried, and they certainly are not substitutes for a functioning asylum system. The experience with in-country processing for refugee resettlement has been mixed, to say the least, for both refugee protection and migration management. For example, the Orderly Departure Program (ODP) from Vietnam and Cuba at least partially stemmed large-scale departures in unseaworthy boats, saving lives and providing a safer avenue for departure. The departures were stemmed, however, because both governments agreed to halt the movements. Bona fide refugees who were afraid to apply for orderly departure, thereby making themselves known to the government, had even more limited options for flight. In Haiti, in particular, the presence of in-country processing was used by the United States as a reason to return interdicted boats directly to Haiti without affording passengers the opportunity to apply for asylum.

From the immigration management vantage, ODP arrangements could hinder the capacity of the receiving country to set its own priorities for admission. In the Vietnamese ODP, for example, the U.S. established lists of persons who sought entry and met minimal criteria for admission, and Vietnam set lists of those it would grant exit permission.

Generally, only those who were on both lists were able to leave, but these individuals may not have been as high priorities as were other applicants. Despite these problems, and the necessity for UNHCR continually to reinforce that in-country procedures cannot be a substitute for asylum, they hold one overriding advantage: they provide opportunities for victims of persecution and other abuses to find safety without resort to subterfuge and further violation of their rights. Explore the feasibility of establishing regional protection mechanisms. Regional protection holds promise for helping States balance twin interests: providing protection to refugees without providing admission to persons who do not otherwise qualify for entry. As discussed above, international migration generally requires both push and pull factors. In the case of refugees seeking entry into the highly developed countries of North America and Europe, the push may be persecution or conflict, but the pull is generally better economic opportunities. Regional protection – that is, protection in neighbouring or nearby countries with similar economies to those of the country of origin – offers safety without the potential magnet for unauthorised migration presented by admission to wealthier nations. It also presumably facilitates repatriation when conditions permit because the economic advantages of remaining outside of one's country are reduced.

Regional protection is hardly a new concept. The vast majority of refugees have always found asylum within their regions of origin, generally in neighbouring countries. What is new is the interest of European and North American States in redirecting movements towards regional centres.

This approach was pioneered in Southeast Asia, when a processing centre was established in Bataan, the Philippines, to receive refugees admitted to Thailand, Malaysia, Singapore, and Hong Kong for temporary asylum before they were resettled elsewhere. Because the numbers seeking entry outpaced the resettlement capacity, the processing centre relieved the pressure on first asylum countries, keeping the door opened for protection, and allowed the resettlement countries to examine applications carefully to determine who was admissible. The processing centre effectively served both protection and migration management ends.

A different form of regional protection was used in 1994 to address an increasing number of boat departures from Haiti. In this case, regional protection was offered as an alternative to admission into the United States. Fearing that access to U.S. territory would serve as a magnet to further flight, the U.S. instead offered safe haven at Guantanamo Naval Base and, through a regional agreement, in Panama and the Turks and Caico Islands – but emphasised that there would be no admission to the U.S.

The implementation of this policy led to an abrupt decline in boat departures, but not before about 40,000 Haitians afforded themselves of this regional protection. The need for safe haven lessened considerably when international pressure and the threat of military intervention led to a restoration of the elected government and the presence of peacekeeping forces. The vast majority of those offered protection chose to return home when conditions permitted. A small number were permitted entry into the U.S. to pursue asylum claims or to seek medical attention.

A third example of regional protection, supplemented by humanitarian evacuation to preserve first asylum, occurred during the Kosovo crisis. By far the largest number of refugees from Kosovo remained in the neighbouring countries of Albania and the former Yugoslav Republic of Macedonia. However, to ensure that first asylum was maintained, and in recognition of Macedonia's concern about its own security, other States agreed to accept some refugees for temporary protection or resettlement. A regional approach was hence sustained by international responsibility-sharing.

Migration management regime

While UNHCR's principal focus is on forced migrants who require international protection, it is in UNHCR's interest that a more fully developed migration regime evolve. At present, State obligations towards refugees are spelled out more clearly than are their responsibilities towards other migrants. For a variety of reasons, governments, advocates on behalf of migrants and the migrants themselves have an interest in defining migratory patterns, regardless of cause, as refugee movements. There are policies for handling asylum claims even in countries that routinely deny that they have immigration and, hence, the need for immigration policies. If found to be a refugee, the migrant has far more rights than accrue to others who move across international boundaries. This works two ways.

In some cases, the UNHCR's very presence makes it desirable to label migrants as refugees since some of the responsibility for assisting and protecting the individuals coming through the asylum/refugee system can be shared. In other cases, States refuse to label any migrants as refugees, fearing that they will then be asked to admit them permanently.

Either of these blurring of distinctions between voluntary migrants and forced migrants needing protection makes it difficult for UNHCR to argue for special attention to the populations within its mandate. UNHCR could contribute towards solving this problem in two ways: by encouraging adoption of more comprehensive and transparent immigration policies; and by encouraging and supporting the establishment of a global migration regime to address movements of people who do not fit within UNHCR's mandate.

A fuller range of immigration policies will not necessarily reduce pressures on the asylum systems of receiving countries. Such countries as the United States, Canada and Australia, whose categories for admission of immigrants and temporary workers are well developed and broadly conceived, nevertheless also see significant applications for asylum from individuals with weak claims. When countries have comprehensive and transparent immigration systems, though, the ability to make distinctions among different applicants for admission or relief from removal is enhanced. So too is the ability to place migrants in appropriate categories that reflect their reasons for migrating. And, in the final analysis, decisions to remove those who fit no category – family, employment or humanitarian – are more readily justified. In turn, if UNHCR has greater confidence that all avenues of protection and admission have been explored, the organisation can more readily support such removals.

The development of a global migration regime would be useful as well. Such a regime would include international agreements to govern movements of people and mechanisms for determining the responsibilities of States towards different categories of migrants. Through negotiations, such a regime would likely take into account the interests of all parties to migration, including source, transit and receiving countries as well as the migrants themselves.

The international community is at some distance, however, from having such agreements. The various regional fora for discussion of migration issues, such as the Puebla Group discussed above, are useful vehicles for moving along debate about the rights and responsibilities of migrants and States. UNHCR's active participation in these regional mechanisms, along with the International Organization for Migration, which is serving as secretariat to a number of them, is essential not only to ensuring that refugee issues are properly addressed but to encourage a more comprehensive approach to migration management.

States increasingly are turning towards temporary mechanisms to address migration flows. The growing interest in temporary protection policies, along with the increased use even in traditional immigration countries of temporary work provisions, lead to many situations in which the longer-term status of migrants, including forced ones, remains in doubt for sometimes lengthy periods. There are two likely resolutions to these situations: return of migrants to their home countries or more permanent integration into their new communities. Third country resettlement is a less frequent, though often important, alternative for migrants in some type of temporary status.

At present, mechanisms for determining which solution is appropriate are sorely lacking. States have no agreed upon criteria for determining whether conditions justify return, particularly in the aftermath of conflict. Even in the case of voluntary migration, States differ as to the extent that they should take such considerations as brain drain into account in requiring return.

Resolving status is particularly important if temporary protection mechanisms are to work towards giving refuge to the largest number of persons needing such protection. If governments fear that temporary protection is merely and always a way station towards permanent admission, they may be less likely to be generous in its grant. On the other hand, if governments persist in arguing that all of those granted temporary protection should return regardless of how long it takes for home country conditions to change, they are fighting against the realities of the equities that long-term migrants develop over time. More transparent policies that provide criteria for determining when and how return or adjustment to permanent status will occur will help to resolve some of the most difficult dilemmas now seen in temporary protection policies.

Activities with Regard to International Migration

By virtue of the mandate received from the countries of the region, the Latin American and Caribbean Demographic Centre (CELADE)-Population Division of ECLAC provides cooperation to help ensure that international migration is properly considered in national development efforts. This cooperation includes: (a) support for the compilation and processing of relevant information; (b) analysis of migration patterns and trends; (c) organization of and participation in intergovernmental and expert meetings at the regional and subregional levels; and (d) technical assistance for Governments and international organizations, academic institutions and civil society in training and research on migration.

The work of CELADE in this sphere is geared towards providing timely responses to the countries' requirements by updating and reviewing the data on the regional migratory situation within a development framework. Activities are conducted in close association with national bodies and international agencies, such as the Inter-American Development Bank (IDB), the United Nations Population Fund (UNFPA), and the International Organization for Migration (IOM).

Organization of Information on Migration

Since the early 1970s, CELADE has been working on the Investigation of International Migration in Latin America (IMILA) Project. This is an intraregional cooperation effort that gathers and organizes information on the scale and features of regional migration. The project involves compiling and processing data obtained from population censuses on members of the population born abroad. These data, which are remitted to CELADE by national statistical offices, are used to identify members of the population counted in censuses in countries other than their countries of birth and then to quantify and describe stocks of immigrants and emigrants up to the date of each census.

This information is then used to create 14 basic tables on migrants' sociodemographic and socio-economic features, by gender (age, fertility rates, infant mortality, marital status, education and labour status) and by country of birth. These tables are available in a special area of the ECLAC web site and are published in the Demographic Bulletin, which CELADE issues on a regular basis.

Analysis of Migration Patterns and Trends in the Region

The migration research activities conducted by CELADE form part of the substantive work of ECLAC. One example of its work is the interdivisional document, Globalization and development, presented at the twenty-ninth session of the Commission, which contains a chapter that explores the interrelationships between international migration and globalization and examines a number of proposals for action in this regard. In this same spirit, and in furtherance of its programme of work, in the 2002-2003 biennium CELADE prepared a number of studies on patterns and trends in international migration on the part of Latin American and Caribbean nationals, which may be consulted on the ECLAC web site.

One of these studies, on international migration by Latin American and Caribbean nationals in the Americas, served as an introduction for the Hemispheric Conference on International Migration: Human Rights and Trafficking in Persons in the Americas, which was held in Santiago, Chile, in November 2002. Another, on the sociodemographic and economic features of international migration in Latin America and the Caribbean, was debated at a regional technical seminar held in Caracas, Venezuela, in August 2002. Other more specific documents, which have also been presented at regional and subregional forums and seminars, refer to remittances and their impact on social welfare , regional migration trends and the challenges of the regional migratory agenda .

In September 2003 CELADE concluded a research project on changes in the regional migratory map, using information from the 2000 census round. After analysing a number of stylised facts relating to recent migratory trends -such as perceptions of the "escape valve" effect and concerns about the role of remittances - the study goes on to describe three traditional regional migratory patterns (immigration from overseas and the cessation of this process, intraregional migration and its moderate intensity, and emigration to the United States) together with a fourth, new type of extraregional migration (with Spain and Japan being the most common destinations).

It also refers to migrant returns to the region, which occur with significant frequency. It then explores specifically gender-related traits of international migration, with a particular focus on the quantitative feminization of the phenomenon and the shortcomings and potentials of the information sources used, which raise certain questions about the "invisibility" of migrant women. In addition, the study reviews the structural, social and individual factors underlying women's decisions to migrate and presents findings with regard to their employment status, human rights and the vulnerability of their position in their destination countries.

Organization of and Participation in meeting on International Migration

Together with IOM and with the collaboration of seven international agencies, ECLAC, through CELADE (with the support of the secretariat of the Commission and the Social Development Division's Human Rights Unit), organized the Hemispheric Conference on International Migration: Human Rights and Trafficking in Persons in the Americas, which took place in Santiago, Chile, from 20 to 22 November 2002. The main objective of this meeting was to strengthen cooperation among Governments with regard to international migration and to identify mechanisms that can help to protect and promote the human rights of migrants, help to combat and prevent trafficking in persons and contribute to fulfilment of the relevant international mandates.

The Hemispheric Conference sparked a great deal of interest in the countries, as was apparent from the reactions of government agencies, academic institutions and civil society and from the press coverage it attracted. This may be attributed to the fact that the meeting convened official delegations from the Governments of all the ECLAC member countries, experts from international organizations, academic figures and representatives of civil society organizations; this last group also held a side event. The summary report of the meeting presents a review of the facts highlighted in the debate and a summary of the presentations and discussions of each session; the annexes contain the conclusions signed by the government delegates and the declaration issued by the civil society organizations. CELADE participates regularly in regional and national meetings on matters relating to international migration.

In 2003, in particular, CELADE participated in: (a) the First International Forum on the Latin American Diaspora in the United States and Canada, organized by the State of Puebla and the Foundation for Rural Productivity, with the sponsorship of a number of Mexican and international institutions, at which a document on remittances in the region was presented; (b) a seminar on migration and integration, organized by IOM and the Governments of Ecuador and Chile, at which a lecture was given on trends in international migration; (c) The First Paraguayan Population Congress, organized by the Paraguayan Association of Population Studies (ADEPO), at which a lecture was given on international migration in the region and the challenges for an agenda on migration; and (d) the seventh Jornadas Migratorias de Chile (Santiago, September 2003), a roundtable on migration organized by Chilean Catholic Institute for Migration (INCAMI) with the support of IOM, at which a document on migration and human rights in Latin America and the Caribbean was presented.

Collaboration on Training, Research and Information Use

In its capacity as an observer agency, CELADE has continued to participate in the two intergovernmental dialogues on migration in the region: the Regional Conference on Migration (known as the Puebla process) and the South American Conference on Migration. At the eighth Regional Conference on Migration, CELADE and IOM reported on the progress of the Statistical Information System on Migration in Central America (SIEMCA) Project, whose purpose is to help improve understanding of migratory processes in order to facilitate the adoption of government policies and measures; to this end, in 2003 CELADE generated a set of special tabulations using the information on migration contained in the censuses conducted by the Central American countries.

In April 2003, CELADE participated in a second technical consultative meeting, held in Asunción, Paraguay, in preparation for the Fourth South American Conference on Migration and collaborated with IOM in setting out project priorities and profiles in the different areas identified in the plan of action adopted at the Third Conference; the Fourth Conference is to take place in Montevideo in November 2003.

Technical cooperation provided to the countries of the region by CELADE in 2003 has included support to the Government of Chile in designing its policy on migration and to the Government of Nicaragua in incorporating migration issues into its national poverty eradication strategy. Technical guidelines are also being furnished to the Government of Paraguay for the analysis of information on migration contained in the 2001 national population and housing census with a view to redefining its policies in this regard.

CELADE also provides intensive advisory assistance to public and academic institutions, non-governmental organizations, researchers and students in the countries on a number of aspects of international migration, as well as responding to queries from the press in the different countries. As a part of these responsibilities, the web site on migration is updated on a regular basis.

6

Migration and Security

In an era of growing security concerns and heightened State efforts to curtail immigration to the developed world, Western democracies are increasingly caught between their liberal ethos and their ability to effectively and securely control their borders. An examination of policy implementation in the United States and Europe reveals that liberal States have responded to these cross-pressures by: a) reinventing their modes of immigration regulation; and b) adopting strategies which are converging. States have shifted the level of policy-making to non-State actors, who have the economic and/or political resources to facilitate or curtail travel, migration and return. These include a complex web of actors incorporated by the State, and the transfer of State functions to non-centralized jurisdictions.

Liberal States have been able to extend their realm of action, and overcome certain constraints by changing the gatekeepers at external and internal sites, to include: private (i.e., airlines, travel companies, employers), local (i.e., civic actors, such as churches, elected officials, trade unions), and international/supranational agents (i.e., the EU, Mexico,

ICAO). Together they reflect an enlarged 'migration playing field' in an increasingly global world. State agencies have thus been able to solve the control dilemma in ways that can at once appease public anxieties over migration and security, short-circuit judicial and normative constraints and still promote trade and tourist flows.

The expansion of an immigration regulatory playing-field has been evident in the United States and countries of the EU, since the 1980s when immigration began to be linked with law-and-order concerns. These approaches represent a trade-off of certain democratic values, sanctioned by citizens - a willingness to compromise civil liberties and personal freedom for a greater sense of security from immigration, terrorism, and globalization. They are consistent with an older repertoire of mechanisms liberal States employ when security looms large.

Security is a powerful issue that motivates voters to transfer such authority to bureaucracies and other non-State actors in the name of law and order. It is important to examine the sources (i.e., public opinion constituencies, media framing) and rationale that inspire these dynamics, as well as the implications for immigration, rights-based norms, and democratic values. Assuming that convergence of these modes has taken place among democratic countries, to what degree are the outcomes similar in the U.S. and the countries of the EU, and why? What are the lessons that liberal democracies may offer each other regarding policy instruments? Does the impact of 9/11 promise more continuity or change?

On September 11, the alarm bells of terror reverberated beyond the borders of the United States. The implication of foreign networks was much discussed in the media, raised the specter of populism and led to arguments that liberal democratic governments would be compelled to dramatically rethink their border controls in a global world full·of 'people on the move'. A marked increase in bilateral and multilateral activity on international migration, that include two UN experts' Coordination meetings, and the launching of an independent Global Commission on International Migration bear witness to the changing nature of migration.

In the language of international relations, migration issues have shifted from the technical domain of 'low politics' to those related to security or 'high politics'. The growing tendency to view international migration-related questions through a national security heuristic has also coincided with the re-emergence of anti-immigrant politics on the extreme-right. The question posed especially since the tragic events of September 11 2001 has been, what has changed?

The link between migration and security is not new. Security in its various forms has assumed various meanings across cultures and time. The traditional security agenda has been embedded in the notion of protection from external aggression, or national interests in foreign policy, and has thus been linked to State sovereignty and identity. The term however has been broadly attached to societal, personal, national, or more basic human security, including economic, physical, health, environmental, cultural and political dimensions. A few scholars developed the link between international migration and security as early as the 1980s. While Myron Weiner was the first political scientist to address the relationship between immigration and security issues, several scholars indirectly captured this linkage in their work on immigration and refugees in the US foreign policy.

More recently, scholars of European politics have broadened their security-migration focus to include demographic, societal and cultural conflicts as well as identity politics. Although the security ramifications of immigration have thus been evident for a long time, the broad security agenda that has emerged more recently makes clear that there is still no consensus regarding the scope and definition of security as it relates to international migration. Similarly, the mechanisms States adopt with regards to migration control when security concerns loom large do not appear so new. In face of security and global pressures, States in the post-Cold Wars system are embracing an older repertoire of strategies they employ when seeking more effective immigration control. They incorporate and enlist actors at the private, local and international levels in gatekeeper functions. There are two innovations here.

First, globalization has afforded migration control an extraordinary degree of sophisticate and extensive new technology. Second, the post-WWII context of liberal judicial norms that States have to overcome in order to pursue these national interests is also unprecedented. That is, formal constitutional guarantees as well as activist administrative and constitutional courts have significantly circumscribed both the authority and the capacity of States to prevent family unification or to dispose of migrants at will. The "liberal epoch" of human rights norms that facilitated humanitarian migration alongside labor recruitment (family unification and asylum) strikingly contrasts to earlier periods.

One only needs to recall the expulsions of 400,000 Poles from Germany in 1885-1886, or the exclusion of Chinese immigrants before the turn of the century in the United States to realize the normative evolution that has taken place in the migration policy domain. Moreover, liberal States concerned with promoting modern trade and commerce cannot unambiguously embrace policies that hinder the movement of people across borders. Free trade requires a degree of openness that impedes calls for tighter border controls.

In an era of growing security concerns, Western democracies are increasingly caught between their global market and rights-based norms on one side, and political and security pressures to effectively control their borders, on the other. The extent to which immigration regulation has converged throughout Europe and North America reinforces the commitment towards immigration regulation. The most striking policy developments towards.this goal include tighter border controls, increased visa requirements, readmission agreements, carrier sanctions, accelerated return procedures, employer sanctions, labor enforcement, detention and removal of criminal aliens, changing benefits eligibility, and computer registration systems. These initiatives were evident by the late 1980s, but soared after 9/11.

Europe has adopted buffer zones, Eurodoc fingerprinting and Schengen Information System databases, 'safe third country' principles and increasing coordination. In a similar vein, American observers have witnessed the Patriot Law of 2001 and the passage of the Enhanced Border Security and Visa Entry Reform Act in 2002. Direct legislative responses to the terrorist attacks, these acts paved the way for electronic innovations, visa screening, racial and ethnic profiling, acceleration of procedures, unprecedented security checks, the modernization of immigration controls with the latest technology, such as the use of biometrics, the SEVIS database for foreign students, as well as the formation of a new Office of Homeland Security to coordinate activities with a reorganized INS. The latter represents the first significant addition to the US government since1947, when Harry Truman merged the various branches of the US Armed Forces into the Department of Defense to better coordinate the nation's defense against military threats .

While national legislation and immigration reforms represent the most obvious policy responses to immigration, administrative decisions and policy implementation may provide more practical implications of the character of immigration control. What has gone unnoticed in all these policy developments has been the reliance on third-party, non-State actors who provide services, resources and non public practices that are otherwise unavailable to central government officials. More specifically, policy implementation has relied on the enlistment or collaboration (also known as 'burden-sharing' in political jargon) of non-State actors, who have the economic, social and/or political resources to facilitate or curtail immigration and return.

They represent efforts of States to extend the burden of implementation away from central governments and national borders, and to the source of control, thereby increasing national efficacy and reducing the costs to central governments. Most of these processes have relied on reinvented modes of 'remote control' mechanisms that enable States to control migration. The development of the relationship between States and non-State actors in meeting security goals captures a global era marked by both a political desire to control movement and agents willing and able to play on the link between migration, crime, and security. Thus, any analysis of an enlarged migration 'playing field' needs to go beyond the typical analysis of State policies in terms of legislation and focus on implementation structures.

Table 1. Non-State Actors in Remote Control Immigration Policy

International	Public	Private
EU	Local jails	Employers
NAFTA	Mayors	Sponsors
Schengen	Schools/universities	Families
Consulates		
(visa policy)	Health care	NGOs
Foreign countries		Hotels
Airlines		Schools/universities
Security agencies		Travel agencies
Ship/transport carriers		

Liberal States have been able to extend their realm of action and overcome certain constraints by shifting the liabilities to: international and supranational actors; private actors (through privatization); and local agents (through decentralization). The proliferation of non-State actors in regulating immigration is evident on both levels of policy-immigration (intake) and immigrant policy (integration).

Three types of actors - private, local, and international - have been incorporated by liberal States to monitor external and internal sites, including questions of entry, stay and exit of migrants. Despite substantial structural and cultural differences between the EU and US, which mediate policy organization, implementation and effectiveness, a comparative analysis of the American and European cases reveals that policy tools are transferable. It suggests that an international regime on immigration is possible; however, unlike regimes for capital and goods, an international migration regime may be more oriented to protectionism, with some adverse effects on civil liberties.

Private actors, or independent authorities who rely on market forces have become crucial immigration agents in extending the area of what is referred to as "remote control" immigration policy. These actors include airlines, shipping carriers, transport companies, security services for entry; employer groups for work; universities, propriety schools such as language or aviation facilities, hotels, health care services and civic actors, such as churches, families, trade unions and NGOs for immigrant stays. They also include detention centers, for-profit security services and space for deportation and exit. Often constrained by international agreements, these actors are either incorporated by the State or contracted out.

To the extent that their functions have evolved from contractors into regulators - from the public to the private sphere, we can speak about these processes as a 'privatization of regulation'. The incentives for cooperation are economic; the constraints are sanctions or fines. Thus, with little training investments, private carriers and agencies are able to partake in an enlarged migration control as agents of the State. In return for government cooperation, they are assured a smoother flow of business, trade, labor, and tourism.

A core actor in the enlarged control system at the entry level is transport or carrier companies. This is not new. Carriers have long been obliged, at their own expense, to transport inadmissible passengers back to their countries of departure. Sanctions against ships have been in force in the United States, since the Passenger Act of 1902. However, since the adoption of guidelines established by the 1944 Convention on International Civil Aviation (ICAO), transport companies have been increasingly forced to assume the role of international immigration officers imposed on them by States. The standards of the convention established.the airline's responsibility to ensure that passengers have the necessary travel documents. Apart from ICAO guidelines, many countries have introduced laws that increase the responsibilities of carriers and levy fines against them for non-compliance.

In 1994, all EU countries, with the exception of Spain, Ireland, and Luxembourg passed laws increasing carriers' responsibilities. The abolition of internal borders critical to European integration has been essentially mitigated by the flurry of legislation and implementation of the carriers' liability to check passengers. Indeed, more stringent security checks at airports-of identity cards, tickets, boarding passes, baggage, and so on-have made the absence of passport controls virtually irrelevant. International instruments have further sanctioned the role of States in controlling their borders. In the European Union, member-States refer to their obligations to Article 26 of the 1990 Supplementation Agreement of the Schengen Convention in relying on carriers to serve as immigration officers.

Although private actors have long been incorporated in European policy-making through neo-corporatist arrangements, even in the United States, independent commissions to regulate inter-State commerce had been established by the late 1880s. Devolution of inter-State regulation to expert bodies in the US may be traced back to federal government adoption of the InterState Commerce Act regulating the railways and setting up a corresponding regulatory body (InterState Commerce Commission).

The United States Congress, thereby delegated its own power to regulate an important part of interState commerce, namely railway traffic to an agency designed especially for the purpose. This was an important institutional innovation at the federal level. It represented the transfer of activities of State interests to private actors. In this way, market activities may be generally regulated in areas which are considered important, and in need of protection as well as control.

Security concerns have laid the grounds for enlistment of private actors in State regulations, and have been justified to compromise certain civil liberties. In the wake of September 11, the Transportation Security Administration (TSA) has threatened to use its power to issue a security directive to force airlines to hand over passenger information so that the federal government could screen reservation records for possible terrorists.

These options place private companies in delicate positions, as exemplified by the notorious JetBlue Airways outrage, which has led to a 2003 class action lawsuit on behalf of 5 million passengers, for giving personal information to a Defense Department contractor.Such episodes tap into the ideological conflict that exists between protecting privacy rights and security interests.

Furthermore, in a corporate culture, travel industry groups have voiced concern that new airport security systems could hurt the industry. Security concerns however have prevailed, and are a powerful motive to justify the incorporation of non-State or private actors who can help with monitoring functions in ways otherwise unavailable to central government officials.

At the internal level of immigration control, the private counterpart to admissions regulation lays in the employment sector, where immigration control may be equally effective. Increasingly, approaches to stem illegal migration at the work site have been developed to extend and redistribute the liabilities of migration control outside of the central State, and make employer groups more significant actors. In the early to mid-1970s, most advanced

European countries instituted similar provisions adopted by the French as early as 1926, and have adopted and refined employer sanctions.

The French approach to stem illegal migration at the work site has been considered a model of emulation for other Western countries, including the United States. Premised on the assumption that the battle for immigration control would be won or lost at the local level, in particular in industries and places of employment, the French model of department-level commissions, brings together concerned enforcement services, elected officials, and representatives of employers and employees. Similarly, the agreement in the 1990s between the U.S. Department of Labor and the Immigration and Naturalization Service to allow labor inspectors to check I-9 compliance represented a step towards the French approach.

There are substantial differences, which derive from conceptual distinctions between European and American systems of labor control. Despite considerable structural variations, in most European countries, the agency with the most labor market expertise, the labor agency, has responsibility for detecting and removing unauthorized workers from the workplace. Europe, for example has a long history of protecting her workers by controlling access to her labor market by illegal migrants. Her labor agency thus regards the removal of undocumented workers as a means of protecting legal workers.

In contrast, in the United States, inspectors from the Immigration and Naturalization Service have traditionally been concerned about the workers' legal status, rather than about their wages or working conditions, while the State labor inspectors are concerned about wages but not about the workers' legal status. Over time, controversies involving

State labor inspectors who have failed to cooperate with federal officials have led to a rethinking of coordination.

Broadly-speaking, these cross-cultural differences have meant that liabilities have been governed by different conceptual schemes, generating disparate outcomes even when similar policy tools have been adopted. In the United States, worksite sanctions have fallen in the framework of (illegal) migration rather than within the rubric of employment standards. In contrast to France, where employer sanctions have been part of labor laws since as early as 1926, in the United States, before IRCA, illegal aliens were considered to violate Federal law by entering the country and working, but employers were not.

Employer sanctions corrected this asymmetry and made the knowing hire of illegal aliens a violation of Federal labor law for the first time. In addition, employers have now been required to verify the status of their new hires by examining a selection from a large variety of documents and keeping records of their examinations. Nonetheless, due to the European system's heavy social safety net, which sets employer payroll taxes and related overhead costs at higher levels than they are in the United States, the fine structure in Europe is often far greater than in the United States.

Although much of the enforcement capacities of work control systems depend on the verifiability of documentation, there are dramatic differences between the U.S. and its European counterparts that stem from different civic traditions and political cultures. Although France for example does not have a mandatory national identification document system, it is believed that over 90 per cent of Frenchman carry a national identity card.

Lacking in such traditions, American strategies to regulate the worksite have been hampered in addressing the problem of fraudulent and/or counterfeit documents. Moreover, a political culture adverse to business or corporate intervention makes the role of employers less vulnerable to liabilities than their European counterparts. Nonetheless, there are incremental changes on this front.

In 1989, the INS revised the "green card" and in 1996, began replacing some of the older work authorization forms with a new "tamper-resistant" Employment Authorization Document (EAD), based on a Social Security number (SSN), and on improved breeder documents to establish identity. The INS also began to develop and test databases and access systems for businesses to use in verifying employment eligibility.

In November 2003, new legislation was passed to expand the 1996 law used by employers from six original States to the country-wide level. Under the program, employers can check with the Social Security Administration and the INS to confirm that Social Security numbers and alien identification numbers are authentic.The adoption of a worker authorization system has been viewed as a first step towards a national ID card, and unsurprisingly has come under substantial ammunition from civil rights advocates and those who oppose the expansion of federal government power to give employers permission for hiring.

Since 9/11, renewed calls for national identity cards have gained more legitimacy, and public opinion has been more sympathetic to the option. The system of work-site control of immigration represents a coordinated effort to stem migration at the source, while ensuring a necessary supply of workers needed to maintain a competitive economy. In both Europe (especially Germany) and the United States, there have also been a growing number of tripartite agreements between governments, employers, and trade unions, or coordinated activities that emphasize the central role of employers in immigration control. These agreements have coincided with the reemergence of guest-worker programs, a feature of the initial 30-year post-War period until 1973. At the core of this system are quotas, negotiated between government, employers and trade unions. Although reminiscent of the Bracero program of 1942-64, and its unintended consequences, an amendment to the 1996 US Illegal Immigration Reform and Immigrant Responsibility Act granted temporary work visas for approximately 250,000 foreign farm workers. Such initiatives have been designed to stem illegal migration flows and target sectors with shortages. In interest-matrix terms, these dynamics mean that seasonal workers obtain skills and earn a salary which can then be used on return, in their country of origin.

The sending country benefits from the influx of resources and more highly skilled work force. The company hiring these workers profit through lower wage rates and freedom from heavy fines imposed by hiring illegal migrants; and the host country reduces illegal immigration, the costs of border control and resource-draining legal procedures for eventual deportation. In addition, the State can also derive benefit from taxes and social welfare contributions of these temporary or seasonal workers.

The devolution to private actors over immigrant control or issues of immigrant stays has emerged in many forms, both officially and unofficially. These strategies are less novel than they are more formally enforced. In the United States for example, foreign students have long been required to sign a waiver permitting their registered institutions to provide information to immigration officials as a condition of most education visas.

In the U.S., before the last breath of the Immigration and Naturalization Service proper in March 2003, the increasing focus on immigration enforcement, came at the expense of its service component.The Service's functions of processing had increasingly been redelegated to churches and trade unions that have operated as go-betweens in legal services, educational programs and information campaigns between immigrants and legislation. Moreover, the absence of INS offices or federal legal services in certain areas of the vast country have contributed to the expansive role of municipal officers, jails, security services and detention centers in regulating migrants on behalf of federal inspectors.

States have also shifted the onus of regulation to private individuals and civil actors in monitoring stays through deportation and enforcement of exit rules. The 1996 U.S. bills granted new authority to State and local police officials to detain aliens when there is an outstanding order to depart and they imposed increased penalties for document fraud on illegal migrants, such as civil fines and the barring of future entry (a serious penalty for someone with close or nuclear family members). The "contracting out" of detention centers and guards to private for-profit security services, companies, and space has been deferred to private, State, and local actors, with the support of government sums. These trends have coincided with increasing emphasis on detention, and have prompted all types of civil rights criticisms, as well as uprisings at apparently underinspected facilities.

In the U.S., the Illegal Immigration Reform and Responsibility Act of 1996 put into motion a shift in liabilities away from courts and toward individual migrants. Eliminating the authority of federal courts to review decisions by the INS in deportation and legalization cases the Act essentially stripped both the rights of non-citizens to file complaints against the agency in court; and the rights of courts over what in the past has been considered the last line of defense against abuse of official power. It practically placed the INS beyond judicial scrutiny.

Since 9/11, indefinite detention is valid without an initial court hearing, as part of the anti-terrorist campaign. With the US Patriot Act, Attorney General John Ashcroft put into effect sweeping changes that include the indefinite detention of those who enter the country illegally. While in the past, denial of release required a court ruling that the person was dangerous or would flee if released, since 2001, an illegal immigrant could be denied release if he/she raised national security fears (not necessarily a risk) among US government agencies.

The focus on detention of immigrants has been speculated to become a lucrative business,and has comer under attack by civil rights advocates who have repeatedly lost the battle to security interests. Thus, for example, in the US, the Supreme Court has consistently upheld the government's secret detention hearings, where the foreigner was deemed to be a "special interest" case. The Court has rejected appeals from the American Civil Liberties Union over the government's surveillance powers, and those from the international community over the detention of hundreds of prisoners picked up in Afghanistan and held at Guatanamo Bay, Cuba without formal charges or access to lawyers. These decisions were made on the grounds that national security concerns outweigh public access to such hearings.

At the core of privatizing regulations for immigrant stays has been the role of the family and private citizens. In the United States, the burden on families has emerged in the form of more restrictive sponsorship rules and practices that are now enforceable. New sponsorship rules affect legal immigrants who are typically sponsored by relatives or by business.Until the recent Immigration bills, sponsors of immigrants were typically required to assure that anyone they brought into the country would not become a 'public charge'. Since these pledges had become unenforceable in court, the more recent bills aimed to make this support binding.

Sponsors, rather than taxpayers, are required to provide a more substantial safety net for immigrants by making the sponsor's affidavit of support a legally enforceable document (up to 10 years or the immigrant becomes a citizen). For the first time, the notion of "becoming a public charge" has been carefully defined with the intention of making this a realistic ground for deportation. Similarly, the controversy in France over a proposed Government law aiming to prevent illegal immigration reflects State efforts to "transform all citizens into police informers". The new bill proposed that French hosts who have foreign guests on special visas inform the town hall when their guests leave, allowing the French government to compile computer records on the movements of foreigners.

The role and liabilities of non-State actors in sharing the burden of regulation has developed almost uniformly in the countries of Europe as well as the United States, and are manifest in the use of more stringent deterrent methods such as sanctions. On the one hand, these shifts in liabilities represent an incorporation of private actors in State regulatory functions; on the other they constitute more general trends occurring in other policy areas, namely to shift the externalities of policy-making outside of the central government.

Privatization, loosely defined as the shift of a function from the public sector to the private sector, involves a dependence on market forces for the pursuit of social goods, and may turn local actors or contractors into regulators. Both the incorporation of private actors through sanctions and the privatization of migration regulation through 'contracting out' of implementation functions involve the extension of State control over migration outside and beyond its borders. These strategies which operate before the border or at the control site facilitate the movement of tourists and businessman while preventing unwanted migrants.

In this way, liberal States can respond to the consequences of globalization: sustained migration pressures, tourism, free trade flows, and global terror networks. While many of these instruments are not new, their novelty lay in the current context of liberal norms. They are now deployed to circumvent legal constraints absent in the early twentieth century. However, these areas are where the most significant problems occur, as exemplified by the notorious JetBlue Airways episode. They challenge the Western commitment to civil liberties and democratic values amidst a climate of heightened threat.

Local Actors

Local actors too have gained a bit of prestige from their expanded jurisdiction. Through processes of decentralization, national governments have delegated substantial decision-making powers to local elected officials, in ways that have been considered to be exclusionary and detrimental to foreigners' rights. A major reason behind this kind of decentralization is that national elected officials concur and depend on local elected officials, who under financial and political pressure to attract more funds and votes by adopting exceptionally harsh measures against immigrants.

In France, for example, mayors have become actors in migration control through their authority over marital and residential certificates. City halls have the prerogative to inspect the veracity of marriages between nationals and foreigners. A 1993 law granted mayors the possibility to refer a marriage involving an alien to the Procureur de la République, who can delay the marriage for a month and then, if they see fit, prevent it. A 1996 survey on this measure revealed significant geographical diversity in its implementation, and a use of the measure to arrest illegal aliens.

Since 1982, when the Deferre laws on decentralization were voted in France, mayors have gained in clout and local political debate has intensified even outside electoral campaigns. Mayors in urban areas or in the Southeast, where the National Front has made electoral headway have used their new monitoring role in migration control policy to the fullest.

In the trend in liberal democracies to use integration policy to affect immigration flows, national governments have increasingly shifted monitoring functions of immigrant stays and rights downwards to local actors. By devolving implementation of such measures as barring the children of undocumented migrants from public schools to local actors, the theory is that undocumented migrants will be discouraged from migrating, or from staying illegally. In France, following the passage of the Act on Immigration Control and Conditions of Entry and Residence of Foreigners, foreigners living in the country illegally no longer qualify for social security (i.e., child allowances, health insurance, old age pensions, and unemployment benefits). In these cases, local governments are bearing the direct costs.

In the United States, Proposition 187, and the Gallegly Amendment, measures to bar the undocumented and their children from public schools and welfare programs, while ultimately failing, focused on the liabilities of local actors for implementation. These demands for more local power concur with national plans for restrictions of foreigners' rights. The 1996 Welfare Reform Act marked the end of the sixty-one year-old federal guarantee of cash assistance for the nation's poorest children; it revoked federal benefits like food stamps and Supplementary Security Incomes from non-citizen immigrants. This new law also gave States vast new authority to run their own welfare programs with lump sums of federal money. It thus represented renewed efforts to grant States (local actors) more control over traditionally unfunded mandates, creating a mechanism for uneven integration policies among States and regions.

Of course, the incorporation of local actors in migration regulation is not new. In the United States, State and local governments have long regulated the movement of people across legal borders, through the use of criminal laws, vagrancy laws, quarantine laws, registration, and before 1865, throughout the law of slavery. Until the middle to late nineteenth century, States still carried a number of prerogatives in the area of migration, including the rights granted to aliens, and the bestowing of nationality.

Part of the explanation stems from the fact that States with slave populations wanted control over nationality and hence, it was not surprising that courts rescinded these State rights after the Civil War. Increasingly, during the twentieth century, Supreme Court decisions emphasized the exclusive federal prerogatives in the area of immigration regulation, via the plenary power doctrine, and the dangers of State encroachment.

Thus, although some argue that the devolution of immigration policy to States is a growing reality, and a legitimate one, given the handful of States that are major fiscal and political stakeholders of immigration, from a historical perspective, contemporary political demands for a State role in immigration policy is a call to turn back the clock. In many cases, although the complicity between national and local actors to surveil foreigners have been evident at the informal level, increasingly the delegation of competence has taken a legal forum, through laws and the enactment of circulars, and implemented by decentralization measures.

In France, substantial controversy was generated by the prerequisite "housing certificate" administered by city hall in order to be eligible to host a foreigner. The 1982 creation of the certificate became a migration control tool in mayors' hands in 1993. Since the law of 24 August 1993, the certificates could be refused by the mayor after ordering an investigation by the International Migrations Office (OMI).

In fact, some mayors refused to distribute the forms or systematically did not deliver them, and over 50% were reported to seek papers not required by law. Before these changes, there had been a number of instances in which mayors had exceeded their authority to target aliens, but they had been condemned in court.

The novelty in the 1990s is therefore not the attitude of local authorities, but the new means that they have been granted to play a role in migration control. To be sure, the devolution of mandates, downward to States, municipalities, and local actors, to monitor immigrant stays are old strategies employed when nations look to impose more stringent control over migration. Immigrant policy, long delegated to State and local governments to implement and fund, often with unfunded mandates from federal legislation and court decisions, is marked by increasing formalization of legal controls and responsibilities imposed by central governments.

By reinforcing the local authorities' responsibilities and autonomy in immigrant policy, federal governments have been able to effectively enlarge immigration control through burden-sharing exchanges. Still, as legal scholars have argued in the American case, it is ultimately up to the U.S. Congress to authorize States to play a role in immigration policy, as the latter did in 1996 with respect to welfare benefits. In part, these trends have led to renewed conflicts between federal, State, and local mandates.

Thus, the 1996 Illegal Immigration Reform and Immigrant Responsibility Act, which permitted the INS to train and deputize local police officers to enforce immigration laws has received uneven political reception. In New York City, home to one of the most diverse immigrant populations in the U.S., Mayor Bloomberg, for example, under pressure from immigration groups and the City Council was forced to revise his immigration policy to make it more difficult for city agencies to report illegal immigrants to federal authorities. Such political wranglings are seen not only to heighten turf wars, and contradictory goals of different arms of the State (i.e., the police, judiciary, public administration), but also the lines between national and local mandates.

International and Transnational Actors

International and transnational actors have become important agents in the State's coordination of migration regulation. There is a misguided tendency to understand the role of intergovernmental groups (such as Schengen in Europe), international conventions or bilateral agreements (e.g., U.S.-Mexico) as constraints to national interests in managing migration. In fact, the collaboration between foreign actors and private and local ones may be interpreted to buttress State interests in securing their borders.

In policing and border control, for example, competition between different types of police at the national level makes participation in international fora an important source of domestic recognition, and may be a means of expanding national jurisdiction. The devolution of immigration regulation to these actors beyond the State level has served to extend State control over immigrant rights, and in certain cases, have enabled States to regain some control that may have been lost because of national jurisprudence.

In Europe, where the movement towards complete free movement of persons is critical for European integration, abolition of checks at internal borders have been somewhat offset by the proliferation of intergovernmental and supranational actors (i.e., the EU 'third pillar', the Ad Hoc Immigration Group, TREVI, EUROPOL, the coordinating Rhodes Group and the Schengen Group) who promote a more effective migration control regime.

Bolstered by the European project of regional integration, these actors and types of arrangements have now evolved in the image of the Schengen Group, representative of the administrative culture of traditional immigration decision-making, where decisions have been typically made behind closed doors, with little or no formal debate in a public forum.

Many intergovernmental cooperation groups do not have to answer to a more representative body or international courts such as the European Parliament or the European Court of Justice. The lack of transparency of these negotiations not only makes it difficult for certain national actors to oversee the process, but may be used to circumvent even the most liberal national constraints on migration control. This proliferation and diversification of instruments used to restrict immigration in Europe are considered to fortify the State apparatus in immigration control, leading some to insinuate evolving images of police States.

Border extensions may be said to exist in Europe as a result of "Schengland," which makes each member country the beneficiary of police screening efforts of the others, long before incomers arrive to national borders. European integration has produced the 'securitization' of internal and external controls through collaborative policy agency work, and the extension of police and gendarmerie activities. An empirical study in France has suggested that increased competition for budgets has forced these agencies to develop strategies for the expansion of their jurisdiction by appealing to EU networks, both as a source of legitimacy and efficiency.

In an attempt to control illegal migration across Europe's southern borders following the 2002 Seville meeting, Operation Ulysses was deployed among five EU countries (Spain, Britain, France, Italy and Portugal) to coordinate police, customs and navy ships. This represents the first time that EU members have formally coordinated their efforts in this way, and according to Spain's interior minister, Angel Acebes, the operation "could be and should be" the precursor to a common European border police force.

In the U.S, success has been marked by a significant reduction in petty crime and street vending, which has been said to derive from strong public support (even within the Mexican-American community) and the perception of enhanced public safety (as a result of the discontinued chases of border patrol and undocumented aliens near the border.

While negotiations between American President Bush and Mexican President Vicente Fox on the eve of September 11 2001 for 'an amnesty program came to a crashing halt, a new focus was directed at the Canadian border. The revelation that several hijackers entered surreptitiously across the Canadian border led the US to opt for some type of "joint security perimeter" in lieu of compromising a friendship and economic interest by resorting to physical and administrative barriers along the border. In an effort to get the Mexico deal back on the table, resumed talks with President Fox have also proposed the inclusion of Mexico along with Mexico into a security perimeter that covers all NAFTA territory.

The fortification of external controls is reinforced by these kinds of international agreements, cooperation, and the creation of transnational spaces. International agreements have also generated substantial visa harmonization among EU countries, and have expanded the role of third States in fortifying external controls. The joint visa list of the EU States established through the Dublin Convention in 1993, imposed visa requirements on travelers from 73 of the 183 non-EU States. A list of 110 countries whose nationals require visas to enter the EU region was established at the EU Justice and Home Affairs Council meeting on 25 September 1995. In addition to the uniform pan-European entry visa regime, where "problem countries" are identified, countries such as Germany, station immigration officers at overseas airports to ensure that documentation is correctly checked.

These measures may not only be interpreted as a border shift outward (i.e., 'Schengenland', or U.S-Mexico joint border patrols and shift from apprehension after crossing to deterrence before entry). These strategies also mean that governments may rely on "remote control" immigration policy or the creation of international zones (i.e., in airports) where intervention by lawyers and human rights associations is almost impossible and thus foreigners' civil rights are less likely to be respected in these juridical "no man's land" or transnational spaces.

International cooperation and the incorporation of third-State actors have also created transnational spaces in the employment sector, where they may circumvent national protection of foreign workers' rights. One critical trend in shifting levels and liabilities in the employment domain comes in form of bilateral contracts or work agreements between EU or Eastern European firms, who are authorized to move with their foreign workers in order to complete a project. In these cases, the workers are physically present in France, for example, but they cannot claim pension or social insurance benefits nor be protected by labor law there. In these ways, States have been able to delegate functions out to other States and third-party actors, and thus shift levels of policy elaboration upwards to international and transnational political spaces

The potency of international actors and rules in sanctioning States to adopt all types of restrictive migration policies has greatly been underestimated by theorists of globalization and policy-makers, who have overlooked the role of international agreements in bolstering national interests. Indeed, when national interests coalesce, favorable conditions leading to the pooling of sovereignty may lead to migration coordination in order to "upgrade common interests". European regional integration for example represents a prevalent supranational order which consists of strong States committed to pooling sovereignty, based on restrictive migration policies and more effective control.

Unlike international regimes for capital, goods, and services, international cooperation on migration matters may be less than "liberal," serving to inhibit immigration rather than to promote it. Indeed, up to date, cooperation predominantly exists in the prevention of migration. While a shift in regulatory functions upwards to international or foreign State actors is in an infant State, it is becoming increasingly institutionalized as reflected in the 1997 Amsterdam and 1999 Nice Treaties in Europe.

The proliferation of transnational and international actors, agreements and cooperation may be interpreted as national efforts to more effectively control migration. Through international and transnational cooperation, liberal States have managed to use foreign actors to fortify and extend their borders, well before immigrants even arrive, and even after, by circumventing more liberal national jurisprudence. The interests of international actors, particularly civil servants and emergent institutions, are to expand the agency's recognition and jurisdiction, while gaining more national prestige back at home. For States, of course, it offers an essential border shift outward.

For local authorities such as elected officials, the extension of their domain of jurisdiction may often coincide with a scapegoating of foreigners when budgetary crises emerge. Financial or political compensation may serve as both a carrot and a stick for vigilant policy implementation. While the constraints for private actors are sanctions or fines, the incentives are economic. Thus, with little training investment, private carriers and agencies (i.e., airline and shipping companies) are able to partake in an enlarged migration control system as agents of the State.

Private security agencies expand their range of action through their participation in migration control with little training investment. These strategies provide the State with the technological and resourceful means to effectively differentiate between the 'legal' passages of travelers or economic tourists and would-be-overstayers or migrants.

At the international level, civil servants and third-State actors may enhance the degrees of freedom of national policy-makers while reaping the benefits of legitimacy and participation through expanded jurisdiction. The result may include enhanced political capacity of States to all types of migration pressures, and more effective State legitimacy. The expenses are clearly imposed on individual migrants, at the price of liberal migration regimes. Cases of stowaways thrown abroad to avert heavy carrier fines, reversals of due process of law, human right violations, corruption and abuse abound. The risk to the State in these devolution processes lays in the appearance of expropriated control, a gamble that lends support to more nationalist movements of the extreme right.

Since 9/11 however, this risk has been tempered by heightened security threats. That is, new norms have emerged because public perceptions of national interests are likely to shift under conditions of heightened threat. As cross-cultural research shows, when immigration policy becomes linked to physical security, the public favors more restrictive immigration policies to coalesce around a common national interest. Indeed, there appears to be a link between countries that have experienced terrorist attacks and border restrictions, as illustrated in the Israeli case which has cyclically prevented Palestinians from working in the country.

In addition to physical insecurity, threats to national community and identity have.been shown to accompany general immigrant intolerance and rejection. Threat increases ethnocentrism, in-group solidarity, and xenophobia. It promotes intolerance and a willingness to forego basic civil liberties, and leads to closed-mindedness. Indeed, public opinion polls have revealed that since September 11, the role of civil liberties and human rights have been seen as a price of shifting security concerns - a trade-off of certain democratic values, sanctioned by citizen or a willingness to compromise civil liberties and personal freedom for a greater sense of security from immigration, terrorism, and globalization.

In the United States, since 9/11, Americans have reported support for racial and ethnic profiling of Arab Americans, greater FBI invasion of citizens' privacy and a close monitoring of legal immigrants. They are more likely to entertain national identity cards and to be inconvenienced by surveillance schemes for more security.

To what extent have security concerns opened up new channels and opportunities for State regulation over migration? In view of the evidence presented above, it appears that liberal democracies can go very far in the pursuit of their national security interests. Well before 9/11, but particularly after, with more public support, liberal States have been oriented not only in rhetoric but also in capacities toward more restrictive immigration policy. In efforts to reconcile the cross-pressures between economic liberalism and security protection, States have delegated implementation and enforcement functions upwards to intergovernmental forums and cooperation, downward to local authorities, and outward to non-State or private actors.

Under heightened threat, immigration policy has shifted to older, more nuanced forms of control. The image of governments simply making and then implementing policy simplifies the process of contemporary migration practice. Establishing bureaucratic instruments through which to implement and monitor policy is a major activity, and such acts are especially important. However, equally fundamental to increased State commitment to control immigration is a tendency towards pursuing burden-sharing norms that rely on international/transnational, private and local actors and spaces. This is not only elaborately developing in the EU countries, which have a rich history of neo-corporatist arrangements, but also in the United States, which has openly called for "burden-sharing" in its Report of the Commission on Immigration Reform.

Consistent with the EU trend of liberal democracies, US policy (similarly 'constrained' by NAFTA considerations) is increasingly pursuing inter-agency coordination not only within and among its own national institutions, but also with civil rights groups, outreach programs and international police forces, of which the coordination of Mexican-US Border Patrols has been most notably promising. While in all cases, these strategies represent the revival of old approaches towards immigration regulation, their adoption in the 1990s reflect a formalization and institutionalization which rely on such third party actors, as industries, services, companies, local governments, and particularly other States-as extensions of State borders.

These arrangements are based on mutual bargaining exchanges: the promotion of movement, particularly for legal migrants, favoring businesses, and certain social sectors; for assistance in combating and deterring illegal migration. By bringing in private actors, for example, the State itself may be said to reverse the process closer to its favor and diffuse the costs of immigration-more specifically, that of a hostile anti-immigrant public opinion.

The State may thus diminish the political fall-out of migration controls through a diffusing strategy that relies on a variety of third-party actors. In an era of a prevail security agenda, liberal States can go fairly far in regulating migration not only because of the help of non-State actors, but also because of public support. Under heightened conditions of threat, the ability of governments to tie immigration to law and order, and to frame the immigration debate in that context has yielded restrictive and exclusion outcomes. They are sanctioned by their public and by the modes of regulation to compromise their rights-based norms.

7

Reproductive Health

Reproductive health is not merely the absence of disease or disability. It is a state of physical, mental, and social well-being in all matters related to the reproductive system and to its functions and processes. Reproductive health therefore implies that women and men have a right to a safe sex life, and to reproduce if and when they wish. This includes the right of men and women to be informed about and to have access to safe, effective, affordable, and acceptable methods of regulating childbearing. The reproductive health approach requires health services that enable women to go safely through pregnancy and childbirth and provide the best chance of having a healthy outcome for both mother and child. It also encompasses information and services to improve reproductive and sexual health through disease control and increasing gender equity.

The Programme of Action adopted by the 1994 International Conference on Population and Development (ICPD) represented a major departure from conventional thinking on population and development. Among the international community concern has extended beyond the numbers of people and demographic targets, and now explicitly places human beings at the center of all population and development activities. Investments in people, in their health and education, are seen as the key to sustained economic growth and sustainable development. The strategies supported by the World Bank include:

— providing access to and choice in family planning;
— caring for women before, during, and after pregnancy;
— preventing and controlling sexually transmitted diseases (STDs), including Human Immunodeficiency Virus (HIV), which leads to AIDS;
— preventing and treating cervical cancer;
— promoting the health of adolescents; and,
— supporting positive health practices.

These objectives are pursued through a range of comprehensive activities in World Bank-supported projects in population, health, nutrition, and education, though specific components of projects are always determined in consultation with government officials and beneficiaries to take account of specific country needs.

Problems of Reproductive Health

The problems are widespread and serious:

Illness and death from unwanted pregnancies

Birth rates are still very high in much of the world, and frequent pregnancies are correlated with poor health and poverty. One in five births is unwanted, in part because safe and effective methods of fertility regulation are not available. About half of the 45-60 million abortions performed per year are unsafe, and over 65,000 deaths from unsafe abortions occur annually, most in developing countries.

Illness and death from complications of pregnancies

At least forty percent of the 200 million women who become pregnant each year experience complications that require treatment from a trained provider, and one in ten requires hospitalization. But most women in developing countries lack access to basic prenatal and delivery care. As a result, countless millions suffer from preventable or treatable conditions, 15-20 million develop long-term disabilities, and 600,000 die. One-half of all infant deaths could also be prevented by improving maternal health care.

Illness and death from STDs

Sexually transmitted diseases are a major cause of serious illness and death. They usually affect people in the 15-44 age group, the most economically productive years. In some countries, congenital syphilis is one of the principal causes of illness and death of newborns. The presence of STDs— especially those associated with genital ulceration— speeds the rate of transmission of HIV, substantially increasing both the susceptibility to HIV and AIDS, and the infectiousness of an HIV-infected individual. Some 23 million people are infected with HIV worldwide and nearly two-thirds of them live in sub-Saharan Africa.

Illness and death from preventable cancers

Cervical cancer, which is preventable at low cost if signs are detected early, is among the most common cancers in the developing world, causing 200,000 deaths a year. As developing country populations age during the coming decades and the incidence of HIV infection increases, the number of cervical cancer cases can be expected to increase. Women with HIV-induced immune suppression are at increased risk of developing cervical cancer. Breast cancer, which is more difficult and costly to treat, causes 322,000 deaths every year.

Traditional practices harmful to health

Two million young girls are subjected to circumcision and other forms of genital mutilation every year. These practices can lead to death, acute pain, recurrent urinary tract infections, mental trauma, painful intercourse, and complications during childbirth. Discrimination in the way girls are treated can damage their reproductive health—for example, inadequate feeding during childhood may stunt growth, bringing higher risks of complications during childbirth. Early marriage and adolescent pregnancy are serious problems because of the greater health risks of pregnancy for adolescents than for women in their 20s and early 30s, as well as the adverse effects on education and employment opportunities. Poor nutrition is also harmful to women's health. Insufficient nourishment and inadequate iron not only reduce productivity and well-being, but also increase the likelihood of pregnancy-related complications and poor infant outcomes.

Adolescent Reproductive Health

The largest generation of adolescents in history—1.2 billion strong—is preparing to enter adulthood in a rapidly changing world. Their educational and health status, their readiness to take on adult roles and responsibilities, and the support they receive from their families, communities and governments will determine their own future and the future of their countries.

Nearly half of all people are under the age of 25—the largest youth generation in history. *The State of World Population 2003* report examines the challenges and risks faced by this generation that impact directly on their physical, emotional and mental well-being. Today millions of adolescents and young people are faced with the prospects of early marriage and childbearing, incomplete education, and the threat of HIV/AIDS. Half of all new HIV infections occur in people aged 15 to 24. The report stresses that increasing the knowledge, opportunities, choices and participation of young people will enable them to lead healthy and productive lives so that they can contribute fully to their communities and to a more stable and prosperous world.

Today's adolescents and young people have diverse experiences given the different political, economic, social and cultural realities they face in their communities. Yet there is a common thread running through all of their lives and that is the hope for a better future. This hope is bolstered by the Millennium Development Goals agreed to by world leaders in 2000 to reduce extreme poverty and hunger, slow the spread of HIV/AIDS, reduce maternal and child mortality, ensure universal primary education and improve sustainable development by 2015.

Within the framework of human rights established and accepted by the global community, certain rights are particularly relevant to adolescents and youth and the opportunities and risks they face. These include gender equality and the rights to education and health, including reproductive and sexual health information and services appropriate to their age, capacities and circumstances. Actions to ensure these rights can have tremendous practical benefits: empowering individuals, ensuring well-being, stemming the HIV/AIDS pandemic, reducing poverty and improving prospects for social and economic progress. Addressing these challenges is an urgent development priority.

Investing in young people will yield large returns for generations to come. Failing to act, on the other hand, will incur tremendous costs to individuals, societies and the world at large.

In every region, there is a need for positive dialogue and greater understanding among parents, families, communities and governments about the complex and sensitive situations facing adolescents and young people. The report examines such factors as changing family structures and living conditions, rapidly changing norms and social behaviours, the growth in orphans and street children, the impact of urbanization and migration, armed conflict, the lack of education and employment, and the continuing toll of gender discrimination and violence.

Just as they need guidance, young women and men need supportive relationships and institutions that respond to their hopes and concerns. By taking concerted and comprehensive action to address the challenges faced by adolescents and young people, governments can meet their commitments and international development goals, and give greater hope to the world's largest youth generation. UNFPA, the United Nations Population Fund, is working with a wide range of partners and with young people themselves to address the needs of adolescents and young people in a way that is culturally sensitive, locally driven and in line with international human rights standards.

Neglecting young people's health will reduce or negate the benefits of past government expenditures in child survival, childhood communicable diseases, and education as well as curtail future economic and social development. Despite their fundamental importance, programs and policies for young people remain lacking. The needs of young people are often only recognized when it is too late: when they become pregnant, need abortions, or are infected with HIV or other STDS. Services — if provided — are delivered through conventional Maternal Child Health/ Family Planning (MCH/FP) programs which are not specifically geared toward younger age groups.

Ensuring the reproductive health of young people makes social and economic sense: Health complications related to STDS, abortion, or teenage pregnancy can place a substantial burden on individual welfare and scarce government resources. Adolescent childbearing can lead to economic setbacks for young people, their communities, and the national economy. If adequate public investments are not made in the health of the younger generation, these personal and societal costs will only increase.

Risks to Good Health

Low mortality rates among young people have falsely labeled them as a healthy age group. This traditional health indicator — often used by health planners, policymakers, researchers, and program staff — grossly underestimates that young people are disproportionately affected by reproductive health problems and ignores the future costs of morbidity.

High Prevalence of Sexual Activity

The majority of young people are sexually experienced by age 20. Much of this sexual activity takes place within marriage; however premarital sexual activity is common, varying among gender and within countries and regions.

Among unmarried adolescents, very few use contraception at first intercourse. Contraceptive use among married adolescents is lower in Sub-Saharan Africa than among unmarried teens. In Latin America, trends are variable. Little information exists about the contraceptive practices of unmarried youth in Asia.

Whether married or not, young people who engage in sexual intercourse without contraception are at risk of adverse health effects.

Low Contraceptive Use

Although knowledge of contraception among young people is increasing, contraceptive use remains low among married and unmarried young women and men.

Increasing STD/HIV/AIDS infections

Sexually transmitted diseases are most common in youth ages 15-24. Incidence rates are higher among young women than men in countries where STDs are a major health problem. In many developing countries up to 60% of all new HIV infections are among 15-24 year-olds. Approximately one-half of all people infected with HIV are under age 25. The majority of new infections will occur among young women.

Increasing Adolescent Pregnancies

Fertility rates for all women, including adolescents, are declining. However, growing population sizes will lead to an increase in adolescent births in many regions of the world. In Sub-Saharan Africa, for example, an approximate 23% increase in adolescent births is predicted for 1995-2020.

Unwanted Pregnancy Pregnancy-Related Complications

Pregnancy in adolescence carries a relatively high risk of death or long-term complications.

Pregnant teens are more likely to suffer from malnutrition, pregnancy-induced hypertension, and eclampsia than women over age 20. In addition, an immature birth canal may prolong labor, increase the risk of vesicovaginal fistula, cause permanent damage to bladder and bowels and to the infant's brain, or lead to death of mother and child.

Young mothers, ages 15-19, are twice as likely to die of pregnancy-related causes than women ages 20-24. The risk of death may be five times higher for girls ages 10-14 than for women 20-24.

Infant Mortality and Morbidity

The mortality and morbidity rates of infants of young mothers are higher than for older mothers.

Abortion Complications

Young women suffer disproportionately from abortion complications. Teenagers are more likely than older women to have clandestine or illegal abortions because of legal, social and financial reasons. Estimates of abortions performed on teenage women range from 1 to 4.4 million. Data from 13 studies in seven Sub-Saharan African countries show that adolescents comprised 39-72% of all cases of abortion-related complications.

Female Genital Mutilation

85-115 million girls and women have undergone FGM. Two million or more girls undergo FGM each year. FGM is most often practiced in 26 African countries, a few Asian countries, and is increasingly practiced in Europe, Canada, Australia and the US.

Impacats of HIV/AIDS

Since its onset in 1981, when the first AIDS cases were reported, the human immunodeficiency virus (HIV) epidemic has become not only the deadliest epidemic in contemporary history but also a major demographic, humanitarian and development crisis. As of end-2002, 42 million people were infected with the HIV and 22 million had already lost their life to the disease. More than 13 million AIDS orphans are currently living in sub-Saharan Africa. The HIV/AIDS epidemic is leading to a reversal of hard-won gains in life expectancy of the previous decades. Moreover, the HIV/AIDS epidemic has been threatening the social fabric of societies in the most affected countries and eroding the social and economic safety net.

Demographic Impacts

The AIDS epidemic is taking and will continue to take a devastating toll on human lives. According to the 2002 Revision of the United Nations World Population Prospects, life expectancy at birth has already fallen by more than 10 years in the most affected countries, those with an adult HIV prevalence of 20 per cent or more. In most of the countries that are severely affected by the epidemic, HIV/AIDS is responsible for stopping or even reversing the long-term decline that had been registered until recently. The impact on population size is most marked in Africa.

In 38 African countries for which the United Nations Population Division explicitly incorporates the impact of AIDS into its 2002 Revision of the official United Nations world population estimates and projections, the population size is estimated at 603 million in 1995, 16 million less than it would have been in the absence of AIDS. By 2025, the population of these 38 African countries will reach 983 million, 14 per cent fewer than in the absence of AIDS. In the 7 countries with an adult prevalence of 20 per cent or more, all in Africa, the impact is more striking. By 2025, the population of these countries is projected to be 35 per cent lower than it would have been in the absence of AIDS.

Life expectancy at birth, a measure indicating the average number of years that a newborn child would live if mortality remained constant throughout his lifetime, is estimated at 47 years in 1995-2000, 6 years lower than it would have been in the absence of AIDS in the 38 African countries. It is projected to reach only 52 years by 2020-2025, 10 years lower than it would have been in the absence of AIDS. In the seven countries with an adult HIV prevalence of 20 per cent or more, life expectancy at birth is estimated at 49 years in 1995-2000, 13 years lower than in the absence of AIDS. By 2020-2025, the difference between the life expectancy with AIDS and the life expectancy without AIDS will reach 29 years, a 41 per cent difference. The age-differentiating characteristic of the AIDS epidemic makes its impact especially devastating for the affected populations.

Impacts on Households

The impact on households and families begins as soon as a member of a household starts suffering from HIV-related diseases. In this regard, three kinds of impacts can be distinguished. The first one is the loss of the income and household production of the family member, in particular if he/she is the breadwinner. The second impact is the increase in household expenditures to cover the medical costs. The third impact is the indirect cost resulting from the absenteeism of members of the family from school or work to take care of the patient.

When the person dies, the temporary loss of income becomes a permanent loss; funeral and mourning costs are incurred; and the family may compensate by reducing investments in productive activities (e.g. removing children from school to save on expenses and increase household labour). Households may lose most of their savings in order to pay for the high costs of HIV/AIDS-related health care and funeral expenses. Furthermore, community attitudes towards helping needy households may contribute to the impact of the disease. For example, households in the more urbanized areas may suffer the worst impact because of the lack of community support.

In societies where stigmatization of the HIV-affected individuals and households is common, the impact of the HIV/AIDS epidemic may be even more severe. The change in the composition and structure of households caused by the HIV/AIDS epidemic may be not only quantitative but also qualitative. Thus, the number of impoverished female-headed households will increase when the male breadwinner of the household dies of AIDS. Where the AIDS patient in the household is female, the impact of the HIV/AIDS epidemic on the household can take a form that is different and of even greater magnitude.

Indeed, the (often culturally determined) position of women can affect the household impact of an illness such as AIDS in males. One of the striking features of the economic impact of AIDS on affected households and families in Zambia, for example, is the rapid transition from relative wealth to relative poverty. Haworth's survey of AIDS-affected families found that the shift into poverty was most visible in families in which the deceased father was both the breadwinner and tenant of a house provided through his job. Many such families were forced to move after the death of the father, with a majority of those families reporting economic difficulties.

In the early 1990s, the International Children's Centre in Paris launched a multi-country field study of the socio-economic evolution of children and families affected by HIV/AIDS in three countries: Burundi, Côte d'Ivoire and Haiti. In each of these countries, about 100 households affected by HIV/AIDS were followed longitudinally for a year. In Côte d'Ivoire, the study showed that marked differences occurred in the economic activities of households, with a steady decline in the number of economically active household members throughout the course of the study. In this study that tracked 107 households with at least one adult AIDS patient, it was found that per capita consumption dropped in households where the AIDS patient either died or moved away.

In households in which the AIDS patient remained relatively free of symptoms, per capita consumption remained stable over time. In a longitudinal study carried out in Kagera, United Republic of Tanzania in 1991-1993, households that experienced an AIDS adult death in the year prior to the first wave of the survey spent, in relative terms, more on funerals and health expenditures than did households which did not experience an adult death, although households without an adult death had higher total expenditure on all goods and services than those with an AIDS adult death.

A more recent study in Zimbabwe showed that heavy expenditures, substantial loss of income and erosion of capital assets associated with terminal illnesses are seriously undermining the economic viability of households. In another longitudinal study conducted in the Free State of South Africa, it was found that affected households allocated more of their resources to food, health and rent and less to education and clothing than nonaffected households. Outside of sub-Saharan Africa, the AIDS epidemic is also taking its toll on affected households. In a study carried out in Thailand, Pitayanon and others compared the direct and indirect costs of an adult HIV-related death with those of an adult death from other causes.

The impact of an AIDS-related death on the household was substantial and greater than the impact of a death from other causes. While the direct costs of an adult non AIDS-related death are slightly higher than those of an AIDSrelated adult death, the indirect costs associated with an AIDS-related adult death are on average 30 per cent higher than those of a non-AIDS adult death. This is because AIDS deaths occur mainly at the prime working-age years, resulting in a higher number of years lost than deaths due to other causes.

Other socioeconomic impacts of a HIV/AIDS-related death included the loss of the family labour production. The production loss in the households was almost 50 per cent leading to about a 47 per loss in the household income. Orphans are paying a heavy toll from the AIDS epidemic. Until recently, the impact of AIDS on orphans had been studied only peripherally. But, a few studies are now trying to fill the gap. For example, in a recent study, Monasch and Snoad showed that the death of parents affected orphans' living arrangements and schooling.

The study of survey data in 40 sub-Saharan African countries found that orphans were less likely to attend school than non-orphans, especially in countries with lower overall school attendance. These results are confirmed by other studies. An earlier study using data collected in 28 countries in sub-Saharan Africa, Latin America and the Caribbean points to considerable diversity in the findings. According to the author the diversity in the findings demonstrates that the extent to which orphans are under-enrolled relative to other children is country specific, at least partly because the correlation between orphanhood and poverty is not consistent across countries.

A study in Eastern Zimbabwe found that maternal orphans were more likely to drop out of school than paternal orphans in Eastern Zimbabwe. However, the studies that are based on nationally representative sample surveys have found that orphanhood affects girls' and boys' schooling approximately equally. Another aspect of the impacts of the disease is the change in the structure and composition of households. In many affected regions in developing countries, more and more older persons are taking care of AIDS orphans. This has implications for the welfare of the children as well as for that of their caregivers.

Studies conducted in Zimbabwe (WHO, 2002) and Thailand showed that older caregivers are under serious financial, physical and emotional stress due to their caregiving responsibilities. The AIDS epidemic not only puts more stress on older persons, but it also impoverishes them at the very same time they themselves may need to be taken care of. This is especially true in societies where the younger relatives are responsible for the care of older persons. The empirical evidence, although sketchy, points to a tremendous impact of AIDS on households.

Indeed, households and families bear most of the burden since they are the primary units in which individuals cope with the disease. Few studies have documented how the impact varies according to the characteristics of the household. Moreover, the impact on orphans has only started receiving attention. Similarly, the effects of the AIDS deaths of children have only begun to be studied.

Impacts on Firms and Private Sector

The HIV/AIDS epidemic is imposing serious costs on the private sector in the most affected countries. AIDS deaths may lead directly to a reduction in the number of available workers, since the deaths occur predominantly among workers in their most productive years. As younger, less experienced workers replace experienced workers, worker productivity may be reduced. The impact of AIDS will also depend on the skills of affected workers. If skilled workers who occupy important positions in the firm become sick or die from AIDS, the company may lose its institutional memory-that is, the "know-how" accumulated through many years of experience. The absence of workers in the company may also have an impact on the morale of the remaining workers, which could lead to declining productivity.

HIV-infected workers also are likely to become less productive as infection progresses to AIDS. In Namibia, NamWater, the largest water purification company, announced in 2000 that HIV/AIDS was "crippling" its operations. They reported a high staff turnover due to HIV-related deaths, increasing absenteeism and a general loss of productive hours. A study in Kenya showed that tea pluckers who died of AIDSrelated causes produced a quantity of tea roughly one-third less in their last two years of life than other healthy workers. The AIDS patients who died had also suffered an earning loss of 18 per cent in the last year before their death.

Firms that have a health programme to help workers who become sick may find themselves responsible for substantial medical costs. The insurance scheme of the firm may become more expensive as insurance companies increase the costs of coverage as a response to high HIV prevalence rates in firms. This could impede any savings for investment by the firms. A study on Lonrho companies in Malawi found that deaths-in-service benefits increased by more than 100 per cent between 1991 and 1996. The study also found that AIDS-related costs were 1.1 per cent of the total costs and 3.4 per cent of gross profits of these companies in 1992. Another study of five firms in Botswana found that the impact of HIV/AIDS depended on the type of business, the skill level of employees, the type of benefits provided, and the amount of savings.

Many businesses will also suffer a shrinking market for their goods when HIV/AIDS epidemic in the community leads to the impoverishment of households which can no longer afford to purchase goods. Businesses that produce "luxury goods" are more likely to experience a decline in the demand of these goods. A South Africa furniture manufacturer (JD Group) projected an 18 per cent reduction in its customer base as a result of HIV/AIDS. The impact of HIV/AIDS on firms depends partly on the age structure of the workers in the firm.

For example, a study conducted in Zambia in Barclays World Bank showed that mortality peaked in the 30-39-year age group. The death rate rose from 0.4 per cent to 2.2 per cent between 1987 and 1991, and the bank paid more than ZK 10 million (US$ 58,140) in the form of ex-gratia payments to the families of employees who died from HIV/AIDS. The study also showed that medical expenses and training costs were on the increase whereas man-hours were reduced. Not only does the absence of infected workers contribute to revenue losses at the firm level, but absence of healthy workers taking care for infected family members or attending funerals of co-workers of family members can also be detrimental for companies.

It has been estimated that extension workers in north central Namibia spent at least 10 per cent of their time attending funerals. In summary, the available studies of the impact of HIV/AIDS on firms point to an impact of the epidemic on the labour force, costs and productivity of most firms depending on the skills of those who are affected and whether they are replaceable or not. The evidence available also points to a greater impact of the HIV/AIDS epidemic on small firms, those with less than 10 employees. The loss of a few employees in key positions in these firms can lead to their disappearance. It may be noted that many studies are conducted by firms for their own use and are still not in the public domain. Their publication would aid in assessing the economic impacts of the epidemic, and in devising sound public policies in response.

Impacts on Agriculture

HIV/AIDS is also having a dramatic impact on the agricultural sector, partly because the great majority of the infected population in the most affected countries lives in rural areas. In many African countries, farming and other rural occupations provide a livelihood for more than 70 per cent of the population. A number of studies have been conducted to assess the impact of HIV/AIDS on agriculture. Most of these studies were conducted under the auspices of FAO. Indeed, of the AIDS impact studies conducted so far, the majority have dealt with the rural world. A study conducted in Burkina Faso in 1997 found that the HIV/AIDS epidemic had led to shifting work patterns and an overall reduction in food production. Revenues from agricultural production had decreased by 25 to 50 per cent.

A study among agricultural workers in the United Republic of Tanzania showed that a woman whose husband was sick was likely to spend 45 per cent less time working than if the husband were healthy. In Kagera, a survey showed that, on average, adults in households that experienced a death spent five hours less in farming during the previous week than those without a death. In Kenya, a study found that the commercial agricultural sector is facing a severe social and economic crisis due to the impact of HIV/AIDS. The loss of skilled and experienced labour to the epidemic is a serious concern. But it is difficult to quantify the impact of the epidemic in terms of increasing costs.

The impact of HIV/AIDS on agriculture may also depend on the level of prevalence in the country or area. For example, production loss in AIDS-affected households was reflected in a survey conducted in Zimbabwe, a country with an adult HIV prevalence of more than 25 per cent. According to this survey, conducted in 1997 by the Zimbabwe Farmers' Union, agricultural output in communal areas declined by nearly 50 per cent among households affected by AIDS. Maize production by smallholder farmers and commercial farms declined by 61 per cent because of illness and deaths from AIDS. These production losses could result from a number of factors including shifting production patterns. But according to the same author, the data did indicate a dramatic switch from cash to subsistence crops up to the time of the study.

The impact of AIDS is expected to increase in the future. FAO has estimated that in the 27 most affected countries in Africa, 7 million agricultural workers died from AIDS between 1985 and 2000 and that 16 million more deaths are likely to occur in the next two decades. In the ten most affected African countries, labour force decreases ranging from 11 to 26 per cent are anticipated. In summary, the studies available show that HIV/AIDS is having a detrimental impact on the agricultural sector.

Since, in many of the most affected countries, this sector occupies most of the population, this impact will be far-reaching and in the long run threatens the food security of areas or entire countries. However, the future impact will depend partly on the possibility of mechanizing agricultural production and reducing reliance on labour-intensive means of production. It is therefore important to review periodically the impact on this sector. It is also important to point out that the agriculture sector in the most affected countries is already facing a number of other crises, such as desertification and the neglect of the traditional farming sector by governments. FAO observed that the HIV/AIDS epidemic was intensifying labour bottlenecks in agriculture; increasing malnutrition; and adding to the burden of rural women, especially those who head farm households.

Impacts on Health Care System

The HIV/AIDS epidemic is posing tremendous challenges to the healthcare systems of the developing countries, especially the most severely affected countries. HIV/AIDS increases the overall health expenditures at the same time it is claiming the lives of doctors and nurses in the developing countries. The impact of HIV/AIDS on the health sector may operate in many ways. First, there may be an increase in the number of health workers affected with the HIV virus. Indeed, epidemiological surveys from sub-Saharan Africa have shown that HIV/AIDS prevalence has been disproportionately higher among doctors and nurses, as well as teachers. This loss of health workers will affect the supply of public health services.

Occupational exposure may also affect the supply of health care, as more health workers may contract the disease in the workplace through injuries with HIV-positive patients. The increasing mortality of health professionals in some countries poses a serious threat to the replacement of those who are deceased. Training of new professionals will certainly cost more money, while the accumulated experience of those who die is lost forever. The morale of health professionals may also be affected. Indeed, staff taking care of HIV-infected patients may suffer greater stress than other health workers. This may lead to greater staff absenteeism and staff refusing to be transferred to high-prevalence regions within countries.

A shortage of nurses and doctors has been observed in the high-HIV-prevalence countries. This shortage is particularly pronounced in rural areas. The AIDS epidemic is also responsible for diverting expenditure towards higher levels of care needed for the AIDS patients. Although anti-retroviral therapy is not readily available in the most affected countries, the treatment of opportunistic infections can be costly. The latest anti-retroviral therapy costs more than US$10,000 per person a year. Although countries are exploring generic drugs that may cost US$300 per person a year, according to the latest estimates, this figure is still hardly within reach of many African countries.

On average, treating an AIDS patient for one year is about as expensive as educating ten primary school students for one year. The World Bank estimated that a country with a stable 5 per cent adult HIV-prevalence rate can expect that each year between 0.5 and 1 per cent of its health care providers will die from AIDS. In contrast, a country with 30 per cent prevalence would lose 3-7 per cent of its health workers to the HIV/AIDS epidemic. A study conducted in Rwanda showed that HIV-positive outpatients visited the hospital 10.9 times on average as opposed to only 0.3 times for the general population.

The study also revealed that the increased demand for out-patient services was characterized by a considerable inequality-reflecting differential access and command over income. In summary, the studies conducted on the impact of HIV/AIDS on the health sector show that the magnitude of the impact is high. Absenteeism and deaths of health workers pose a serious threat to the health system of the most affected countries. Moreover, because the treatment of AIDS is expensive, few public health sectors in the developing world can afford it with the meagre budget devoted to health. Overall, the studies conducted have shown that the health sector in the most affected countries is stretched beyond its limit with the increasing demand due to the HIV/AIDS epidemic. Coping strategies need to be devised by Governments to avoid the collapse of the health system in these countries.

Impacts on Education

Like every other sector of the social and economic life of an AIDS-afflicted country, the education sector has been feeling the impact of the HIV/AIDS epidemic. Indeed, an increasing number of countries in sub-Saharan Africa have been facing a shortage of teachers as the pool of qualified educators is shrinking. Deaths and illnesses have also been affecting the education sector administrators, planning and finance officials. Hence, the HIV/AIDS epidemic is threatening the achievement of the commitment to Education for All made by the international community at the April 2000 World Education Forum in Dakar, Senegal, as well as the Millennium Development Goals for education.

HIV/AIDS affects the education sector through three main routes: the supply of education through the availability of experienced teachers, the demand for education (number of children enrolled in school) and the quality of education. The absenteeism of teachers from school and ultimately their death affects the supply of education. Teachers who are infected with the HIV virus may try to transfer to another area or, once visibly ill, disappear. Other teachers may also want to transfer out of heavily affected areas or refuse to be posted to them, thus decreasing the supply of education available in the region.

The deaths of children or parents may affect the demand for schooling, as a smaller number of children will be entering the school system and more children will be dropping out of school to take care of sick parents or siblings after the death of their parents. The number of children entering the school system is expected to diminish if AIDS orphans do not enroll, delay enrolling, or leave school in large numbers. Equally important is the possible decrease in educational quality as teachers may be absent from school and may not be able to provide the same quality of schooling they were providing before becoming sick.

Many studies have been conducted to estimate and predict the impact of AIDS on education. A number of studies undertaken under the auspices of UNICEF reached the conclusion that because of AIDS, many **countries will** be facing a shortage of teachers in the near future. For instance, a study conducted in Zambia using a model developed by UNICEF showed that of around 1.7 million primary school students, 56,000 would have lost a teacher to AIDS in 1999. The study also found that the number of teachers' deaths in 1998 was equivalent to the loss of about two thirds of the annual output of newly trained teachers.

The same UNICEF study estimated that 860,000 children have lost a teacher to AIDS in sub-Saharan Africa Among them, children from South Africa, Kenya, Zimbabwe and Nigeria are the most affected. In Malawi, 10 per cent of education personnel in urban areas are estimated to have died of AIDS by 1997, and by 2005, it is projected that this figure will increase to 40 per cent. HIV/AIDS is also affecting the demand for education. For example, focus group discussions with AIDS-affected households found that these households were unable to meet the costs of children's education as a result of AIDS.

Furthermore, an analysis of 49 case studies of families affected by AIDS throughout Zambia found that 56 of 215 children had been forced to leave school. In most countries affected by the HIV/AIDS epidemic, the school-age population is projected to continue to grow in spite of HIV/AIDS. But in a few countries, some projections show that the population aged 15 years old and under in 2010 will be smaller than it was in 2000. For example, recent projections of the United Nations Population Division suggest that some of the countries most severely affected by HIV/AIDS will show a reduction in the school-age population.

In Zambia, projections yield a population under age 15 and below at 5.8 million by 2010, 1.4 million less than it would have been in the absence of AIDS. Despite the limitations in the availability of reliable data, the currently available evidence points nonetheless to a tremendous impact of the HIV/AIDS epidemic on the demand for education, on the education supply and, to a lesser extent, on the quality of education.

Many questions remain unanswered, though. For example, is there any difference in the school attendance of children whose parents have AIDS but are still alive and children who are AIDS orphans? Does the situation of AIDS orphans regarding schooling change over time? What are the mitigating factors? Follow-up studies need to be conducted to document these changes over time. Because most of the studies conducted so far have used small samples, their results may be hard to generalize. It is therefore important to undertake studies using large samples so as to allow in-depth examination of factors affecting the supply, demand and quality of education. Although some studies have mentioned that teachers are dying of AIDS at a higher rate than the general population.

Impacts on Economy

The impact of the HIV/AIDS epidemic on the economy as a whole is an issue that has been addressed since the beginning of the pandemic. There have been claims that the HIV/AIDS epidemic is responsible for slowing the rate of growth of the gross national product (GNP) of many heavily affected countries and that in some cases, GNP could decrease by more than 1 per cent for every 10 per cent HIV prevalence. Others claim that HIV/AIDS has had no impact on the macroeconomy so far. Indeed, it is difficult to estimate the effect of HIV/AIDS on a country's economic growth because so many factors other than the HIV/AIDS pandemic affect the longterm economic growth.

The most affected countries in the world are also faced with drought, war and other problems. There are a number of ways in which the HIV/AIDS epidemic could affect the economy: First, the AIDS epidemic may reduce the labour supply, leading to reduced productivity. This may be particularly true in the labour-intensive sectors where replacement of workers is not easy to achieve. Following are some of the mechanisms in action leading to the impact of HIV/AIDS on economic development.

— The AIDS epidemic will reduce the labour supply. The economic impact can vary according to the sector of the economy, the degree to which HIV/AIDS affects hard-to-replace skilled labour, and whether or not there is a substantial pool of "surplus labour".

— Savings of families will be reduced due to the increase of HIV/AIDS-related health expenditures (drugs and hospitalisation), leaving less income to invest in the economy.

— The AIDS epidemic may also divert investment fund from other vital sectors to health expenditures, leading to a slower growth of the gross domestic product (GDP). Foreign private investment may also decline, if potential investors become convinced that the epidemic is seriously undermining the rate of return on investment.

— The HIV/AIDS epidemic may also deepen the poverty of the most affected countries by decreasing the growth rate of per capita income and by selectively impoverishing the individuals and families that are directly affected.

A variety of economic modeling approaches have been employed to estimate the macro-economic effects of the

HIV/AIDS epidemic. In most cases the focus is on estimating effects on growth of GDP or GDP per capita. Sometimes effects on intermediate outcomes, such as saving and investment, are also estimated.

In interpreting the estimates of the epidemic's effects on the macro-economy, it should be borne in mind that economic forecasting is not an exact science. "It cannot be said that econometric modelling...has a good track record. Also, it should be readily admitted that we know relatively little about those structural relationships which are important for estimating the impact of HIV on development". Despite the controversies and uncertainties that surround such estimates, there remains a need for policymakers to try to understand the impacts that HIV/AIDS may have on overall performance of their economies and their budgets.

Results of these estimation and modelling exercise vary, depending on the modelling approach as well as on the national context. Dixon, McDonald and Roberts reviewed 11 studies that attempted to quantify the effect of HIV/AIDS on GDP per capita in Africa. Some of the studies employed a neoclassical growth model fitted to the data of a particular country, and others used cross-national data and regression analysis. "The consensus from these studies is that the net effect on growth of GDP per capita will be negative and substantial.

The more recent studies show greater effects; and the most recent estimates indicate that the pandemic has reduced average national growth rates by 2-4 per cent a year across Africa". How large are these effects in comparison to other factors affecting economic growth? Some analysts note that other factors can produce effects on economic growth that are at least as large as those estimated to result from the spread of HIV/AIDS. For instance, Greener notes that a reduction in the rate of growth of GDP by between 0.5 and 2.6 percentage points, which encompasses the size of the effect indicated by most studies, "is within the range of variation that could be caused by poor economic management or fiscal policy. This implies that the macroeconomic impacts of HIV/AIDS, in themselves, can be substantially reduced by appropriate policy interventions".

However, the longer-term effects on the economy may be more serious than most macro-economic estimates suggest. Estimates of AIDS' effects on macro-economic performance usually take no account of the loss of "social capital" or of the long-term damage that is accruing to human capital, as children's education, nutrition and health suffers directly and indirectly as a consequence of HIV/AIDS. The effects of lowered investment in the human capital of the younger generation will affect economic performance over future decades, well beyond the timeframe of most economic analyses (MacPherson, 2003; Bell, Devarajan and Gersbach, 2003).

While many of the studies discussed here deal with quantifiable economic effects of the HIV/AIDS epidemic, the concept of "development" implies more than material advancement. A nation's achievement of a long and healthy life for its population is itself one of the main defining features of successful development, as is highlighted, for example, by UNDP's Human Development Index (HDI), which is a combined measure of mortality, education and per capita income. Cohen and Gaigbe-Togbe show that HIV/AIDS affects the HDI through its impact on life expectancy at birth. Based on empirical evidence of societies' economic valuation of a death, the epidemic's effect on mortality itself represents a loss of welfare that dwarfs the estimated effects of HIV/AIDS on GDP.

AIDS and Mortality Trends in Asia

The estimation of the risk factors underlying mortality also suffers from significant uncertainty. Low levels of interest in the measurement of adult mortality have made reliable information on this indicator difficult to obtain. However, the unfolding of the epidemiological transition, particularly the marked recent decline in child mortality, is now contributing to changing this situation. The validity of cross-country comparisons within Asia can be impaired by the huge differences in population sizes among the countries of the region, as well as differences in the age structure of their populations. The comparative interpretation of absolute and relative figures therefore needs to make allowances for these differences. The Asia region presents a great deal of variety, with widely contrasting mortality situations and examples of virtually all the stages in levels of development, and stages in demographic and epidemiological transition, all of which influence mortality levels.

The current mortality picture

The current mortality picture examines commonly used measures of general mortality and age specific mortality: life expectancy at birth and the probability of adult death (between ages 15 and 59), the latter indicator being particularly meaningful in the context of AIDS mortality.

Life expectancy at birth

This indicator essentially reflects population health conditions and levels of health development. It is, however, closely correlated with the CDR and presents a very wide range of values (almost two-fold) among the countries of the region. In 2001, three countries had a life expectancy above 78 years for both sexes: Japan, which is both the world's and Asia's leader with 81.4 years, Israel and Singapore. In a few countries life expectancy was above 70.

Most countries of the region had values comprised between 60 and 70. The four countries with the highest CDR values had a life expectancy below 50, again highlighting the close correlation between the two indicators. The post-conflict countries of Afghanistan (42+) and East Timor (48) ranked at the bottom with respect to this indicator. Age patterns of mortality at the sub-regional level show marked differentials favoring women in virtually all age groups. Higher male mortality prevails in all adult age groups, except among the population aged 70 and above in WprA and SeaB.

Differences between males and females with respect to life expectancy at birth range widely. The female advantage of 7 to 8 years typical of most industrialized countries is found in Sri Lanka, the Republic of Korea, the Philippines and several Central Asian Republics. This advantage narrows to 6-7 years in Japan, Mongolia and Thailand and to less than 3 years in Bhutan, Brunei, China, India, Indonesia, the Lao People's Democratic Republic and Maldives. In two countries the sex differential actually reverses itself to a slight male advantage. This reflects the combined effects of higher child mortality among girls and high maternal mortality.

b. Adult mortality levels

This indicator refers to the risk of dying before age 60 among those who have reached age 15. Premature adult mortality is closely correlated with life expectancy at birth, though exhibiting an even wider range of values in 2000. The same two countries that had a life expectancy above 78 had premature adult mortality levels below 100. The same four countries that had a life expectancy above 70, plus Viet Nam, had premature adult mortality levels between 100 and 200.

Most countries of the region were in the range 200-300. The highest levels of premature adult mortality were found in Cambodia, the Lao People's Democratic Republic, Myanmar and Nepal, which rank among the poorest countries of the region. With respect to adult mortality also, sex differentials range widely. Differences are widest in Armenia, Georgia, Israel, Kyrgyzstan and the Republic of Korea. There is virtual parity between the sexes in Bangladesh, Nepal and Pakistan, three countries with extremely high levels of maternal mortality.

Table 1 displays the values of ${}_{45}q_{15}$ for males and females in 1999 and 2001 for the countries of the Asia region with HIV prevalence of 0.1 and above. Male adult mortality shows little correlation with HIV prevalence rates, although Cambodia has the highest values for both indicators. In all countries, irrespective of HIV prevalence rates, ${}_{45}q_{15}$ values are significantly higher for males.

Recent trends in mortality levels

On the whole, overall life expectancy has improved moderately in the countries of Asia over the last few years. This stands in contrast to child mortality levels, which have fallen markedly between 1990 and 2000 in all countries of the region. This should not be surprising, however, as reductions in adult mortality, being much more difficult to achieve, are typically less extreme.

Table 1. Probability of dying between ages 15 and 59 by sex in Asian countries with HIV prevalence of 0.1 percent or above (1999-2001)

Country	*HIV prevalence (adult rates), 2001*	*45Q15 Males*		*45Q15 Females*		*% women HIV +,2001*
		2001	*1999*	*2001*	*1999*	
Cambodia	2.7	394	385	323	268	46
Myanmar*	2.0	253	364	231	258	n.a.
Thailand	1.8	261	272	181	148	34
India	0.8	275	291	217	222	39
Papua New Guinea	0.7	377	308	325	250	26
Nepal	0.5	297	302	274	293	n.a.
Malaysia	0.4	172	194	125	108	27
Viet Nam	0.3	225	201	153	132	27
Bahrain	0.3	137	123	99	89	15
Armenia	0.2	166	216	81	99	20
Singapore	0.2	126	92	67	54	25
China	0.1	170	157	125	106	26
Fiji	0.1	247	212	141	152	30
Indonesia	0.1	240	246	197	213	23
Israel	0.1	101	115	59	55	n.a.
Maldives	0.1	214	276	208	213	n.a.
Oman	0.1	135	182	94	106	15
Pakistan	0.1	194	229	147	203	21
Yemen	0.1	288	289	257	234	15

Trends in life expectancy at birth: In the last decade of the 20Century, life expectancy at birth has increased in every country of the region. Notable exceptions can be found in the Democratic Republic of Korea (decrease of 4 years for both sexes) and Sri Lanka (decrease of 1 year for males only). The highest gains (6 to 8 years) were achieved in Bangladesh, Bhutan, the Lao People's Democratic Republic, Nepal and Viet Nam. The smallest gains were made in Thailand and Cambodia, where progress was hindered by slight absolute declines in life expectancy among the male population. This trend reflects the incipient effect of AIDS deaths in these two countries. Recent trends in $_{45}q_{15}$ as shown in table 1 male adult mortality increased in 11 of the 19 countries between 1999 and 2001. This increase was most marked in Myanmar. Female adult mortality increased in 8 of the 19 countries. As a result of these trends, sex differentials in $_{45}q_{15}$ have been increasing slightly in a majority of the countries. This trend is consistent with the much lower HIV infection rates among women. Women are estimated to make up 23 per cent of the HIV positive adult population in East Asia and the Pacific and 37 per cent in South and South East Asia, as against 58 per cent in Sub-Saharan Africa.

Causes of death: patterns and trends

The epidemiological transition is typically marked by a decline in the relative importance of childhood diseases and infectious diseases preventable by vaccination and by an increase in the relative importance of chronic diseases more common at older ages. Just in the short time interval between 2000 and 2001, changes in causes of death discernable from the statistical data for each of the four WHO epidemiological sub-regions appear to have been consistent with the unfolding of the epidemiological transition.

a. *Leading causes of death:* The top five causes of death in 2001 in SearD (High-child and High-adult mortality countries, including India) included two chronic diseases, ischaemic heart disease and cardio-vascular disease, which together accounted for about one fifth of all deaths. They also included three diseases related to poverty: lower respiratory infections, peri-natal conditions and diarrhoea, which together accounted for about one-quarter of all deaths.

In WprB (Low-child and Low-adult mortality countries, including China), the two major causes of death were cardio-vascular disease and chronic obstructive pulmonary disease, which together accounted for nearly one-third of all deaths. Others among the top five were ischaemic heart disease, lower respiratory infections and stomach cancer. There were no significant changes in major causes of death between the two reference years.

b. AIDS as a comparative cause of death Worldwide, HIV/AIDS is the fourth highest cause of mortality. In Asia, the contribution of AIDS to overall mortality levels is substantially smaller. According to WHO estimates for 2001, AIDS figured among the top ten causes of death in only two of the four epidemiological subregions for Asia. In SearB, it ranked as killer number 10 and accounted for about 2 percent of all deaths (60,000). In SearD, which includes India, it ranked number 8 and was responsible for 3 percent of all deaths (385,000). In the other two WHO sub-regions (WprB and WprA), AIDS ranked 30th and 57th respectively among causes of death, and its impact on overall mortality rates was barely discernible, despite an absolute number of 53,000 deaths attributed to the disease in WprB (which includes China).

While AIDS is making headway as a global killer, it is not at this point a major cause of death in the Asia region, except in SearD, where it accounted for nearly 400,000 deaths, up from none recorded in 1995. As of 2001, the toll it exacts still lags far behind that of deaths by chronic disease. For example, deaths attributable to tobacco overuse reached 800,000 in 2000 and are bound to continue to increase rapidly in view of the more widespread tobacco use of the last few decades. Yet, the exact place of AIDS in adult mortality continues to be surrounded by uncertainty, not only because of frequent misattribution of causes of death, but also because the impact of the disease is only gradually unfolding in Asia.

AIDS impact on overall mortality

As AIDS is nearly always fatal, an HIV/AIDS epidemic will almost inevitably end up affecting mortality levels to some extent. However, the long asymptomatic phase of the disease after initial infection and the lag of one to three years between the appearance of AIDS symptoms and death mean that the impact of AIDS on mortality may not be apparent for quite a few years, even in countries with rapidly rising HIV incidence. The UNAIDS report for 1997 provides estimates of cumulative numbers of AIDS deaths for adults and children together up to late 1997. South and South-East Asia as a whole was estimated to have lost a cumulative total of 730,000 persons to the disease, while East Asia and the Pacific was estimated to have lost 11,000. In absolute terms, the most severely-hit countries of the Asia region at that time were India (350,000 deaths), Thailand (230,000), and Myanmar (86,000). For the year 1997 alone, the two UNAIDS sub-regions lost 250,000 and 5,000 persons to the disease respectively.

The largest national losses for that year were also in India (140,000), Thailand (60,000) and Myanmar (29,000). Four years later, annual death numbers had increased considerably but the geographic distribution of AIDS deaths had probably changed little. South and South-East Asia registered some 400,000 deaths and East Asia and the Pacific 35,000. India and Myanmar did not release official estimates for that year.

Table 2. AIDS related deaths, total population and AIDS mortality rates in Asian countries with adult HIV prevalence rates of 0.1 percent or above (2001)

	HIV prevalence	*AIDS deaths*	*Total Population (th.)*	*Crude AIDS Death Rate*
Cambodia	2.7	12,000	13,441	0.89
Myanmar	2.0	48,000	45,064	1.07
Thailand	1.8	55,000	63,584	0.86
India*	0.7	310,000	997,663	0.31
Papua New Guinea	0.7	880	4,920	0.18
Nepal	0.5	2,400	25,593	0.09
Malaysia	0.4	2,500	22,633	0.11
Viet Nam	0.3	6,600	79,175	0.08
Singapore	0.2	140	4,108	0.03
China	0.1	30,000	1,284,972	0.02
Indonesia	0.1	4,600	214,840	0.02
Pakistan	0.1	4,500	144,971	0.03

Elsewhere, the largest national losses were in Thailand (55,000 deaths), China (30,000) and Cambodia (12,000). Table 2 presents estimates of AIDS-related deaths, total population, and crude AIDS mortality rates in Asian countries with adult HIV prevalence rates of 0.1 percent or above. Total AIDS deaths are somewhat correlated with population size, while AIDS-related death rates are correlated with HIV prevalence rates. In both cases, China is the most notable negative residual.

*Impact on adult mortality:*AIDS has markedly increased the probability of premature death among the young adult males of some countries of the Asia region. Worldwide, HIV/AIDS disproportionately affects young adults and adult mortality is therefore affected more strikingly than overall mortality. But this pattern, which prevails worldwide, is more clearly marked still in the Asia region. In the South and South-East Asia region, 89 percent of the AIDS-related deaths in 2001 were adult deaths. In East Asia and the Pacific, the percentage was 95 per cent (table 3).

Table 3. AIDS-related deaths and proportion of adults among HIV-positive persons, 2001

deaths	*AIDS-related deaths (adults)*	*AIDS-related deaths (children)*	*Percent adult HIV/AIDS*	*Adults as % of those living with*
South and South - East Asia	350,000	42,500	89	96
East Asia and Pacific	34,000	1,700	95	81
Sub-Saharan Africa	1,800,000	515,000	78	90

These figures markedly contrast with those in sub-Saharan Africa (78 per cent) and reflect the relatively small role of mother to child transmission in the region, as well as the lower rate of infections among women compared to men. The impact of AIDS on mortality is much more noticeable in young adult age groups, especially in the 25 to 34 age groups, than in the population as a whole. HIV prevalence and AIDS deaths are highest in these age groups, which additionally tend to have very low mortality from all causes. Table 4 presents estimates of AIDS-related adult deaths, adult population and crude AIDS mortality rates among adults in Asian countries with adult HIV prevalence rates of 0.1 percent or above. The correlation of adult HIV prevalence rates with crude death rates among adults, not unexpectedly, is somewhat stronger than that with overall mortality rates.

Table 4. AIDS deaths in adults, adult population and AIDS adult mortality rate in Asian countries with adult HIV prevalence rates of 0.1 percent and above, 2001

	Adult Population (th.)	AIDS Deaths in Adults	Crude Death Rate per 1,000
Cambodia	6,314	10,050	1.59
Myanmar	25,855	42,000	1.62
Thailand	36,636	63,000	1.72
India	509,007	250,000	0.49
Papua New Guinea	2,491	800	0.32
Nepal	11,106	2,100	0.19
Malaysia	11,868	2,350	0.20
Viet Nam	43,343	6,150	0.14
Singapore	2,324	130	0.05
China	726,031	32,500	0.04
Indonesia	118,163	4,250	0.04
Pakistan	67,964	4,050	0.06

Projections of AIDS mortality: Short- to medium-term mortality from AIDS in Asia has been estimated in two sets of projections. One set was prepared by the United Nations for the 4 countries of Asia with the highest adult prevalence rates (Cambodia, India, Myanmar and Thailand) taken together. Total excess deaths in these countries were estimated to reach nearly 1.5 million for the period 1995-2000, or a 3 percent increase relative to a no-AIDS scenario, and were projected to reach over 2.2 million for the period 2000-2005, or a 5 percent increase. The second set of projections, by WHO, covered a larger number of countries.

Based on a standard survival time of 9 years from initial infection, it yielded a figure of 784,000 AIDS-related deaths for the year 2005 alone for the region as a whole. It suggested that annual deaths in the age groups 15 to 49 could possibly increase by 40 percent in countries such as

Cambodia, Myanmar and Thailand. In other countries of the region where adult prevalence rates are still under 1 percent, the increase in annual deaths could be up to 5 percent. The two sets of projections from the UN and WHO are broadly compatible.

Impact on life expectancy: On the global level, the United Nations has estimated the average relationship between HIV prevalence and life expectancy based on 45 countries for which projections were available. The correlation is very high and an increase of 1 percent in the adult prevalence rate is associated with a decline of almost one year in life expectancy. For the four countries of the Asia region with the highest prevalence rates taken together, the decline in life expectancy at birth attributable to AIDS was estimated at 0.6 years for the period 1995-2000 and at 1.2 years for the period 2010-2015. Life expectancy in individual countries would be affected differently, depending on their HIV prevalence rates. The decline would be about 4 years in Cambodia (from 60 to 56), 3 years in Myanmar (from 59 to 56), 2 years in Thailand (from 73 to 71) and 1 year in India (from 65 to 64).

Impact on population size: In at least some countries of Asia, the increased mortality due to AIDS will eventually have an effect on the population growth rate and, ultimately, on population size. The slowing down of population growth rates caused by AIDS is not due to increased mortality alone, however. Indirectly, it also results from the fact that infected women who die early in their childbearing years bear fewer babies, thereby lowering fertility. But this effect will only be visible in the longer term, when births that did not happen combine with premature deaths to affect population size. Even in African countries with extremely high prevalence rates, AIDS only started having a visible effect on population size in the early 1990s.

In Asia, where current prevalence rates are significantly lower than in sub-Saharan Africa, this effect is likely to be less marked and to be delayed even further. For the four countries of the region with the highest prevalence rates, the United Nations has projected a 1 percent difference in population size by 2015 relative to a no-AIDS scenario, as against a 10 percent difference in Africa. By the year 2050, the differences would be 2 percent and 15 percent respectively.

The large population sizes of some Asian countries have raised serious concerns that even relatively low adult HIV prevalence rates could translate into huge unmanageable numbers of infected persons, and ultimately deaths. China (1.3 billion persons) is widely thought to be on the brink of a widespread HIV/AIDS epidemic and in India (1 billion persons) reported numbers of AIDS cases are already substantial. These two countries were recently the objects of a projection exercise whose results can be instructive. For each country, three scenarios based on mild, intermediate and severe epidemics were used to project numbers of AIDS deaths and related changes in life expectancy for 5-year intervals to the horizon 2025.

China: In China, the three scenarios were based on prevalence rates rising from 0.17 percent in 2000 to 1.5 percent, 3.5 percent and 5 percent by 2025. By 2005, for instance, numbers of annual AIDS deaths were projected to range from 150,000 to 190,000, while cumulative AIDS deaths over the first decade of the century would reach 370,000 to 410,000.

India: In India, prevalence rates were assumed to increase from 0.57 percent in 2000 to 1.5 percent (mild scenario), 5 percent (intermediate scenario) and 7 percent (severe scenario). Annual AIDS deaths by 2005 would reach between 320,000 and 360,000 and cumulative AIDS deaths could be as high as 980,000 to 1,030,000. In both countries, the projected yearly death tolls then increase very fast between 2005 and 2010, being multiplied by 3 or 4 in the case of the mild epidemics and by up to 10 in the case of the severe epidemics. Also the gaps between mild and severe scenarios widen as time goes on.In the case of the milder scenarios, the impact of such mortality levels by the year 2025 would be to slow down gains in life expectancy, though not to reverse them. The intermediate scenarios would result in a slight absolute decline in life expectancy in India (from 62 years in 2000 to 61.5 in 2025) and a near stagnation in China (from 70.5 to 71). Only the severe scenarios would bring about an actual reversal in the gains in life expectancy achieved in the last few decades (down to 69 in China and around 58 in India).

The weakness of this interesting projection exercise stems from its lack of an assessment of the plausibility of the assumptions made with respect to the evolution of prevalence rates, on which everything else obviously depends. Nor are certain arbitrary but crucial choices explained, such as why a "severe" epidemic in China would be defined by an adult prevalence rate of 5 percent, whereas the same "severe" epidemic in India would be defined by a rate of 7 percent.

BARRIERS TO GOOD REPRODUCTIVE HEALTH

Why do young people disproportionately suffer from reproductive health problems?

— *Lack of Information:* Many young people lack knowledge and have misleading information about sexual issues.

— *Lack of Access*: Legal barriers often prohibit or limit provision of information or services to young people.

Financial and geographic barriers prevent many young people from paying for services or being able to access clinics.

— *Cultural and Social Restrictions*: Unequal power relations and sexual coercion between boys and girls and older men and girls often prevent girls from negotiating the timing of sex and contraceptive usage.

— Attitudes toward sex, particularly premarital sex, often result in the restriction of information and access to services for young people. Low levels of female education lead to less reproductive decision-making power and earlier childbearing among many young women.

Actions Required

Ensuring young people's reproductive health is not solely the responsibility of the health sector, but also that of the education, poverty, and population sectors.

Young People's Health is a Population Issue:

Young people represent a large and growing population group. Associated with the demographic transition is an absolute and relative increase in the population of older people. Investments in the human capital of youth are necessary to build a healthy workforce that can support and ensure the welfare of the elderly population.

Young People's Health is an Education Issue

The health of young people has a direct impact on their educational potentials. Schoolgirls who become pregnant are either forced to leave school, risk unsafe abortions to avoid leaving school, and are prevented from returning to school after giving birth, because they have to take care of their child. Young women who become pregnant at an early age, therefore, achieve lower levels of education than women who delay childbearing until their 20s.

Young People's Health is a Poverty Issue

Improving young people's health is critical to the goal of poverty reduction: Young people comprise an increasing percentage of the workforce, are the workforce of the future, and contribute to the economic production in the home through paid and unpaid work. Obstructed labor, HIV infection, and chlamydia infection rank among the leading ten causes of disability-adjusted life years (DALYs) lost among young people ages 10-24 living in developing regions.

Cost-effective Interventions

As background work for the 1993 World Development Report, the World Bank, in collaboration with the World Health Organization (WHO), carried out a comprehensive analysis of the disease burden—the amount of premature death and disability attributable to specific diseases and injuries. In combination with information on cost-effectiveness of health interventions, these estimates help set priorities for the health sector and guide governments in directing public spending.

The 1993 World Bank report assesses the cost effectiveness of a wide range of health interventions and identified a minimum package of essential health services. Reproductive health interventions— including family planning services, prenatal and delivery care, and case management of sexually transmitted diseases—are a fundamental part of this minimum package. Clustering services can further increase their cost-effectiveness. For example, providing STD management and prenatal care services, or postpartum family planning and infant care, at the same place and time often promotes positive interactions in health benefits and reduces service delivery costs and women's time and travel costs.

Quality family planning services can eliminate the health risks of unwanted pregnancies. Extending prenatal, delivery, and postpartum care to the underserved, particularly the management of obstetric complications, would substantially reduce the death and disability associated with childbearing. Because STDs increase the ease with which HIV is transmitted, controlling STDs is one of the most important interventions for containing the spread of AIDS.

Prenatal screening and treatment for syphilis and iron supplementation have been recommended for the minimum package, because of the health benefits for mother and child and the low cost of treatment. In developing countries with the financial resources and political will to go beyond the minimum clinical package, a more comprehensive set of services could include appropriate screening and treatment for cervical cancer.

Reproductive health is fundamental to improving human welfare, reducing poverty, and promoting economic growth. Investments in reproductive health have multiple payoffs for families, communities, and the national economy. In particular, reproductive health has a significant effect on the health and productivity of the next generation, in addition to the benefits for the current generation. In contributing to sustainable development through improving equity, quality of life, and economic potential, investing in reproductive health confers widespread benefits to the society as a whole.

Integrated approaches to reproductive health are more likely to succeed when adequate account is taken of the specific needs of a country, its cultural values, and its financial and institutional constraints. In most cases, an incremental approach will be needed that works toward provision of the essential services on the basis of existing capacity and with emphasis on closing the most serious gaps in the reproductive health needs of its population.

Bibliography

Abernethy, V. *Population Pressure and Cultural Adjustment.* New York: Human Sciences Press. 1979.

Abernethy, V.D. *Population Politics: The Choices That Shape Our Future.* New York: Plenum. 1993.

Bartlett, Albert A. "Reflections on Sustainability, Population Growth, and the Environment." *Population and Environment* 16(1). 1994.

Catton, W.R. *Overshoot: The Ecological Basis of Revolutionary Change.* Urbana: University of Illinois Press. 1980.

Cohen, J.E. How Many People Can The Earth Support?. New York: W.W. Norton, 1995.

Daly, H.E. Beyond Growth: The Economics of Sustainable Development. Boston: Beacon Press. 1996.

Deffeyes, K.S. *Hubbert's Peak: The Impending World Oil Shortage.* Princeton: Princeton University Press. 2001.

Duncan, Richard C. "World Energy Production, Population Growth, and the Road to the Olduvai Gorge." *Population and Environment* 22(5). 2001.

Ehrlich, P.R. and A.H. Ehrlich. *The Population Explosion.* New York: Simon and Schuster. 1990.

Fuller, Gary, "The Demographic Backdrop to Ethnic Conflict: A Geographic Overview." in *The Challenge of Ethnic Conflict to National and International Order in the 1990s: Geographic Perspectives.* Washington D.C.: Central Intelligence Agency. 1995.

Hardin, G., *Living Within Limits: Ecology, Economics and Population Taboos.* New York: Oxford University Press. 1992.

Holdren, John. "Population and the Energy Problem." *Population and Environment* 12(3). 1991.

Longwell, Harry J. "The Future of the Oil and Gas Industry: Past Approaches, New Challenges." *World Energy* 5(3). 2002.

Malthus, T.R. *An Essay on the Principle of Population.* 1798. Norton Critical Edition, edited by P. Appleman, 2nd ed. New York: W.W. Norton. 2004.

Moffett, G.D. *The Global Population Challenge: Critical Masses.* New York: Viking Press. 1994.

Pimentel, D. et al. "Will Limits of the Earth's Resources Control Human Numbers?," *Environment, Development and Sustainability* 1: 19-39, 1999.

Ponting, C. A. *Green History of the World: The Environment and the Collapse of Great Civilizations.* New York: Penguin Books. 1993.

Smail, J.K. "Confronting a Surfeit of People: Reducing Global Human Numbers to Sustainable Levels." *Environment, Development and Sustainability* 4: 21-50, 2002.

United Nations Population Division, World Population Prospects: The 2002 Revision. New York: 2003.

World Urbanization Prospects: The 2003 Revision. New York: 2004.

Wackernagel, M. and W. Rees. *Our Ecological Footprint: Reducing Human Impact on the Earth.* Gabriola Island. BC: New Society Publishers. 1996.

Wilson, E.O. *The Future of Life.* New York: A.A. Knopf. 2002.

World Bank, Intensifying Action Against HIV/AIDS in Africa: Responding to a Development Crisis. Washington. D.C.: 1999.

World Health Organization, Global Prevalence and Incidence of Selected Curable Sexually Transmitted Infections. Geneva: 2001.

Index